THE PICASSO RANSOM

THE PICASSO RANSOM

and other stories about art and crime in Australia

Mark S Holsworth

First Printing, 2023

paperback ISBN 978-0-646-87307-7
ebook ISBN 978-0-646-87308-4

A catalogue record for this book is available from the National Library of Australia

Mark S. Holsworth is the author of *Sculptures of Melbourne*, the long-running blog, *Black Mark: Melbourne Art & Culture Critic*, articles, short stories, plays and various hack writing jobs.

Aboriginal and Torres Strait Islanders readers are advised that this book contains the names of people who have died.

CONTENTS

Introduction – At the intersection of art and crime

What follows are forty-five true-crime stories at the intersection of art and crime – stories about some of the usual suspects of the art world, along with a few notorious underworld names. Con artists selling millions of dollars in fake art, forgers painting in secret studios, criminally creative art galleries, and collectors gloating over stolen art. Political corruption, forensic detection, art conservation nightmares, courtroom dramas, surprising judgements and even more surprising attributions. Salacious reports of visits to art galleries by the vice squad, ransom demands, trials and tribulations, the sacred and the profane, from the sublime to the criminal. Troc signs off a graffiti piece – "The secret ingredient is crime."

Like white-collar crimes, everyone thinks they know what 'art crimes' are. However, no crime statistics are kept for them. Art theft may be burglary or even extortion. Art forgeries are recorded among the fraud figures. And other art crimes may be classified as vandalism, pornography, illegal imports or exports, blasphemy, obscenity, desecration, treason, or *lése majesté* (although not all of these are crimes in Australia).

In dollar terms, art crimes rank alongside illegal drugs and weapons sales. It destroys people's lives, careers, reputations and cultures for those dollars. For art is more than just an asset; it is history, sacred traditions – culture.

Most people who write true crime have a connection to the underworld: former crime reporters, retired police officers or convicted criminals. I am none of these. Instead, I know the art world, from the artists' studios and aerosol-painted laneways to the high-end commercial art galleries. My first book was about Melbourne's public sculptures, but I knew I wanted to write about art and crime for my second.

My interest in art crimes started with the theft and ransom of Picasso's *Weeping Woman*. It fermented my interest in visual art's underworld, a brew of art, money, violence and politics that bubbled along for decades. Who were the Australian Cultural Terrorists? Why were they holding a painting hostage? Would they destroy it? It was such a bizarre crime, and even more intriguing, it remains unsolved.

I clipped out newspaper reports, first about the *Weeping Woman* and then other art thefts and forgeries. It was not the only remarkable crime in Australia. Entire exhibitions were stolen, forged or accused of being child pornography.

I was writing about the subject, reporting on a couple of criminal trials involving the visual arts, so earlier versions of some parts of this book have appeared in various publications. This was an excellent way to source additional information on several occasions. I knew I was getting somewhere when the daughter of a man who had taken a Picasso and a convicted art forger emailed me in the same week.

Then there was more research, including searching through newspaper databases and archives, hundreds of newspaper articles with the words "stolen" and "painting". "Stolen paintbrushes" also came up in my search – before mass production made them less expensive, many paintbrushes were stolen from signwriters. As well as interviewing people, I visited locations and retrospectively cased joints. Unlike most people, artists and criminals create a lot of records.

All the crimes in this book start or end in Australia. Some involve art by internationally known artists, others art by locals. This geographic focus resulted in a greater variety of crimes rather than focusing on price or notoriety. It was also convenient for me.

Australia's art world is, more or less, like many other countries, a mix of local and international content, emerging artists and old masters, Indigenous and colonial. A place of white-walled galleries, auction houses and artists' studios on streets with commissioned public art and unauthorised graffiti and populated with artists, collectors, dealers, educators and others, drinking wine at exhibition openings. Most of them are honest, decent people. Some are very rich, and others want to be very rich, including brazen thieves, deceitful forgers and dodgy art dealers.

I selected crimes from the colonial era to the present to tell an art history with the piquant flavour of the illegal, and to show a variety of art, crimes and their legal, political and commercial significance for Indigenous peoples' struggle for cultural survival. Some crimes are known internationally and involve millions of dollars; others are almost trivial in comparison.

The stories are grouped into five parts. I have given abusive names to them to be clear about my sympathies. *Thieving Ratbags* is about art thieves who are as variable as their motivations. *Bullshit Artists* has cases of art forgery and fraud. *Self-righteous Pricks* refers to the accusers and looks at the politics of what can be shown. *Bloody Vandals* looks at both the vandalism of art and graffiti vandals. Finally, *Other Bastards* covers other brushes with the law, especially artists who changed the law or almost did.

Nobody mentioned in this book should be presumed guilty unless convicted; not everyone who takes art from an art gallery without permission is a thief, nor is everyone who copies art a forger. There are plenty of colourful characters in both art and crime. And as in any story of true crimes, plenty of greedy, selfish, narcissistic, destructive people. But unlike most true crime books, there are many people with irrepressible creativity, passionate love, and extreme generosity.

All dialogue is taken word for word from newspaper reports, court transcripts or police recordings.

All amounts are in Australian dollars unless otherwise stated.

For reasons of cost, copyright and taste, there are no photos in this book. If you want to see an image, in the words of Greens' Leader Adam Bandt, 'Google it, mate.'

Timeline of events

1885 Break-in at the Art Gallery of SA
1897 Person stabs portrait of James Patterson at the NGV
1908 Jury in the fraud trial fails to reach a verdict
1926 Wilkie's *The Gentle Shepherd* stolen from the NGV
1931 Vice squad seize the magazine *Art in Australia*
1933 Noel Counihan was arrested for obstructing traffic
1947 Two stolen Streetons left under a bench in Bondi
1949 Victoria police seize Rosaleen Norton's paintings
1950 SA Police investigate fake Namatjira watercolours
1959 Statue of Poseidon castrated
1966 Mike Brown convicted of obscenity
1967 A Picasso is taken from the Queensland Art Gallery
1975 Ivan Durrant's *Slaughtered Cow Happening*
1977 Exhibition by Grace Cossington-Smith stolen
      Peter Sparnaay convicted of art fraud
1978 Tom Robert's *The splitters* held for ransom
      "Paintings by Jackson Pollock" opens in Perth
1979 Eighty paintings from Joseph Brown
      Six bark paintings were taken from Hogarth Gallery
1980 Renoir painting stolen from Loti Smorgon
1982 Police seize Davila's painting *Stupid As A Painter*
1986 Picasso's *The Weeping Woman* held for ransom
      Robbery at the New Norcia in WA
      Paintings were stolen from Carrick Hills in Adelaide
1988 Twenty-four paintings stolen from Smorgon's home

Cath Phillips jailed for exhibiting 'obscene' art
1994 Ethel Carrick-Fox's *In the Nice Flower Market* stolen
1995 *Larry La Trobe* by Pamala Irving stolen
Liz and Phil Down by the Lake is decapitated
1997 Vandals attack Serrano's *Piss Christ* at the NGV
1998 Nine paintings stolen from Cyril-Stanley's home
Max Joffe convicted of stealing from Albert Tucker
2000 O'Loughlin convicted over fake Tjapaltjarri paintings
2002 Sissons convicted of handling stolen Tucker painting
2004 Brett Williams steals John Opit's art collection
2006 Police take and return *Proudly unAustralian*
2007 Ivan and Pamela Liberto convicted of forgery
Renks jailed for multiple graffiti offences
A Cavalier stolen from the AGNSW
2008 NSW police seize and then return works by Henson
Thieves steal idols from the temple in India
2009 Police raid Ronald Coles Investment Gallery
Fay Plamka fined for contempt of court
2013 Victoria Police cut out parts of Yore's installation
2016 Ether arrested, imprisoned and deported
2017 Gant and Siddique's convictions overturned

Thieving Ratbags

The Abstraction at the Adelaide Art Gallery

Shots rang out in a nameless alley in Adelaide in 1885. A young dressmaker was startled, but she knew who was doing the shooting. Arvid Hilarion Wistrand was a twenty-six-year-old Swede and opiate addict who lived next door in the alley between Sydney and St Helen Place, off Halifax Street. He often disturbed her firing his gun or pestering her; she wasn't sure which was worse. She went to the police to lodge a complaint.

It joined other, more serious, complaints about Wistrand to the police. Before the end of the year, he would be "arrested for an abstraction" at the Art Gallery of South Australia (AGSA).

The AGSA was established in 1881. It was housed in what is now the magazine room in the public library building on North Terrace.

On Sunday morning, November 15, 1885, the art gallery's caretaker noticed that one of the windows was broken and its wirework screen torn away. The chain locking the front door was open. Inside he found an empty but otherwise undamaged frame on the floor.

It was a wide, gilded frame for a little painting about a foot square. Missing from the frame and the gallery was its smallest painting. *Avant in Procession* is an oil painting by Vincent Jean-Baptiste Chevillard, a French artist alive at the time. It was a recent acquisition, purchased that year from French Gallery in London for £200 (an amount worth over $26,000 today).

The painting depicted a monk enjoying a drink with a gendarme beside a stone building with Gothic arches. The monk is holding a bottle and a glass while the gendarme is lighting his pipe. In the nineteenth century, it would have been described as "a study of life", but today considered a sentimental illustration.

The mystery of the theft of *Avant in Procession* was revealed that evening by Wistrand. He walked into the offices of the *South Australian Advertiser* and said a friend had taken the painting. He then inquired about getting a receipt for the painting if he returned it to *The Advertiser*. Ernest Govett, a twenty-nine-year-old sub-editor, agreed to issue a receipt. When Wistrand left to collect the painting, Govett notified the police.

Wistrand returned with the painting around 10 o'clock and was shown into Govett's office. He explained that he had taken the painting to demonstrate that the security was inadequate.

On Saturday night, the doorkeeper at the art gallery shut at 5.15 p.m. and locked its double doors with a brass chain and padlock. Wistrand was already inside the building, hiding in a cleaning closet near the front door. The closet had a glass door, but Wistrand went unseen amongst the mops, brooms and lumber stored there. When the building's caretaker locked and bolted the outer front door, Wistrand left his hiding spot. He went to the gallery door and prised apart the metal chain's links; it was easy as the links weren't even soldered.

Wistrand selected the smallest painting because it was the easiest to carry. Taking great care, he removed the canvas from its frame. It was only fastened to the frame with half a dozen small nails and paper pasted over to keep the dust out. He was less careful when he forced the window open breaking the glass in the lower part. He then made a hole in the wire-netting screen large enough for him to squeeze out.

At the end of his story, Wistrand gave Govett the painting, saying: 'You will see it is in good order. You will be kind enough to give me a receipt for it, and you will kindly publish my statement, as I wish it to be understood I have done everything in a straightforward manner. Now you quite understand my motive for doing it.'

Wistrand was arrested upon exiting the front door of the *Adelaide Advertiser*'s offices in Rundle Street by Detective George Thorn. Thorn had listened to Wistrand's confession to Govett from an adjoining room.

The following morning Wistrand gave an interview from his cell to a reporter from the *Advertiser*'s rival, *The Adelaide Observer*. In the reporter's now antique words, he explained how he had 'abstracted the picture' ('abstracted' meaning 'to remove).

His motivation was further emphasised on Monday in a long-winded letter received by the Commissioner of Police, postmarked Saturday:

> *"Adelaide, November 14, 1885*
> *To the commissioner of Police, Adelaide, South Australia*
> *Sir,*
> *The course of action I have decided upon makes it imperative to me for more than one reason to communicate with a man of high intelligence and one able to give an unprejudiced opinion, and willing to do so even when public sentiment takes a different view. I do mean to say that I expect or believe that the public opinion will differ from my own. In fact, I strongly hope and believe that the people of Adelaide will to its fullest extent appreciate my action in this matter, for even the vilest of tongues, whilst they may attempt to prove to themselves and others that when interesting myself in this matter to this extent I only had in view what I might possibly gain by proving to*

the colony that I have saved it from a possibility of great loss – I say that whilst they may say this, they cannot deny that the service done to the people of the colony is real, and of the greatest value. I have chosen you, sir, among many I have thought of, because I believe you will see that fairness is done me. In a case of this kind also a man has to defend himself from any charge of criminal intentions on his part, and I believe you will think this sufficient. I will now tell what I refer to. I, a short time ago, saw two men in the vestibule of the Art Gallery handling the chain that keeps it locked. After they had left I went up to it and saw that the links were so open that anyone could simply unlock them. I then formed a plan to prove to the country and the committee of the Art Gallery that it was not safe, and I knew I would not succeed to do that unless I undertook to take something out of the Gallery myself; therefore tonight I intend to enter the Art Gallery and to take out one of the smallest oil paintings. If I am caught on the spot I trust this will clear me; if I succeed, I shall call at the Detective Office on Sunday and see you. If I am not arrested on the spot, I shall be very thankful to you for keeping this private until you see me on Sunday, the 15th instant. I hope I can rely on your sympathy.

Yours respectfully, A. H. Wistrand. St. Helena Place, Halifax Street

P.S. - I have posted a similar letter to another gentleman in Adelaide."

The other gentleman was Edwin Thomas Smith, a brewer with a beard like a hops shovel. He was also the member for East Torrens in the South Australian House of Assembly. He received a letter at his Kent Town Brewery, also postmarked Saturday, November 16; both letters were in good handwriting on blue-lined paper. The only difference was that his envelope had postmarks from Adelaide and Norwood.

> *"Adelaide, November 14, 1885*
> *Mr. E.T. Smith.*
> *Sir,*
> *I have written to the Commissioner of Police appraising him of the fact that I intend for a certain purpose, to remove tonight from the Art Gallery a picture. In case called upon I hope you will acknowledge the receipt of this.*
> *Yours most respectfully, A. H. Wistrand."*

On Tuesday, in the Police Courts, Wistrand pleaded guilty to damaging a window to the value of £1 and a picture to the extent of 10s. He offered no defence. He was ordered to pay the damage, £1 10s, a fine of £2 and costs, £4 12s. in all (just over $500 in today's value). Reporters following the case noted that two other charges, unrelated to the abstraction at the art gallery, were withdrawn by the prosecutor: having unlawfully pawned a Bible for £3 15s and an album for 15s.

Rowland Rees, MP and Chairman of the Board of Governors of the Adelaide Art Gallery, took the opportunity to once again draw reporters' attention to the lack of security at the gallery. Rees was an archetypical Victorian engineer and architect with an enormous moustache and mutton-chop sideburns. He told the reporters that he had wanted iron bars, not wirework, across the windows and was getting frustrated at the lack of action about security. None of the reporters suggested that this honourable gentleman would ever have considered hiring a henchman like Wistrand to demonstrate this point.

The Art Gallery of South Australia still has *Avant in Procession* in its collection.

A swag of art thefts

Here is a swag of stories about art thefts that illustrates some aspects of stealing art. Art has been stolen from ships, hotels, universities and from artists' homes and studios. Art has even been stolen from the High Court in Canberra. But most often, it has been stolen from art galleries and private homes because that's where most of it is.

Hanging in the National Gallery of Victoria was David Wilkie's *The gentle shepherd*, a work of considerable appeal to the numerous Scottish immigrants in Melbourne. Wilkie was a nineteenth-century Scottish artist who painted sentimental scenes set in romantic landscapes. Its full title is *A scene from Ramsay's 'The Gentle Shepherd,* a pastoral comedy that became the libretto for the first Scottish opera.

It was not the original painting, which is in the National Galleries of Scotland, but an etching based on Wilkie's painting. It might seem odd today for a state art gallery to exhibit a print of a famous painting. However, in the nineteenth century, it was not uncommon for major art galleries to acquire high-quality copies of works of art; the Metropolitan Museum in New York also has an etching of *The gentle shepherd* in its collection.

On Friday, August 20, 1926, at one o'clock in the afternoon, the gallery attendant made his usual rounds of the three galleries and noticed nothing suspicious. The attendants were the only security for the state's art collection. When they locked up at five o'clock, they failed to check all the galleries. Possibly they were in a hurry to leave because it was a Friday night.

The following day, on opening, the attendants discovered that *The gentle shepherd*'s frame had been turned around and the etching removed. It would not have been difficult; a screwdriver or pocket knife would have been all that was needed to remove the back of the frame and the paper tape that secured the etching to the mountboard. Moreover, the paper with the etching on it was not large, only 30 × 40 centimetres. Rolled up, it would then have been easy to conceal, allowing the thief to stroll casually past the attendant, down the stairs and out onto the street.

The police were called, and Detective Percy William Lambell investigated the theft.

Detective Lambell was five foot nine with brown eyes, brown curly hair, and a fresh complexion. He was born in Victoria in1890 and had been a soldier before joining the police in 1910. He was a good detective and could spot a pickpocket at Flemington Race Track. He had arrested a gang for forging £1 notes at Black Rock, the Zoological Garden's payroll robbers, pickpockets at Princes Bridge Railway Station (aka Flinders Street Station), conmen selling salicylic acid as cocaine, magneto thieves, a fratricidal 14-year-old from Springvale, and charged the gangster 'Squizzy' Taylor with threatening a witness.

Lambell believed that the thief might offer the picture for sale. So he told the reporters they should, "warn anyone against buying it". A reporter from *The Argus* helpfully included the description, "A shepherd seated on a bench outside a cottage door. He is playing a flute. On his right are a dog and two village women with bare feet, while on his left are his staff and a wooden table."

However, Lambell didn't know if he was looking for a thief who intended to sell the etching or keep it. He didn't know if the larceny was planned or merely opportunistic. Was it an inside job? About 80 per cent of art thefts are inside jobs. Understanding the motivation is key to a successful investigation and necessary for a successful prosecution. Without a motive, Lambell could only hope that a potential buyer would recognise the etching if the thief tried to sell it. Greed is not the only motive for art theft, and if the thief intended to keep it, then there was little hope of ever finding it.

The theft attracted little public interest, and in this particular investigation, Detective Lambell's intelligence and dogged perseverance failed to uncover the thief or locate *The gentle shepherd*.

It is a fizzer, but it is all too common in stories of stolen art, and I don't want to give a false impression by only writing about art thefts where the art is recovered.

What has happened to all of the stolen art? Most stolen goods go through a network of family and friends, which is true for most stolen art. Some may still be hanging on someone's wall, and eventually, some will enter the art market again.

However, even when stolen art is found, the original owners don't always get it back. Under Australian law, civil claims for the return of the stolen property acquired by another in a good faith transaction must be brought within six years of the theft. Otherwise, after six years, the original owners lose the property.

In 1930 Detective Lambell crossed paths with Melbourne's art world again when he was the first detective on the scene of the murder of Mollie Dean, the lover and model of the artist Colin Colahan. However, his inability to catch Melbourne's first art thief or Dean's killer did not slow down Lambell's career. By the time he retired in 1950, he had been promoted to inspector.

For most of the twentieth century, security at galleries relied primarily on human surveillance; there was no other option before the development of closed-circuit television, motion detectors, intrusion alarms, perimeter alarm systems, and sonic-radar sensors. Contrary to what you might see in movies and TV shows, most art thieves do not have to overcome elaborate security systems, and many high street shops have better security. A pipe or a brick has been the equipment of choice for smashing gallery windows or glass doors. Many art thefts are not publicised because art galleries don't want to expose problems with their security, and private collections don't want to draw attention to the value of their collection.

On Saturday night, September 10, 1938, a thief broke in and took a gold cup and some antique coins. Security at the Art Gallery of South Australia had not improved much since Wistrand stole *Avant in Procession*.

Two weeks later, in Melbourne, Detective R. L. Loane arrested a 49-year-old man going by the name Walter Godfrey Radcliffe. Radcliffe had the gold cup and some of the coins. He had tried to sell the antiques to a second-hand dealer in Melbourne, who had reported him to the police. Australian art thieves, burglars and art forgers continue to follow Radcliffe's example of moving stolen art and antiques interstate or internationally. Detective R. L. Loane brought him back to Adelaide, where Radcliffe pleaded guilty and was sentenced to four years.

Radcliffe (aka Walter Godfrey Reeves, Walter Keating, Walter George Ratcliffe, Arthur William Dowding, John Jackson, Charles Jackson, and Bernard Godfrey Walter Leahan) was born in Australia in 1890. He had done time in a prison in England in the 1920s, so Scotland Yard had a complete description of him: Five foot eight inches tall with a fresh complexion, brown hair, blue eyes, a nose inclined to the right, a scar on his right jaw, a scar on the back of his right wrist and first finger, tattoos of clasped hands, crossed flags with a boat in the centre, a cross and a woman on his forearm.

A painting was cut from its frame during a burglary at the Exhibition Building in Melbourne on Friday, April 29, 1932. Cutting an oil painting from a frame so that the canvas can be rolled up to easily transport is a move seen in many art-heist films. It also causes two kinds of severe damage – it crops the image, which loses its edges and original dimensions, and the stiff surface of an oil painting on canvas is not designed to be rolled up, and the paint cracks and flakes.

The missing painting, a 'Rembrandt' belonged to the late politician and celebrity medical practitioner Dr L. L. Smith. Smith claimed it was given to him in 1901 by the Duke of York. It was described as Rembrandt, *The Wayfarer*; however, before we mourn the loss of a masterpiece from the golden age of Dutch painting, remember that attributions are not an exact science. Some attributions are very wild and free. There were thousands more paintings attributed to 'Rembrandt' in 1932 than there are now. The inaccuracy may have been a reason to steal it, saving the owners from future embarrassment.

The accurate attribution of art is often an essential aspect of all art crimes for both criminals and the law. After Leslie Richmond Board died in 1942, two oil paintings went missing from his home at 18 Macleay Street in Potts Point, Sydney. One was *Boy*, attributed to the sixteenth-century Florentine painter Bronzino (aka Agnolo di Cosimo). The other was a nude woman, *Eve,* by a little-known, modern English painter, Allan Davidson.

Nine years later, Leslie's son, Gregory Board, was told where he could buy a Bronzino in Sydney and from the description, it sounded like the same one his father owned.

The Bronzino was being sold by Albert George Briskie, a licensed collector of firearms and antique dealer living above his shop on King Street. Briskie had worked as a houseman for Leslie Board before his father's death.

It was enough for a police raid on Briskie's shop and home. They discovered the two paintings. Briskie was charged with the theft of the two paintings and possession of eleven unlicensed firearms.

The case fell apart in court. Briskie claimed that the Board family was short of cash, hadn't paid his wages, borrowed small amounts of money from him, and asked him to sell some paintings on commission, for which he wasn't paid. He had retained the two paintings to make up for these losses. The unlicenced firearms were antiques, including an elaborate eighteenth-century, brass-mounted, sixty-centimetre Turkish pistol.

Was it even a genuine Renaissance painting by old master Bronzino? Briskie's lawyer doubted its authenticity, and the police had no expert witnesses to call. After all, its late owner was the chief scenic artist for J. C. Williamson Ltd's theatre productions, and the value of the painting was listed as ten shillings on his probate affidavit. The 'Bronzino' might have been a piece of theatre scenery that Briskie had been trying to sell for a thousand guineas.

At the end of the prosecution's case, the judge ruled that there was no case to answer. After being arrested and put on trial, Briskie gave the two paintings to Gregory Board. Was this a generous and forgiving act? He hadn't been able to sell them in nine years, and now that he had cast doubt on the authenticity of the 'Bronzino', what else could he do with them?

A surprising amount of stolen art is returned or abandoned – call it a thief's remorse or simply restitution, and there are many more examples. There always is the chance that stolen art will just be returned, sometimes in the most surprising ways. In February

1947, a package containing two stolen paintings sat under a garden seat on Campbell Parade at Bondi Beach. A man phoned the NSW police to tell them the two paintings' location, and they were recovered undamaged.

Both *Street in Cairo* and *Seller of Drinks* were painted by Arthur Streeton (aka Smike) during his five months in Egypt in 1897. They were valued at £250 and £175 ($28,000 today if they had been sold in 1947 because the value of Streeton's paintings has increased far more than inflation).

The paintings were first noticed missing on December 20, 1946, but it was only reported to police on January 2 because university staff thought that it might only be a student prank. Their owner, Dr Oscar Paul, was relieved, as was the University of Sydney. Dr Paul had lent them to the University, and they had been hung in a room in the Union Hall. The room was locked, but the windows had been kept open to air it.

In 1966 burglars broke down the door of the composer and conductor Camille Gheysens's house in Sydney. They neatly cut paintings by the Australian artists Drysdale and Dobell from their frames and stole works by Van Gogh, Gauguin, Toulouse-Lautrec and other European artists. They took Gheysens's entire art collection in a smooth operation on Sunday, November 5, when he was away on a four-day visit to Brisbane. He returned home to find furniture overturned and twenty-five of his paintings missing.

The three investigating police officers told Gheysens that they could recover his paintings if he paid a reward for information. On their instruction, Gheysens and his insurance company transferred $7000 ($90,000 today) into a Sydney bank account. And in January 1967, most of his paintings were recovered from shrubbery in Centennial Park.

You might think the story ends when the art is returned, but this becomes more about extortion and corruption than burglary. There were allegations that two detective sergeants and a detective senior constable pocketed part of the reward money and gave the rest to a known criminal. A year after the paintings were recovered, Police Commissioner Norman Allan's (aka Norman the Foreman) report on police corruption allegations was kept secret. And Liberal Premier of NSW, Robert Askin (aka Robin Askin), was asked questions about it on the floor of Parliament. Not that this damaged either man's career – Premier Askin and Commissioner Norman Allen were in charge of notoriously corrupt organisations. There are often more complex motives for taking art, and political corruption intersects with many art thefts.

La belle Hollandaise

A record for the highest price paid for the work of a living artist was broken in Sotheby's auction room in London on May 6, 1959, when Pablo Picasso's *La belle Hollandaise* (*The beautiful Dutch woman*) sold for £50,000 ($1,550,210 today). It was purchased by Major Harold de Vahl Rubin of Queensland. The odd thing is that he had bought it from himself; Major Rubin had first purchased *La belle Hollandaise* for £6000 ($477,880 today) in 1940.

The painting depicts a plump young woman wearing nothing but a traditional Dutch lacy-cloth cap. The twenty-four-year-old Picasso painted it on a visit to Holland in 1905. He was between his early 'Blue period' with its downbeat subjects in blue paint, and his 'Rose period', when he focused on pleasant scenes in a primarily pinky hue. It is painted on cardboard mounted on wood, 77.1 × 65.8 centimetres, in gouache, a water-based poster paint.

Major Rubin was at the Sotheby's auction with his dark-haired fiancée, Julie Muller (aka Julia Eleanora Gvozdic, Julia Eleanora Hanselman). He was a 60-year-old multi-millionaire; she was a 30-year-old divorcee from Sydney; it was his fifth and final marriage.

Some people say that Major Rubin was eccentric; one of his grandsons describes him as "barking mad". Whichever it was, it didn't matter because he was super rich. Rubin had inherited a multi-million fortune made in the Western Australian pearl business and invested in pastoral properties in Queensland. He also acquired a collection of modern European and Australian art, including paintings by Albert Tucker, Norman Lindsay, Jeffery Smart and several Dobells.

Why did Rubin buy a Picasso from himself? Some reports say that Rubin wanted to know its current value, so he put it up for auction and repurchased it. This ostentatious demonstration was part of Rubin's dispute with Australia's prohibitively high import tax on modern art. Instead of banning modern art, Menzies's government had made it impossibly expensive to import, and Australian customs wanted millions from Rubin to bring his own art collection into the country. In a negotiated compromise, the Queensland Art Gallery acquired a Degas, a Renoir, a Toulouse-Lautrec, a Vlaminck and three works by Picasso, including *La belle Hollandaise* from Rubin. And Rubin was allowed to import his art collection.

After Rubin's death in 1964, his widow, Julie Rubin, was worried about the Queensland Art Gallery administration. In 1967 she had heard a flying report that the gallery might sell *La belle Hollandaise* to raise money for its new building on the southern bank of the Brisbane River. She wasn't the only one who had heard the speculation; it was so widespread that university students held a sit-down demonstration in front of the painting to raise awareness of the issue.

Queensland University Professor C. F. Presley wrote an open letter calling for an inquiry into the gallery's trusteeship to the acting Education Minister (and later premier) of Queensland, Joh Bjelke-Peterson. It was signed by fifty other Brisbane residents, including Julie Rubin, but she did not trust Bjelke-Peterson. As far as she was concerned, her husband had just loaned the Picasso in perpetuity, and any move to sell it would dishonour this deal.

In attempting to dismiss the rumours, the chairman of the art gallery's trustees and Liberal Party state president, Sir Herbert Leon Trout, ended up giving them further credibility. Instead of denying any intention to sell the Picasso, Trout decided to explain that the law gave the gallery's trustees the right to dispose of any painting in their possession.

Rumours of the Picasso's potential sale were not the only issue for Trout; he was swimming in them. The choice of James Wieneke as the new gallery director had already caused two of the trustees to resign in protest. Wieneke had no academic qualifications, and as the director of a commercial gallery in Brisbane, he had an obvious conflict of interest. Furthermore, acting director Robyn Hill had also resigned over a separate dispute about the paintings requested for the new Government House by the Governor of Queensland, Sir Alan Mansfield.

So Julia Rubin turned to a good friend, and less than twenty-four hours later, Queensland Art Gallery no longer had *La belle Hollandaise* in its possession.

Very early on Monday, June 5, two men climbed up some scaffolding on the outside of the gothic revival brick building on Gregory Terrace in Bowen Hills. A top-floor window was forced open with a screwdriver. The building is now known as the Old Museum Building, but back in 1967 it housed the Queensland Art Gallery.

One of the two men was Robert Ronald Richard Ferguson, a twenty-two-year-old New Zealander. If there is a local equivalent to the fictional Arsène Lupin, then Ferguson is the gentleman art thief. A polite, discreet man born into a family of ophthalmologists, he is the great-grandson of Sir Lindo Ferguson, the first ophthalmologist in Australasia. Ferguson had been in Australia for the past five years and was a good friend of Julia Rubin. He says they met when he saved her son from being run over by a car. At the time, Ferguson was living in the coastal suburb of Margate and working as a labourer in Brisbane, although that could be a cover story.

Neither of the men was interested in art, and probably neither had visited the gallery before that night. But they had Julia Rubin's detailed information on the gallery's layout and security. They knew there were no burglar alarms in that part of the gallery and removed the Picasso painting without any problems.

Ferguson stored the Picasso at another one of Rubin's properties in Brisbane for a few days before taking it over to Rubin's mansion, 'Toorak House', in Brisbane's inner-northern suburb of Hamilton. At the time, it was one of the largest and most expensive houses in Brisbane and included two reception rooms, a combined dining and ballroom.

Unfortunately, the other man breaking into the gallery was a paid police informant. And the police had Rubin's mansion staked out, waiting for the painting to be delivered. So on Monday, June 12, the Chief of the Brisbane CIB, Inspector Wilhelm Herman Raetz, and three other detectives arrived with a search warrant and found *La belle Hollandaise* in her bedroom.

Julie Rubin claimed that a strange young man knocked on her front door in the middle of Sunday night. However, she let him in as he was carrying a familiar painting. The stranger wanted her to reconsider her late husband's gift and begged her to keep it for a month before reporting it to the police. Julie Rubin told the police that she had agreed to this and hadn't asked the young man any questions. She didn't give the police any information about the young man, she could not describe him or his clothes, except to say that she didn't know him.

The following day, after an examination for damage or substitution, *La belle Hollandaise* was back on public display.

Ferguson wasn't arrested until Saturday, June 24. The police claim to have found a loaded Colt 45 Auto under Ferguson's mattress. Ferguson claims Detective McSporan stuck his revolver to Ferguson's temple and said, "Move you bastard, I'll blow your brains." Ferguson was remanded for eight days while his father flew over from New Zealand to help arrange bail.

Ferguson's defence was that he never intended to permanently deprive the gallery of the Picasso painting because he intended to return it. He claimed to have been motivated by idealism. Ferguson told the police, "I was satisfied the public did not appreciate the painting, so I decided to steal it." His father went along with his son's story, telling reporters he had a passion for art and was a frequent visitor to art galleries.

Rather than reveal where the stolen painting had been stored, Ferguson became creative and claimed that for five days, he hid it wrapped in blankets in the bush on the slopes of Mt Coot-tha before deciding to return the painting to Julie Rubin. It is unlikely the water-based paint would have survived the two days of rain in such conditions.

On Tuesday, August 8, 1967, a jury found Ferguson not guilty of breaking and entering the art gallery and stealing the Picasso. Like Wistrand's abstraction at the Art Gallery of SA, Ferguson was only found guilty of damaging the gallery window. He remained best friends with Julia until her death, and she gave him "a French painting" from her collection.

La belle Hollandaise still hangs in the new Queensland Art Gallery, now in a purpose-built building in the South Bank precinct of Brisbane.

Artnapping

The safari suit-wearing Terry Whelan was open about his sexuality at a time when many gay men were still in the closet. On June 2, 1973, three men broke into his South Yarra home, bashed him and stole thirty-two of his paintings. Whelan knew one of the men who beat him up, Peter Lindsay.

The muscular Lindsay was a twenty-year-old hospital orderly, gym instructor and a Mr Junior Victoria bodybuilder contest winner. And the theft of the paintings was intended to force Whelan to pay the $2500 ($22,700 today) that he promised Lindsay for posing naked and allowing Whelan to 'massage' him.

Two years later, a jury found the trio not guilty of assault occasioning actual bodily harm. But after years of legal troubles, Lindsay was no longer interested in collecting the debt.

Public and private collections are vulnerable to artnapping; stolen art held hostage. While it might be difficult to sell stolen art, thieves know that the owners want it back.

In August 1978, someone walked into the quiet Ballarat Art Gallery and cut Tom Roberts' painting *The splitters* (aka *Charcoal Burners*) out of its frame. They rolled up the almost one-metre-square canvas up and walked out the door.

Was it a man with crutches and a leg in plaster seen in the gallery that day? Nobody knows, but whoever it was, their timing was excellent. The Ballarat Art Gallery had no security systems, a staff of three, and was in the process of being taken over by the City of Ballarat from its previous private management.

The thief had also chosen the right painting to steal. Tom Roberts painted *The splitters* (aka *Charcoal Burners*) in 1886. Although it is not as famous as his *Shearing the rams*, painted four years later, it is still an important work in Australian art history.

The theft was widely reported. Months passed before a ransom demand arrived: $4000 ($19,000 today) for the return of an $80,000 painting. In May 1979, the money was paid, and *The splitters* was left in a Sydney park leaning against a statue. Nothing more was ever discovered about the crime.

Most artnappers aren't so successful. Most are too clever for their own good and end up charged with receiving stolen goods, concealing a serious offence, or corruptly taking a reward to recover stolen property.

It is sometimes said that one of the attractions of art crime stories is the absence of violence; if that is true, then many reports of stolen art have been overlooked. Art has been stolen at knife and gunpoint, leaving owners and gallery staff fearful. Although there has been no death or permanent injury, this has been due to good fortune rather than the benevolence of any of the criminals involved.

The most violent art robbery in Australia occurred on the night of July 10, 1985, in the town of Narbethong, in central Victoria. Two career criminals, Douglas Frederick Robinson and Victor Campbell Loughnan, drove to a remote farmhouse in a hired van. Robinson had a brutal plan.

Wearing balaclavas, equipped with walkie-talkies and armed with shotguns, they invaded the home of Frank and Zlata Kastanek. The couple was held prisoner for eight hours as Robinson and

Loughman loaded several million dollars of art into the van. The telephone lines were cut, and Frank and Zlata were left bound as the robbers drove off at dawn.

A few days after the telephone line was repaired, Robinson called the Kastaneks, offering to ransom the art back. He was arrested soon after and was sentenced to eleven years; his accomplice, Loughnan, received eight years.

Later Robinson wrote several true crime books, including one about the six months he spent in Pentridge Prison's H Division: *My Time in Hell Division*.

The Stolen Exhibition

"It's all gone, Gracie! You've lost everything!"

It wasn't the gentlest way for Treania Smith to explain to the 85-year-old Grace Cossington-Smith (aka Grace Smith) her entire exhibition had been stolen.

Treania Smith was one of the partners in Macquarie Galleries, a commercial gallery established in 1925 and still operating in Sydney, along with associated galleries in Canberra and Perth. It has sold art by many prominent Australian artists: Rupert Bunny, Russell Drysdale, Donald Friend, Jeffery Smart, James Gleeson and Grace Cossington-Smith.

Grace Cossington-Smith (aka Grace Smith) was born in 1892 and took her hyphenated name, 'Cossington,' from the name of her family's home in Sydney. A notable Australian modernist, she was inspired by Cezanne and van Gogh. Her painting, *The Sock-Knitter* 1915, was the first post-impressionist art exhibited in Australia. Her iconic scenes of the Sydney Harbour Bridge under construction. Images built up with rows of individual brushstrokes loaded with paint straight from the tube mixed wet on the canvas.

She had exhibited with Macquire Gallery since 1932, and by the time of the exhibition in 1977, her position in Australian art history was secure. The Gallery of NSW had a retrospective exhibition of her work in 1973.

The exhibition in 1977 was challenging to put together. Cossington-Smith stopped painting in 1973 and hadn't painted any significant work in years. A search had to be made of her old garden studio in Tarramurra, and four pieces were "kindly lent" from private collections. Still, it would be worth it as it was likely to be the last chance to buy her art while she was still alive.

Most of it had sold before the exhibition officially opened. Amongst those early buyers, the Australian National Gallery bought six, and the Nepean College of Advanced Education and the John Darnell Fine Arts Collections at the University of Queensland bought one each. Commercial galleries like Macquarie arrange these advanced sales to get the art into prestigious collections. The purchasers and lenders were listed in the catalogue reflecting the prestige of her collectors.

Unlike today's extensively documented and photographed art catalogues, this was just a single typewritten page listing the work in the exhibition. Two pieces in the exhibition were not listed in the catalogue: *The Pink Trees*, an oil painting on board 73 x 59 cm and a pair of works on paper, a drawing and a watercolour, framed together, two unrelated political cartoons depicting the Kaiser and Mr Asquith.

Daniel Thomas, a curator at the Art Gallery of NSW, had taken black and white Polaroid photos of every piece when the exhibition opened. He often did this at exhibitions that he considered significant.

A month after the exhibition opened, shortly after three o'clock in the morning of Easter Monday, April 4, 1977, a person phoned the police. The caller didn't give their name but described seeing a maroon Holden sedan breaking the doors of Macquarie Galleries at 40 King Street in Sydney and four men loading paintings into the car.

At 3:20 am, the police arrived to find the two plate-glass doors smashed and the gallery deserted. The thieves knew the value of the art inside. While they had made off with an entire exhibition of works by Grace Cossington-Smith, they had left paintings by the Italo-Australian artist Salvatore Zoffrea in a smaller gallery space, untouched.

After the robbery, Daniel Thomas provided his Polaroid photos to the police to assist in the investigation. Then Thomas's photos went missing in police evidence. Now the catalogue is the only evidence that the exhibition ever existed.

And there was more bad news from the gallery for Cossington-Smith. The entire exhibition was valued at $24,800, but Macquarie Galleries had underinsured it. After a civil law court case, Cossington-Smith was awarded $8000, plus costs; Macquarie galleries then sued its insurers, settling the matter out of court. Macquarie Galleries would not be the last gallery to have under-insured its exhibition against theft or damages. Some, like Hahndorf Academy, failed to insure their art, losing sketches and preparatory drawings by Hans Heysen with no compensation.

NSW and Commonwealth police investigated, but none of the paintings was recovered, leaving many unanswered questions. Who was the anonymous late-night caller? And what happened to Daniel Thomas's Polaroid photos?

Speculation was rampant, and until the Picasso was stolen from the NGV, no other art theft in Australia attracted as many conspiracy theories about the identity of the criminals. A gloating collector of stolen art? A collector of Cossington-Smith trying to increase the value of their collection by illegally editing existing works? Had an insurance scam gone wrong? Or was it corrupt NSW police?

This was not the only entire art exhibition to be stolen in Australia. In 1991 all forty-two of Pro Hart's paintings were filched on the night of Thursday, August 22, from Evan Mackley Fine Art

Gallery in Melbourne. It was just twenty-four hours before Hart's exhibition was planned to open. And, like the Cossington-Smith exhibition, none of those paintings was ever seen again.

Sky Blue and Joseph Brown

Joseph Brown (aka Josef Braun) was born in Poland in 1918 and migrated to Australia as a teenager in 1933. He wanted to be an artist but had to leave school to work to help support his struggling family. Working in the rag trade, he proved talented at designing dresses and running a business. So, collecting art became his life passion. And along with collecting art, Brown started to sell art. In 1967 he established his art gallery at 5 Collins Street, later moving it to the front hall and three large front rooms of his house in South Yarra.

You can tell the history of art in Australia through Brown's collection: Colonial, Impressionist, Modernist, Indigenous and contemporary. And Daniel Thomas did precisely that in 1974 with his book, *Outlines of Australian Art – the Joseph Brown Collection.* Brown donated his collection to the NGV, and it is now on permanent exhibition, free to the public, at the Ian Potter Centre. A history of Australian art in over 150 paintings, many of which could have disappeared forever in one burglary, very early on January 1,1979.

People were still celebrating the New Year when a stolen VW Kombi van quietly parked on Caroline Street in South Yarra outside Brown's home and art gallery. The Victorian mansion with its ornate façade, one of many on the tree-lined residential street, was unoccupied that night; Brown and his wife were on holiday at their Mornington beach house.

Wires were cut in the switch box to disconnect the mansion's alarm system. An attempt was made to jemmy the french window to the left of the front door. It broke the glass, but the sound went unnoticed amidst the continuing New Year's revelry. Then the window to the right of the door was prised open.

Inside, the burglars removed paintings and works on paper from their frames; larger paintings were moved aside to access smaller works. Ninety-two paintings and drawings, along with Brown's OBE insignia, were loaded into the Kombi.

The haul included works by colonial painters; John Glover, Eugene von Guerard and Robert Dowling. Paintings from the Heidelberg School, including Tom Roberts's *Moorish Doorway*, one of only two known paintings Roberts did on a tour of Spain in 1883; twenty-four Sidney Nolan paintings from that crucial period between 1945 and 1953 before he became famous. And William Dobell's *Study for The Cypriot*, which Brown believed, was more important than the finished painting in the Queensland State Gallery. At the time, the estimated value of the ninety-two stolen paintings was over half a million dollars.

On January 2, one of Brown's daughters came to water the garden, saw the broken window and called the police.

Apart from the broken glass, nothing in the house was damaged. This was a professional heist by experienced criminals who left no fingerprints and few clues. The theft of Brown's OBE insignia showed this was not an opportunistic crime where some burglars stumble across a valuable art collection. They knew what they were doing and who they were doing it to. Brown's assessment of the thieves was, "They were very selective and knew the works unquestionably well." Being professional criminals, the thieves had done their homework and read Thomas's book.

Did the thieves intend to sell the art? The police were ill-equipped to deal with that quantity of stolen art. State treasury made a special grant of $6000 ($27,400 today) to print colour images of the missing art to distribute to city and country police stations, customs offices and Interpol. Ten days after the burglary was reported, the break-in squad had no leads. They didn't even know how many people were involved.

Operation Boney involved fifty detectives from Melbourne, Canberra, Sydney, Yass and Queanbeyan. It was formed after two weeks of undercover work by nine members of the Victoria Police. They were convinced that the stolen paintings had been moved interstate. Around six in the morning of Friday, February 2, 1979, police sledgehammers broke down seven doors in Canberra and Sydney. They only found a copy of Thomas's book on the Joseph Brown collection.

A couple of months later, on Thursday, April 5, it looked like the police were again closing in because a ransom demand had been made. This was not the first or last time art would be held for ransom in Victoria, but it was for something more than money. This time it was political. The woman on the phone threatened to destroy the paintings unless a new inquiry into unlawful physical violence, torture and abuse of prisoners by guards at Pentridge Prison was conducted.

Six years earlier, the 1973 Jenkinson Inquiry into the routine bashings in Pentridge Prison's H Division found that prisoners had been brutally treated. Regardless of the inquiry's findings, the bashings continued; no prison officers were convicted, and some were even promoted. "Ban the Bash" was being painted on walls around Melbourne. It appeared on an overpass on the South-Eastern Arterial, on the walls of Pentridge, and even on Parliament House's steps. (After that, two police guarded the steps twenty-four hours a day.)

The ransom demands gave the desperate detectives some new leads or at least the proof that they were talking to the right person. Detectives recovered a crate in a storage depot in Highbury Road, Burwood. Inside were sixteen paintings by Arthur Boyd, John Coburn, Robert Dickerson, Robert Dowling, Russel Drysdale, John Glover, Eugene von Guerard, Jeffrey Makin, Sidney Nolan and John Perceval. Some were in poor condition. Canvases had been removed from stretcher frames, cracking the paint, and others showed signs of damage from transportation. Russell Drysdale's *Tree Forms*, 1945, was torn when the canvas was removed from its stretcher.

The next day detectives raided an isolated farmhouse on Woodend Road, in Romsey, near Hanging Rock in Central Victoria. When they arrived, there was a bonfire out the back of the house. Several picture frames from the Joseph Brown collection were nearby. Was the fire part of the threat, or was it just a way of disposing of evidence?

The man at the house had good reason to be burning evidence, but he hadn't burnt it all. The detectives found a substantial quantity of Buddha sticks (compressed marijuana from Thailand), a shotgun, a rifle modified for fully automatic fire, ammunition and stolen jewellery. However, he had a strong alibi for the burglary at Brown's house and couldn't tell the police anything. He was, in his way, another victim of the artnappers.

Forensic scientists started shifting through the ashes at the back of a farmhouse, trying to determine what had been burnt. Unlike the police, Brown didn't believe that the paintings had been burnt, perhaps because he had not been told about the ransom demands. "There have been so many theories put forth about the paintings. I don't take them seriously..." Brown told reporters.

Months went by. Detectives continued to raid houses in Melbourne's eastern and northern suburbs to no avail. The stress of the burglary hit Joseph Brown hard, and he suffered a heart attack.

On September 7, Stephen Donald Sellers (aka Steven Jorgic) and his girlfriend and fellow acidhead, Sky Blue (aka Doreen Mildred Jacques), were in Sydney. They were enjoying a Friday night in the iconic beachside suburb of Bondi until they were arrested driving a stolen car.

Sellers was a professional criminal with a formidable record: a standover man, safe-breaker, bank robber and drug dealer. He was first convicted in 1957, aged twelve, and had worked with other hardened criminals, including Russell "Mad Dog" Cox, Ronald "Jockey" Smith and Christopher "Mr Rent-a-Kill" Flannery. But, Sellers was different from his criminal associates in one respect, the drugs he used – psychedelics, marijuana and LSD rather than cocaine and amphetamines.

In 1968 he became an inmate of Pentridge's H Division. Sellers refused to participate in H Division's strict regime; he would not march or break rocks. Sure he screamed when the guards bashed him, but he kept on screaming, shouting and, most dangerously, talking, refusing to participate in the culture of silence. Changing the culture of criminals of not informing on prison and police brutality.

This attitude was reinforced in 1974 when Sellers was hanging out with the notorious painter and docker, Laurence Joseph Prendergast, in a South Yarra flat of John Killick. According to the police, Killick, Prendergast and Sellers planned to rob the Mont Albert Branch of the State Savings Bank. Eleven members of the armed robbery squad arrived at the flat, and in the ensuing struggle, Sellers was pushed through a window falling nine metres face-first onto concrete. While Sellers was lying severely injured on the pavement, he was handcuffed, and a policeman pointed a gun at his head for some minutes. Sellers spent thirteen and a half weeks in the Alfred Hospital recovering from his injuries. He was not charged with anything from the police raid, but he still spent nine months in Pentridge for breaching his parole. In 1976 the Beach Inquiry into police corruption concluded that seven senior police conspired to give false evidence about Seller's arrest.

Out of prison in 1978, Sellers was doing everything he could to end the inhumane treatment of prisoners in Australian jails, even attempting to free inmates of Long Bay's punishment section – the electronic zoo of supermax block Katingal – by armed force. Sellers' views were in line with the 1978 Nagle Royal Commission that called for the immediate closure of Katingal; they only disagreed being on how to do it.

When he was arrested in Bondi, Sellers had a loaded pistol and the address of a warehouse in Essendon on him. Police recovered the remaining eighty of Brown's paintings in two locked metal cabin trunks in the Essendon warehouse.

Sky Blue was found guilty of receiving the Burwood warehouse paintings, the Kombi van, and police uniforms stolen from the Fairfield police station. Sellers was convicted of a far longer list of offences, including the theft of paintings from Brown.

Celebrating his paintings' return, Brown felt that he should do some act of charity for his good fortune. He donated some of the recovered art to the University of Melbourne and sold others, after all, he was running a commercial art gallery. Sidney Nolan's *Desert Storm* c.1955, one of the paintings recovered from the Burwood warehouse, ended up in the Tate collection in London.

Coincidentally, this was not Joseph Brown's only experience with art theft. In 1984 he discovered two stolen Lloyd Rees paintings from the Manly Art Gallery (aka Manly Art Gallery and Museum, MAGAM). It was eight years after thieves had forced the front door of the oldest purpose-built municipal art gallery in New South Wales. Their loot comprised works by some of Australia's most famous artists: Tom Roberts's oil painting, *A Flower Seller*, Norman Lindsay's watercolour *Swans and Peacocks*, William Dobell's drawing *Portrait of Billy Frost*, Arthur Streeton's oil painting *Nude*, and two Lloyd Rees oil paintings, *An Old Barn, Parramatta* and *Grecian Memories*.

Brown discovered he was trying to sell the two stolen Rees paintings. He returned them to the Manly Art Gallery. The vendor who supplied them to Brown also had Streeton's *Nude*. He had offered it to Brown, but Brown hadn't been interested.

The back of a painting can reveal a lot; artists write their name, art dealers add catalogue numbers, and collectors accession numbers. And if Brown or the vendor had turned Streeton's *Nude* over and looked at the back, he would have seen the label stuck on the frame: 'Presented to Manly Art Gallery'.

In the early morning on Tuesday, April 26, 1988, Sky Blue was driving a brown Ford Meteor with NSW licence plates on the Princes Highway near Orbost. Steven Sellers and another man, Hayden Smith, were passengers. Sellers was out on bail for selling 3.3 kilos of hashish and had $1500 in his pocket. Sky swerved to avoid an oncoming semitrailer and collided with a gum tree at Cabbage Tree Creek. Sellers was killed instantly. Sky Blue and Smith were injured and were taken to Sale Hospital; Sky Blue did not recover.

Whose law? Whose culture?

The facts were not in dispute. In 1979 the plate-glass door of Hogarth Gallery was smashed with a brick by two men who loaded six bark paintings into the back of their car.

Hogarth Gallery was Sydney's first commercial art gallery specialising in Indigenous art. The two young men taking the paintings were Cecil Patten, a field officer with the Aboriginal Legal Service in Redfern, Sydney, and William Craigie, a coordinator for the Black Unity Centre.

Patten and Craigie contended that the paintings belonged to "the Aboriginal tribal people and could not be sold under white man's law." The bark paintings were by Yirawala MBE (aka Billy/David Yirawala), a Gunwinggu (aka Kuninjku) religious leader born around 1897 in the Marrkolidjban region on the Liverpool River in the Northern Territory. Yirawala was happy for his paintings to be exhibited because he wanted them to understand the depth of his culture and connection to country. He wasn't pleased with art dealers exploiting his culture, breaking up story cycles, and making huge profits selling them as individual paintings.

In court, Judge Bell was there to deliver NSW law. "The only matter that was really in issue was what is called a claim of right," Bell explained. If the two accused honestly believed they had a right to take the paintings, then they could not form an intent to steal them. Therefore, to return a guilty verdict, the jury had to be convinced beyond a reasonable doubt that the two men did not believe they had a right to take them.

"After 200 years, you have given black people in this country hope," Cecil Patten said from the dock as he thanked the jury for finding him not guilty. Patten wasn't just some random activist; it was a family tradition. His father was Jack Thomas Patten, who founded the Aborigines Progressive Association in 1937 and led the Cummeragunja walk-off in 1939. Cecil Patten became the executive officer of the Aboriginal Legal Service in Sydney.

Patton and Craigie were on the right track. Their dramatic protest highlighted a continuing pattern of injustice around the appropriation of Indigenous cultural artefacts and sites.

Consider another example. Around or before 1000 BCE, the original inhabitants of Tasmania, the Palawa people, carved large circles on a large rock at Sundown Point on Tasmania's north-west coast.

Sometime between October 11 and 15, 1998, a large section of the carved surface was sawn away from the rock. A worker on the Bass Strait ferry claims to have seen a slab of rock in the back seat of a car going to the mainland. It has not been seen since. The petroglyph is listed on Interpol's stolen art database, and Australian Federal Police collected crime scene samples. However, this doesn't mean that it is stolen.

In Tasmania, taking an ancient petroglyph would not result in a criminal prosecution. Only a fine, a very high fine, $1.63 million for an organisation and $815,000 for an individual, but it is not a crime – no time is served, and no conviction is recorded.

Whose laws are protecting whose culture? Tasmanian law does not place a high value on protecting Indigenous culture. Indigenous artefacts are illegally plundered, and Indigenous heritage needs better protection from exploitation and destruction. Removing artefacts from their cultural and archeological context destroys their meaning. And the racist structures behind Australian laws often fail to protect Indigenous people and culture.

The destruction of Indigenous culture in Australia is not treated as a crime, and Indigenous culture, like the petroglyphs on the Burrup Peninsula (aka Murujuga), are being destroyed on an industrial scale. Even the most egregious incidents, like the damage to the Kuyang stones at Lake Bolac or the destruction of Juukan Gorge, only receive official reprimands or a fine.

Loti's Renoir

"Loti, I promise that one day I will buy you a Renoir," Victor Smorgon told his bride when they were married at the East Melbourne Synagogue in 1937. It was an impossible romantic promise from an immigrant kid. When the famous French Impressionist Auguste Renoir died in 1919, he was already regarded as among the top artists of all time. And Victor was twenty-four and working in the family's kosher butcher shop in Carlton North with his father and uncles.

It took Victor forty-one years to keep his promise to Loti. In that time, the Smorgon family business had expanded from meat to packaging, plastics, glass, steel, electronics, recycling, forestry and property. Smorgon Consolidated Industries became the largest family business in Australia. When the company was broken up in 1995, it was valued at $1.5 billion. So in 1978, Victor could afford to pay $218,509 (equivalent to just over $1 million today) for a small Renoir oil painting, *Coco with fan*.

Coco with fan was painted around 1906 when Auguste Renoir was in his sixties. In his later life, Renoir was no longer painted elegantly dressed French women strolling in parks bathed in dappled light. He painted more personal subjects close to home. He had married a young dressmaker, one of his models, and they had three young sons. *Coco with fan* is a sweet painting, but the title should be *Coco's nurse with fan*. The dark-haired woman wearing a shawl and holding a Japanese fan depicted is the children's nurse, Gabrielle Renard, and not Renoir's son. Although Renoir often painted his young son, 'Coco' (Claude), dressed in a smock and with a ribbon in his blond hair, at the time it was the custom to dress young children of both sexes in this fashion. Gabrielle also appears in many of Renoir's paintings and is clearly recognisable in this one.

For two years, the painting hung in Victor and Loti's Toorak mansion along with the rest of their art collection. In 1980 when the couple returned from a six-month holiday, they discovered that Loti's Renoir was gone. There were no signs of a break-in, and Victor suspected one of his four adult daughters and her boyfriend's drug debts were involved.

Coco with fan was now in the hands of professional criminals. They knew Smorgon would want it back, so their first plan was to ask for a ransom. In September 1981, Victor received a phone call from a Kew art dealer, Arnold Philips, who acted as a go-between. According to Philips, the Renoir could be returned for $50,000. Victor was tempted by the offer because of its sentimental value. However, after consulting his insurers and the police, he decided against it. Philips was charged with handling stolen goods.

After that, nothing was heard about *Coco with fan* for five years. Then, on Sunday, 15 February 1985, Dutch police raided a small hotel near Amsterdam airport. They were following a tip-off from the Victorian Bureau of Criminal Intelligence about the painting. At the hotel, the Dutch police found Loti's Renoir *Coco with fan* and arrested five men. One of the men was Jan Stegehuis, a 50-year-old Melbourne resident from Ferntree Gully who had flown into Holland that Friday. Stegehuis was convicted of receiving stolen goods and sentenced to three months in jail.

Victor paid back the money to the insurance company and returned his promised Renoir to Loti.

The Picasso Ransom

On Tuesday October 18, 1938, in the loft of 7 Rue Grands-Augustins in the district of Saint Germain des Prés of central Paris, the 57-year-old Pablo Picasso added the finishing touches to another painting. It was a small 55×46 centimetre oil on canvas depicting the face of his 31-year-old lover Dora Maar. In a typical Cubist strategy, free from the tradition of single-point perspective, her face is shown in both profile and front on. Her nose points to the side while both her tear-filled eyes are visible. It was a postscript, part of a series of paintings and drawings based on the sobbing woman in the window from his masterpiece *Guernica*. Painted the previous year, *Guernica* was a protest against the aerial bombing of civilians in the Spanish town of Guernica by fascist forces in April 1937. The smaller painting, *Femme au mouchoir* (*Woman with handkerchief*), would become widely known as *The weeping woman* when it was hijacked in Australia's most famous art theft.

Melbourne first saw her green face in 1984 at the touring blockbuster 'Picasso' exhibition at the National Gallery of Victoria (NGV). The painting was on loan from a private New York collector interested in selling it. The NGV wanted a Picasso for its collection. For the NGV, *Femme au mouchoir* was more than a single painting; it was a symbolic connection to European modernism. Having a Picasso was seen as essential for telling the story of modern art. There was also an interstate rivalry to consider, as New South Wales and Queensland already had their own Picassos; the Art Gallery of NSW had Picasso's *Nude in an armchair*, and the Queensland Art Gallery had *La belle Hollandaise*.

In 1985, the NGV purchased *Femme au mouchoir* for $1.6 million. Currency fluctuations at the time made the actual price around $2 million; adjusted for inflation, that would be about $3.9 million today. At the time, it was Australia's most expensive work of art, more expensive than the $1.3 million the NGA paid for Jackson Pollock's *Blue poles* in 1974, although adjusted for inflation, *Blue poles* might have been more.

At only 44 years of age, the director of the NGV, Patrick McCaughey, was young for a director of a state gallery. He was only 23 when he became the art critic of *The Age*. Around that same time, he started to wear bow ties, an affectation he continues. McCaughey was a prodigy with a privileged background; his father, Dr Davis McCaughey, would later be appointed Governor of Victoria.

On December 6, 1985, Patrick McCaughey, wearing his trademark bow tie, proudly announced the gallery's latest acquisition. "This face is going to haunt Melbourne for the next hundred years. Everyone will come to know it very well indeed, I hope."

If McCaughey had known how people would get to know that face, he might have chosen different words. *Femme au mouchoir* was not a popular purchase with everyone. Some of Melbourne's public hated modern art, like the writer of this letter to the editor in *The Age* written December 26, 1985:

> *Picasso's paintings are nothing else but a deliberate and pathetic perversion of art and human values in general. They can appeal only to the decadent and degenerate, too many of whom, alas, have elevated themselves by some mysterious process to the position of influential art critics and omnipotent gallery directors.*

The ignorant among us far too often take their decrees as if they were infallible experts.

Picasso's monstrous 'works', at best, have a value as rare curios. Their collection should be left entirely to the rich eccentrics. Not a single cent of the people's money should be squandered on them.

Instead, our tax-funded galleries should concentrate on the acquiring of the best Australian paintings of the past and present. They should also display some vision and search for new talents, and buy their better works now, rather than waiting when they will become very costly and hard to get.

What a fine collection of Australian paintings could have been established for $1.6 million.

G. Korinfsky
South Kyneton

The following is a timeline of events around the theft.

Saturday 2 August 1986

From the outside the NGV is a rectangular, smooth, grey, bluestone bunker, almost windowless except for its famous archway water-wall entrance. It looks impregnable, surrounded by a moat, but the thief inside the gallery did not have to break in.

The thief could have come in through the public entrance or Sturt Street's carpark and service entrance. Fine arts students or staff at the Victorian College of the Arts had access to the Gallery as their studios were connected to the NGV at the time.

There are staff at the entrances, but there were no video cameras to record any of it. Did the thief have a face the security at the staff entrance recognised, even if they weren't on the permanent staff or weren't rostered on?

After-hours security consisted of two attendants with torches walking around every hour. Had the attendants at the NGV checked that all the cubicles in the toilets were empty before it closed at five o'clock? Had they checked cupboards and other spaces?

Was this a copy of the famous theft of the *Mona Lisa* by Vincenzo Perugia in 1911? Perugia, an Italian petty criminal who worked at the Louvre, had hidden in the gallery overnight. He removed the Mona Lisa from its frame and smuggled it out the next day under his large white smock, the uniform of the gallery's staff. He wasn't arrested until November 1913, when he tried to exchange the painting with an Italian art dealer in Florence for a half-million lire reward. Perugia's crime was a mixture of greed, misguided Italian nationalism and an ignorance of art history. He thought that *Napoleon had looted Mona Lisa from Italy*, when Leonardo had willed it to his patron, the King of France.

As with Wistrand in colonial Adelaide, Perugia was not the only art thief to hide out in an art gallery after closing to steal a painting. In 1971 Mario Roymans hid in the Belgium Fine Arts Palace to steal Vermeer's *The Love Letter*. Roymans didn't want it for himself; he attempted to ransom it to aid Bengali refugees of East Pakistan. He was arrested, and the Vermeer recovered a month later.

The thief inside the NGV was both prepared and experienced in gallery procedure. There were no lights on at night, so, like the gallery attendants, the thief carried a small battery-powered torch. Most importantly, the thief had what experienced art handlers have – cotton gloves and a screwdriver with a head that matched the screws holding the painting on the wall. The screwdriver suggests an inside job; someone with behind-the-scenes access to the Gallery; someone who had done this before, such as a casual worker installing a temporary exhibition. There were no alarms on any paintings, not even for the Gallery's most recent acquisition.

The thief then removed the painting from its wooden frame. They did this quickly but with care. Tabs on the back of the frame hold a masonite backing board with a plastic envelope of papers. Beneath the masonite were the wooden stretcher bars and the back of the canvas. The painting and the backing board were most likely either placed in a large bag or slipped inside a long winter overcoat's lining.

The thief then took a typewritten gallery 'registrar's card', which had been prepared earlier, and placed it on the wall where the painting had been. This card, like the screwdriver, indicates that the thief had access to gallery materials and was aware of NGV procedures. Typed on the card were the words: 'Gone to the A.C.T'.

On the way out of the room, the thief placed the frame on top of a display cabinet about 30 metres from the wall where it had hung for less than a year.

Sunday 3 August 1986

At the NGV, nobody noticed that their new Picasso wasn't there. Staff assumed from the fake registrar's card that the painting had been moved to the ACT, meaning the Australian Capital Territory, Canberra.

Meanwhile, in the outer, eastern suburb of Blackburn, a member of the Australian Cultural Terrorists (A.C.T.) posted typewritten letters in hand-addressed envelopes marked 'news tip' to several newspapers with their ransom demand. The letters read:

> *Attention: Rank Mathews (MLA)*
>
> *We have stolen the Picasso from the National Gallery as a protest against the niggardly funding of the fine arts in this hick State and against the clumsy, unimaginative stupidity of the administration and distribution of that funding.*
>
> *Two conditions must be publicly agreed upon if the painting is to be returned.*

1. The Minister must announce a commitment to increasing the funding of the arts by 10% in real terms over the next three years, and must agree to appoint an independent committee to enquire into the mechanics of the funding of the arts with a view to releasing money from its administration and making it available to artists.

2. The Minister must announce a new annual prize for painting open to artists under thirty years of age. Five prizes of $5000 are to be awarded. A fund is to be established to ensure that the real value of the prizes is maintained each year. The prize is to be called The Picasso Ransom.

Because the Minister of the Arts is also Minster of Plod, we are allowing him a sporting seven days in which to try to have us arrested while he deliberates. There will be no negotiations. At the end of the seven days if our demands have not been met the painting will be destroyed and our campaign continues.

Your very humble servants,

Australian Cultural Terrorists

The 'Rank Mathews (MLA)' to whom the letter was addressed was the Minister for Police and Emergency Services and Minister for the Arts – Race Mathews (aka Charles Race Thorson Mathews). Although Race Mathews had a career as a primary school teacher and speech therapist, the tall, silver-haired 51-year-old's main interest in life was the Labor Party. He had joined when he was 21 and served as chief of staff to state Labor leaders and Prime Minister Gough Whitlam before going into state politics as the member for Oakleigh. When the Labor Party, led by John Cain, was elected in 1982, Mathews expected to become Minister for Economic Development. Instead, he was appointed Minister for Police and Emergency Services and Minister for the Arts. With no genuine interest in the arts, Mathews found himself in the middle of Melbourne's art scene. I remember his speech at the opening of St Martins Youth Theatre's

1983 season. Talking about boosting police numbers to the crowd of young actors, directors and playwrights made Mathews look as concerned for the arts as the vice squad.

Monday 4 August

The NGV was closed to the public on Mondays, but work continued behind the scenes. The NGV's head of security became aware of the theft only when reporters inquired about the A.C.T.'s 'news tip'. He had a look for himself and then told the NGV's director Patrick McCaughey.

McCaughey and the head of security went to the European Gallery where the painting should have been. They looked at the registrar's card; 'Gone to the A.C.T.' meant nothing to either of them. The Gallery's conservation department was called in case they had the painting. A search was made of the NGV. After about half an hour, the empty frame was found.

At first, McCaughey thought the reports must be a hoax. It was only after finding the empty frame that the full alarm was raised, the police called, and the Minister for the Police and the Arts informed.

McCaughey held a news conference at half-past four in the afternoon in front of the NGV's waterwall. Inside, police and staff were still searching for the painting.

McCaughey told artnappers through the assembled reporters: "If the picture is damaged or ruined in any way, then this Gallery will never be able to afford another Picasso painting."

Why not? Wasn't the painting insured?

No, none of the art at the NGV was insured.

"We live in a philistine nation but a civilised city," pleaded Mc-Caughey, distinguishing cosmopolitan and progressive Melbourne from the rest of Australia. He was genuinely worried that the Picasso painting was in the hands of people intent on harming it.

Race Mathews ordered an immediate review of the NGV's security and declared that the state government would refuse to meet the terrorist's ransom demands. "Budgeting by blackmail is just not on," Mathews announced. Economically the A.C.T.'s demands made little sense. If they were followed, the cost of paying the ransom on the $1.6 million Picasso would be between $12 and $35 million, depending on how the demands were interpreted.

Tuesday 5 August

The A.C.T.'s 232-word letter, minus a dozen words 'to enable police to identify hoaxers and assist in their dealing with possible offenders', was published on the front page of *The Age*. It was the paper's lead story, occupying four columns on the front page, along with Ron Tandberg's cartoon of a man with an axe about to strike the painting while another man holds him back, saying: "Don't you think she's suffered enough?"

It was a slow news day. The other stories were about British Prime Minister Margret Thatcher offering token sanctions against the apartheid regime in South Africa and Prime Minister Bob Hawke conceding that federal factors caused the swing against Labor in a NSW by-election.

That day the NGV remained closed. Mathews believed the painting must still be in the Gallery, and thirty police cadets searched the building. The moat at the front of the NGV was drained to see if any of the tacks holding the canvas to the wooden stretcher bars could be found, but they only found small change. To aid their search, the NGV's Conservation Department created a mock-up of the painting so that the cadets knew what they were looking for.

So as not to draw attention to the missing Picasso, gallery staff hung a recent abstract oil painting by local artist John Walker, *Carlton infanta II*. It was the opposite approach to how the Gardner Museum in Boston handled the theft of multiple works in 1990 when they left the empty frames hanging on the wall as a reminder to keep it in visitors' minds.

The first new security measure to be introduced by McCaughey was to remove the gallery attendant's chairs. As McCaughey so eloquently and less diplomatically described it, this meant the gallery attendants could not "Repose in a lethargic stupor". Those were fighting words, and the blue jackets of the gallery attendants were off. At noon the eighty gallery attendants went on strike. Their union, the Victorian Public Service Association, claimed that the chairs were a health issue, not a security issue. The gallery attendants suggested elevated chairs.

Other security improvements included leaving the Gallery lights on at night and more rigorous checking bags at the public entrance. The "Thursday service", a sort-of *Antiques Roadshow* affair where the public could bring in art to have it identified, was suspended due to worries that people might take the opportunity to walk out with some of its art.

Thursday 7 August
Several substitute paintings were offered to the NGV in case *The weeping woman* was not recovered. Kew art dealer and pharmacist Brian Pearce offered a replacement Picasso, *Woman in a Riding Costume*. The notable Melbourne-based artist Juan Davila offered his copy of *The weeping woman*, titled *Picasso theft*. Davila was one of the few people who urged McCaughey to respond to the A.C.T.'s letter and address the problems faced by young artists in Australia. That night, Davila's *Picasso theft* was pinched from The Tin Sheds Gallery at the University of Sydney. The thieves left a note: 'We have no demands but wish to be acknowledged as artists. We ask the question "Where does art end?" Theft for art's sake. Artists Confronting Terrorism.'

Friday 8 August

A compromise was found in the dispute with the gallery attendants, allowing the NGV to reopen. The attendants were to patrol actively, and management returned fifteen chairs to them. All new security measures were to be reviewed by a working party with equal representation from gallery management and the Victorian Public Service Association.

In a gesture towards meeting one of the A.C.T.'s demands, the NGV announced two $5000 art prizes for artists under 30, to be sponsored by the printing and engineering company McPherson's Ltd. It was three short of the number of prizes and without the demanded title 'Picasso Ransom'. Would the A.C.T. accept the compromise?

Saturday 9 August

With the A.C.T.'s deadline approaching, Melbourne's art world was nervous. So it is not surprising this was the start of a strange sidetrack in this story.

In the evening, the director of a prominent commercial art gallery, Anna Schwartz, and artist Mark Howson were at a dinner party. Like people that night at dinner parties all over Melbourne, Howson was talking about *The weeping woman*. Mark Howson studied at the VCA and exhibited work at the NGV when he was only 21. He was one of the founding members of Melbourne's first artist-run gallery, Roar Studios, in Fitzroy. In 1982 the NGV bought a large oil painting by Howson (Howson's art is now also in the collections of the NGA, Geelong Art Gallery, Ballarat Art Gallery, Monash University and Parliament House). Given this early success, Howson was an unlikely artist to dislike how the NGV treated younger artists. Still, something he said aroused Anna's suspicion. Later that night, she phoned McCaughey to tell him about her feelings about Howson.

Sunday 10 August

The A.C.T. posted letters to media outlets and one to the electorate office of Race Mathews.

McCaughey met the police to tell them about Anna Schwartz's suspicions. Suspicions alone were not enough for the police to follow, but they suggested that McCaughey try talking to Howson himself.

That wet Melbourne evening, McCaughey, along with gallery trustee and artist Jan Senbergs went to a terrace in North Fitzroy. They met someone, probably Howson's fellow Roar Studios artist and later wife, Karan Hayman, who gave them the address of Howson's studio in a building near the Victoria Market.

McCaughey remembers a few newspaper clippings about the missing Picasso on the wall of Howson's studio, but that wasn't odd or suspicious; at the time, there were the same newspaper clippings on my desk too. Still, McCaughey remains convinced that something about his visit was significant. "I said deliberately, at least twice, that the people who had taken the work could deposit it in a luggage locker at Spencer Street railway station or at Tullamarine airport." If McCaughey's remarks were significant, nobody can explain how, for now, not even McCaughey believes that Howson was involved. In the desperation to recover the Picasso, suspicions had overtaken reasons.

Monday 11 August

Did the A.C.T. even have the painting? They had produced no evidence, charred or otherwise, that they ever had it. Twenty-five police officers and NGV staff searched the gallery again, looking in air-conditioning vents, storerooms and cupboards. Unlike McCaughey, the police had not dismissed the idea that it was an inside job.

The media published the A.C.T.'s second letter:

Dear, oh dear, Race Mathews, you tiresome old bag of swamp gas ...

We have not dumped the painting in a blue-nosed funk. What should have caused us to panic? Perhaps you imagine that the news that Interpol has been alerted will cause us to cower in our ill-lit garrets awaiting the inevitable 3 am knock on the door as the relentless Clouseaux of a hundred nations tirelessly stalk us. What an imaginative fellow you turned out to be. Interpol! Call on Red Adair to read your gas meter, do you?

We hope you enjoy playing the political he-man, unflinchingly refusing the outrageous demands of these cultural crackpots. You continue flexing your political pectorals before an admiring electorate for as long as you can, Minister. Seven days after the painting came into our hands (Sat. 2nd Aug. 10 pm) if our demands have not been met you will begin the long process of carrying about you the smell of kerosene and burning canvas. You are gambling with the State's two million dollar investment in the Picasso industry against our twenty cent investment in Bryant & May. Mind you, we do find your Conan the Barbarian routine terribly diverting.

The people of Australia, and you as one of their elected representatives, should rejoice that a theft involving less risk than shoplifting cotton hankies from David Jones was performed by a group whose first desire is to return the painting. Not that we would really expect a sensible reaction from someone so determined to have others shoulder the blame. The responsibility is entirely yours. Good luck with your huffing and puffing, Minister, you pompous fathead. We remain

Your very humble servants,

Australian Cultural Terrorists

The A.C.T. included a new security device, a number that was not released to the public.

Judging by the number of amusing popular cultural references and its mocking tone, the A.C.T were enjoying themselves. But the insults raise the question: was the real target Mathews rather than arts funding? Why did the A.C.T. feel particularly aggrieved towards him? But if you want someone to blame, then why not Race Mathews?

The copy of the letter to Mathews contained a burnt match and a note: 'Thank you for your support. Phase two begins shortly. Australian Cultural Terrorists'.

Mathews panicked, wondering what 'phase two' could mean. He imagined that the A.C.T. might steal more paintings from regional art galleries in Victoria and told them to tighten security. He was also realistic, predicting that: "The most likely outcome was that when the last possible drop of publicity has been wrung from the situation, somebody will get in touch with the gallery, the police or myself and indicate how the painting can be retrieved."

Tuesday 12 August

Police released photofits of three of the five people they thought might be connected to the theft. It was all based on the theory of criminals returning to the scene of the crime. Some people were seen acting suspiciously at the NGV the day after; four men and one woman, all about 30-something and all about average height.

Not everyone in Australia disapproved of the A.C.T.'s threat to destroy the painting. The Catholic, anti-Communist B. A. Santamaria wrote in his regular newspaper column in *The Australian*: 'If the Australian Cultural Terrorists have really disposed of *Weeping Woman*, they should not so much invite censure as be rewarded with the Order of Australia.'

Thursday 14 August

The ANZ bank announced a $200,000 bicentennial art scheme divided between the eight state and territory galleries. This was the second art prize to be announced since the ransom demands. Even though it was not connected to the ransom demands, many hoped that the A.C.T. would see it as a partial completion and return the painting.

Tuesday 19 August

A ten-cent coin was all you needed to use a locker in the Spencer Street Station underpass for the day. That day a member of the A.C.T. went to the station with a parcel wrapped in brown paper neatly tied up with string and deposited the package in one of the luggage lockers.

At eight o'clock in the evening, as the Federal Treasurer Paul Keating started to deliver his budget speech in Parliament, a man phoned *The Age*. The man said he spoke on behalf of the A.C.T. and quoted the number from the second letter.

"The painting is returned. Go and look in luggage locker number 227 at Spencer Street Station."

"Who are you?"

"The Australian Cultural Terrorists, you remember us? Ta-ta."

The message was relayed to the police, and journalist Margaret Symonds and photographer Rob Leeson were sent to the station.

At Spencer Street Station subway, Symonds tried the locker herself. It was locked; she would have to wait. Patrick McCaughey and three detectives from the Major Crime Squad arrived next, followed by more reporters. Finally, the NGV's chief conservator Thomas Dixon arrived. A small crowd of commuters gathered to observe. A woman recognised McCaughey by his bow tie and called out, "Have you found it yet?"

"Oh, I hope so."

Around nine-thirty that night, forensic scientist Neil Holland dusted the outside of the locker for fingerprints. However, the locker was too greasy to provide any clear results. The assistant station master opened the locker. Rob Leeson photographed Patrick McCaughey looking inside, and then Holland removed the package.

The package was transported in the back seat of a police car to the police forensic laboratory in Spring Street. Holland unwrapped it as McCaughey and Dixon looked on. Inside was another note from the A.C.T. and a painting that looked like the missing Picasso. It was examined for fingerprints, but nothing useful was found.

The painting was undamaged, but was it the real thing or an ingenious fake substitute? After a careful examination, Dixon declared that it was Picasso's *Femme au mouchoir*.

The painting's masonite backing board with the clear polyester plastic wallet attached to it was still missing. The plastic wallet contained labels from the painting's exhibition history and other documentary evidence to support its provenance. 'We have a photocopy of these labels should they be recovered to prove they came from this picture...presumably, these are still with the thieves.' Dixon wrote in his notes.

Wednesday 20 August

So many people at Spencer Street Station wanted to know where *The weeping woman* was found that station staff made a sign for the locker: 'The Picasso was found here.' Unfortunately, the sign had been swiped by half-past four that afternoon. The staff were still being asked the same question.

Copies of the typewritten note found with the painting arrived in the post to the media. 'Of course we never looked to have our demands met... Our intention was always to bring to public attention the plight of a group which lacks any of the legitimate means of blackmailing governments.'

The painting was returned by Mathews to the NGV in a champagne-fuelled media event. Two security guards flanked *The weeping woman*, which sat enthroned on an easel. Mathews proclaimed that the government was offering $50,000 for information leading to the thieves' arrest and conviction.

McCaughey was very complimentary about how the painting had been packed and handled by the A.C.T., and announced it would be rehung by Saturday. "We want to take extra precautions, bolting it to the wall so that next time they will have to take the wall."

Friday 22 August

It was reported that police believed two women were involved. Two women were seen near the lockers at Spencer Street Station at ten o'clock on Tuesday morning. One was carrying a parcel about the right size wrapped in brown paper. The two women were about 35-45 years old; both had light brown hair. One was about 162 centimetres tall, and the other was slightly shorter. With such vague descriptions, it could have been one of the women described as acting suspiciously with the four men in the gallery on the Sunday after the theft – and thousands of others.

Saturday 23 August

Picasso's *Femme au mouchoir* was once again on public display on the wall of the NGV's European Gallery. Meanwhile, crime squad detectives searched a commercial art studio in Abbotsford, where they seized things referred to as 'unspecified items'. Police told reporters there were likely to be more raids.

There were no more police raids. On Tuesday, August 26, the police admitted they had accomplished nothing and the 'unspecified items' seized were returned.

For two weeks, the A.C.T. dominated the news in Melbourne. Day by day, the story played itself out in the newspapers. Every wit and half-wit in Melbourne wanted to comment. In one newspaper advertisement, an empty frame contained the words 'Will a Stolen Picasso Surface at 239 Clarendon Street?'. By Saturday, the ad included: 'See Page 4 for a fantastic office leasing offer.'

After that, nobody seemed to be interested in finding the A.C.T. The police and McCaughey always had different objectives; McCaughey didn't want a prosecution, just the painting back. The police suspected that it had to have been an inside job, but McCaughey refused to consider that. By the end of the week, when the inquiry into the theft completed its report, he was "heartily sick" of the whole affair.

The state government budgeted $600,000 for security at the NGV over the next three years. Cameras and movement detectors were installed. The most important part of the security plan was to compile a central register of the gallery's collection for the first time since the nineteenth century; it would begin the following year and was expected to take two years to complete. By the end of the first year, it had already discovered that 86 oil paintings were missing from the Australian and European collections.

The following year both Race Mathews and Patrick McCaughey moved to new jobs. Mathews became Minister for Community Services, and McCaughey left Australia to become Director of the Wadsworth Atheneum in Hartford, Connecticut.

Was the A.C.T. a success or a failure? It's hard to imagine A.C.T. members looking back at their activities as failures because they didn't make any mistakes. It is also difficult to imagine what they thought they would achieve besides a successful art heist and a lot of publicity. Several people, including Edward Capon, long-time director of the Art Gallery of NSW, described them as immature. Maybe the ridicule of Race Mathews was juvenile, but the A.C.T.

was prepared to compromise on their demands, and the painting was returned in exactly the same condition it was in when it was removed. Their ransom letters sounded arrogant and confident, but after all these years, that arrogance and confidence seem appropriate.

In September 1986, there was another related unsolved art theft. Two plate windows were smashed to gain access to the Canberra Theatre Centre's Links Gallery. An exhibition by first-year students at the Canberra College of Advanced Education School of Environmental Design was on. The burglar only stole one thing, a painting titled *Mourning McCaughey*, a parody of the *Weeping Woman* with a bow tie, part of an installation by Virginia Aylmore and Stuart Bray.

Most people think that the Australian Cultural Terrorists were never heard of again. Some, including Detective Senior Sergeant John Bourke, doubted the group's existence from the start. However, a defamatory letter about a controversy involving the Australian Centre for Contemporary Art (ACCA) was circulating in Melbourne's art world in early 1990, signed by the A.C.T.

Someone comes up with a new theory about the Weeping Woman's abduction from time to time; most are no better than speculative fiction. The best new clue comes from Neil Holland, the former Victoria Police forensic scientist. He examined the ransom notes and the letters of an NGV employee involved in a love triangle. He established that they were done on the same typewriter using the same paper. However, that does not prove they were typed by the same person, and the identity of the Australian Cultural Terrorists remains a mystery.

Stolen art and the
damage done

Counter-intuitively, art is more often damaged in planned art thefts rather than opportunistic thefts. In 1986 there were two major art thefts; the most destructive was the robbery at New Norcia, but the one at Carrick Hills could have been almost as bad save for the bravery of an artist.

On Thursday, 23 January 1986, the summer sun was sucking all the moisture out of the air, roasting the West Australian Wheatbelt and creating mirages that pooled on the black roads. A bronze-coloured Ford Falcon drove into the small town of New Norcia. It was not a particularly memorable sight. There were lots of Ford Falcons on the road: it was Australia's number-one selling car at the time.

Inside the car were two men in their early thirties. They weren't locals; both were from Sydney's western suburbs. They had flown across the continent and made the two-hour drive from Perth to be there. Neither could afford to be tourists; Smith was unemployed, and Weaver was a bankrupt car salesman. They were looking for the New Norcia Benedictine Community Gallery.

Few local art galleries in Australia have a collection like New Norcia's because of the town's unique history. Founded in 1846 by

Spanish Benedictine monks, New Norcia is Australia's only monastic town. Its founder, Bishop Salvador, had acquired some minor works by Italian and Spanish old masters, sixteenth and seventeenth-century paintings by Titian, Murillo, Maratta and Bernini. And over the years, more art was acquired by the monks.

The Ford pulled up in front of the art gallery. Before they got out of the car, the two men checked that they had everything with them: knives, rope and sticking plaster. They looked at the street; no one was around, even though the gallery was across from the post office. The centre of the small town was completely deserted.

Now it was time for the crucial phase in the plan. It was too easy. Inside the gallery, the attendant was an old lady who had her back to them. She was grabbed from behind, bound, gagged, and sticking plaster placed over her eyes and mouth.

The two men took her upstairs to the toilets. Instinctively they went into the men's toilet. Then they thought about it for a moment, changed their minds and sat her down in the women's.

"We will come back for you."

Left alone, bound, thinking about that last remark and listening to the noises from downstairs, Connie McNaughton was terrified.

Downstairs, the art heist became an art wrecker's yard. Canvases were cut from frames and rolled up. Hacking through the canvases with knives, they left a rough twenty-five-centimetre border on one. Breaking frames to rip the canvases off the stretcher bars. They took twenty-six paintings but didn't know what they were taking. Leaving behind some of the more valuable works and taking some by local artists of little value. They also stole $340 ($911 today) from the gift shop.

From upstairs in the women's toilet, Connie McNaughton could hear the sound of canvas ripping and frames being thrown around. Then she listened to the Falcon start and drive off. They hadn't come back for her.

It took her over an hour to free her hands. She then removed the gag from her mouth and the sticking plaster from her eyelids. However, the knots on the rope around her ankles were too tight for her tired old fingers.

Connie hobbled down the stairs. In the gallery, she saw bits of moulding from the picture frames lying on the floor. Fortunately, the canvas by Titian (aka Tiziano Vecellio), that great Venetian Renaissance painter, remained hanging on the wall. Then she hobbled out the door and across the street to the post office for help.

With the Ford Falcon full of old masters, the two robbers drove back to Perth. They laid low at a motel near the airport, unloading their loot and rolling the canvases up in their luggage and returned the rented car before flying back to Sydney.

The robbers left a couple of clues for the major crime squad's forensic team to find in New Norcia. Outside the gallery, the Ford had left distinctive tyre prints. Inside, there was a fingerprint in the gift shop. A couple of days later, the police found the Ford Falcon with flakes of oil paint in the boot.

The fingerprint matched a 32-year-old man in New South Wales, Nigel George Weaver. A man with more than a few financial problems, a bankrupt with a gambling addiction, who had recently sold the family home to pay off debts. When the police caught up with him, he confessed to the robbery, named his accomplice and told them who had the paintings.

Weaver's information came just in time. Eight of the paintings were found at a city airline office, hours away from being sent to the Philippines. By Thursday, February 6, less than two weeks after the robbery, all but one of the paintings had been found.

A 38-year-old company director from western Sydney, Bruce William Cameron, would have considered himself the brains behind the muscle. He had visited New Norcia, taken photographs of the gallery, planned the heist, and recruited Smith and Weaver. From his time in the Philippines he knew there would be a market for the pious and sentimental paintings at New Norcia. He was jailed for a minimum of three years for receiving fifteen of the stolen art.

Weaver's accomplice in the robbery, Noel Smith, was jailed for a minimum of two and a half years. Weaver received the lightest sentence, a minimum of one year and four months.

The paintings had been badly damaged in the robbery. The heist had been fast, but the restoration was very slow. It took art restorer Melissa Guest more years to restore the art than the robbers served in jail.

Her first step was to get the paintings fully documented. Where had they come from? Who purchased them from whom? Next, they were carefully examined. This revealed that the thieves weren't the only ones to have damaged the paintings. There was a lot of amateur restoration work. Someone had added rosy cheeks, and on another occasion, fly specks had been washed off using soap, water and a scrubbing brush. The restorers worked down through the layers of dirt, varnish and previous restorations to the original varnish. Next, the damage was repaired, torn canvas patched, and missing paint filled in. After ten years, they were ready to be exhibited again.

Although the damage to their paintings was significant, New Norcia has done better than many other art theft victims. News of the robbery put it on the map and attracted tourists worldwide to the small WA town for its honey, olives and art gallery.

The other significant art theft in 1986 was another audacious plan to steal four valuable oil paintings by internationally famous artists. Three of the paintings were by the great Post-Impressionist painter and Van Gogh's drinking buddy, Paul Gauguin: *The Shepherdess* (1886), *Tahitian Woman* (1891), *and The Big Tree* (1891). The fourth was by Eugine Boudin, *Unloading Ships* (1875). While Paul Gauguin probably needs no further introduction, the nineteenth-century French Impressionist painter Eugine Boudin might be less familiar. He was amongst the first Impressionists to paint outdoors, *en plein air,* looking directly at the landscape – or the seascape in Boudin's case.

The location was easily scouted as it was open to the public. Queen Elizabeth had officially opened the thirty-nine acres of gardens and mansion of the Carrick Hill Estate earlier that year. It was the former home of South Australia's wealthiest art patrons, Ursula and Edward Hayward (aka "Bill"). They bequeathed their house, gardens and art collection to the state.

Set on the side of a hill is a mock-gothic sandstone mansion surrounded by an enormous hedge that looks down a terraced lawn towards Adelaide and, on the horizon, a shimmering band that is the ocean. The house was created around the salvaged fittings of a Tudor manor in Staffordshire. A grand oak staircase, windows, doors and wall panels were shipped to Australia in an attempt to recreate England in the Adelaide Hills. It was decorated with one of the best private art collections in Australia. British and French modern art by Paul Gauguin, Stanley Spencer and Auguste Renoir, mixed with works by Australian artists William Dobell, Russell Drysdale and Hans Heysen.

The Australian Formula One Grand Prix weekend was selected because police resources in Adelaide would be stretched. All the burglars had to do was break a window, go in, take the four paintings off the wall in that room, and leave before the police arrived. Paint over them with water-based paint, so they don't look like the stolen paintings. Smuggle them out of the country, remove the water-based paint and sell them or maybe they already had a buyer lined up.

Close to 4 am on Saturday, October 25, 1986, the burglar alarm went off at Carrick Hills. The paintings and the burglars were gone by the time the police arrived; everything was going to plan so far.

The thieves' plan was working perfectly until three days later. On Tuesday morning, October 28, the Liberal member of the South Australian House of Assembly seat of Hanson, Heinrich Thomas Becker (aka Heini Becker), received a phone call. The man on the end of the line claimed to have the Boudin. He wanted Becker to act as the go-between in returning all the paintings. The caller told him not to contact the police, or the thieves would know and destroy the art. He asked Becker to meet him and gave him the address of a flat in Adelaide.

Becker was scared that he was being 'set up'. He was also worried that it was a hoax. Before he left, he told his wife to call the police if he wasn't back in twenty minutes (only in Adelaide in the early eighties does that short time frame make any sense).

At the flat, he was met by a man who showed him a painting of an impressionist harbour scene and told him it was the Boudin. Becker thought that he had met the man before and that he was an artist. The man told Becker that the thieves wanted him to paint over the paintings so they could be smuggled out of the country. He contacted Becker because he didn't want any harm to come to the art. He didn't want a reward; he was an art lover.

In theory, it was possible that water-based paint over oils could be removed again with water, but in practice, it would likely damage the underlying painting. Gauguin's *The Big Tree*, a fan-shaped water-based gouache on traditional Tahitian tapa cloth, would have definitely been damaged.

The man wanted to speak to State Premier John Bannon. Becker didn't want to put his party's leader at risk and suggested a more realistic option. He would get the director of Carrick Hill, David Thomas, as he would be able to identify the painting.

Later that day, Becker and Thomas returned to the flat, where Thomas identified the painting as Boudin's *Unloading Ships*. Taking the initiative, Thomas asked the man if he could take the Boudin with him as a sign of good faith. The man agreed and even gave them a bed sheet to wrap the painting in.

Walking through the yard to his car, Becker couldn't believe what was going on. "Keep walking to the car," he told Thomas. Becker was worried that their fortunes might change again in an instant if they stopped or looked back as he left the underworld.

Thomas conducted further negotiations with the man, and it was all over within a week. On Saturday, 1 November, the South Australian police announced that all the paintings had been recovered in good condition and that no charges were laid. The thieves got away, but at least the art was recovered thanks to the courage of one anonymous artist. Authentication after recovery downgraded *Tahitian Woman* (1891) to the "School of Gauguin", meaning that it looks like a Gauguin, but it's not. All of the paintings are still hanging in Carrick Hill.

Australia's Most Wanted

"Good evening, welcome to Australia's Most Wanted; I'm Roger Climpson. Tonight..." Channel Seven's *Australia's Most Wanted* followed the same format as *America's Most Wanted*: graphic crime scene re-enactments interspersed with on-camera interviews. Its host, silver-haired newsreader Climpson, urged viewers to call a toll-free number with information. It led to one arrest per episode.

One time the arrest happened the day before the program was broadcast. That episode was about a robbery in the Melbourne suburb of Toorak on Wednesday afternoon, June 15, 1988, at the home of Sam Smorgon, cousin of Victor Smorgon.

Cue crime scene re-enactment: Sam Smorgon, a member of one of Australia's wealthiest families, leaves home with his family for an unplanned trip to the family's farm. They hadn't set the burglar alarm as Javorka Martin, their 58-year-old housekeeper, remained at the house.

Just before three o'clock that afternoon, Javorka was in the backyard. She saw she was not alone; three men and a woman were on the property. One of the men pulled out a gun. They took the terrified housekeeper into the kitchen, tied her to a chair and gagged her.

The robbers loaded paintings, jewellery, antiques, oriental china plates, vases and other items in Smorgon's yellow Jaguar and drove off in it. The value of the loot was estimated between $1.5 and $2 million. It included thirteen antique Japanese woodblock prints and twenty-four paintings, including works by the French Impressionist Camille Pissarro and notable Australian artists Charles Condor, John Perceval, Arthur Boyd, Ray Crook, Roy de Maistre and William Dobell.

Javorka managed to free herself two hours later and called the police. She could describe the robbers, including making an identikit image of one of them.

Two days later, Sam Smorgon's Jaguar was found abandoned and empty.

On May 29, 1989, Tom Silver, an art dealer from Bondi, bought the two Dobell paintings for $76,500 ($164,000 today). When Silver sat down to watch television a day or two later, the two Dobell's were fresh in his mind. During the ad break, a promo ran for the upcoming episode of *Australia's Most Wanted* about the Smorgon robbery, and there were the two Dobells he had just bought. Silver put a tape in his VCR, pressed record and waited for the next time the station ran the promo.

The square-faced man with a shock of grey hair who sold the two Dobell paintings to Silver had first introduced himself as 'Murray Newton' when he asked Tom Silver about Dobell's *Prima Donna*. It was worth $50,000 if the holes in the canvas could be repaired. Farquhar got that done and returned twelve days later with four more paintings for evaluation. Silver was interested in buying the two Dobells. He recommended that Farquhar take them to Sue Hewitt, at Christie's Auction Rooms in Double Bay, for a second valuation.

Later the man informed Silver that he was Murray Farquhar. He had good reason to be discreet about his identity as Murray Farquhar OBE was well known as the disgraced former Chief Stipendiary Magistrate of New South Wales. In March 1985, he was convicted of conspiracy to pervert the course of justice and sentenced to four years; he served only ten months. But that wasn't all; it had exposed his connections to Sydney crime boss George Freeman and other underworld figures. Farquhar wasn't the most corrupt chief magistrate in the world, but he played in their league.

"It looks like there's no doubt. How much do I owe you?" Farquhar said after Silver showed him a video of the TV promo. Farquhar told Silver that he was shattered and could not believe the paintings were stolen. He agreed to refund Silver and take back the two paintings. Farquhar hoped that he and Silver could go to the police next week. First, he wanted to get a complete list of the stolen paintings and discuss the reward money. Silver didn't see any reason to delay and was on the phone to the police immediately after Farquhar left.

On Sunday morning, June 4, at 10:30 am, the police arrived at Farquhar's home with a search warrant. They didn't have to search. "I will show you what you've come to look for." The former magistrate told them and showed the two Dobells on a spare bed. The game was over; Farquhar told the police about the art dealer, and the auction house where the other paintings he had recently bought were. He was arrested and charged with being in possession of property stolen outside NSW and having and receiving stolen goods.

Farquhar protested his innocence, telling the police, "I have paid out good money for their correct value and not some undervalued amount." This wasn't true; if his sale of the paintings to Silver had gone through, he was going to make a substantial profit from the sale of just two Dobells.

Farquhar wanted the police to delay charging him because of the publicity that this would bring. He still owed 'Michael' and 'Morgan' money for some of the paintings and tried to convince the police that they could catch them. The police weren't interested.

The Smorgon art robbery episode went to air at 7:30 pm the next day.

Hundreds of kilometres away in Armidale on the NSW Northern Tablelands, on the evening of Thursday, June 8, Betty McCully was cleaning in St Mary and Joseph Cathedral. In the brick cathedral's belfry, she found a black plastic bag containing some painted sheets of masonite. There were six paintings in the bag. Betty showed them to the archbishop, who suggested she take them to the police.

The police put the paintings in their evidence room, tagged them A130234, and there they sat for seven months. They were not detected as stolen because, almost a year later, the NSW police still had not circulated the four-page list of stolen Smorgon artworks that the Victorian Crime Squad sent to NSW Police on June 23, 1988. There were photographs of four of the paintings Betty McCully had found on the list. But in the 1980s, criminal investigations often stopped at the state border.

Sergeant Owen Ellem was sorting through the evidence room one day when he noticed the name 'Arthur Boyd' on one of the paintings. Sergeant Ellem realised it was the name of a famous Australian artist and phoned the New England Regional Art Museum for expert advice. He spoke to the curator, Joe Eisenberg, who, of course, knew of Arthur Boyd, and because Eisenberg had seen the same episode of *Australia's Most Wanted*, he knew about the Smorgon art robbery. So after a few minutes of listening, Eisenberg put it all together for Sergeant Ellem. "I think someone stole them, got cold feet and returned them to God, although I don't think they were meant to be found."

A relieved Sam Smorgon phoned Betty McCully to thank her.

In March 1991, Murray Farquhar was in front of Judge Ducker at the Downing Centre District Court. Farquhar made an unsworn statement from the dock, telling his story to the jury and avoiding cross-examination from the prosecution. "To suggest I would take such paintings, if I had the slightest suspicion, to the very people who would identify them as stolen is absurd."

According to Farquhar, in early 1989, he was enjoying a sandwich and a drink at the Royal Hotel, an old colonial pub in Randwick, when he was approached by a 'tall, neatly dressed' man. The man introduced himself as 'Edward Morgan' and they "talked about things from the past as old men will do". They exchanged phone numbers.

Two weeks later, they met again at the hotel, and the man asked Farquhar if he wanted to buy some art. They went to Farquhar's flat on Beach Street, Coogee, for a couple of scotches and to further discuss the sale. The paintings hadn't fallen off the back of a truck. 'Edward Morgan' had told him he owned a textile business in financial difficulties, so he wanted to sell some paintings discreetly for cash. "I was not at all surprised that a businessman with economic difficulties might prefer cash, might prefer things to be relatively anonymous." Farquhar agreed to pay $58,000 ($124,000 today) for the Dobell and the two Fairweather paintings, which 'Morgan' insisted be sold as a pair.

A week later, another man called 'Michael' came over to his unit with some paintings by four notable Australian artists: *Camouflage in Menangle* and *Prima Donna* by Sir William Dobell; *Foo Chow* by Ian Fairweather; *Cobb and Co Coaches of the gold fields* by the colonial artist S.T. Gill; and *Landscape with pond* by Louis Buvelot. 'Michael' also brought another painting, which he claimed was a Picasso that Farquhar described as 'a woman with three eyes'. 'Michael' wanted $195,000 ($417,000 today) for the 'Picasso', but

Farquhar had doubts about its authenticity and wasn't interested. So the other paintings were left with Farquhar on approval.

Farquhar was worried this might be a confidence trick; perhaps the paintings were forgeries, so he went around getting the art authenticated. In April, he had asked Barry Pearce, the senior curator of Australian Art at the Art Gallery of NSW, to authenticate the S.T. Gill painting. If NSW Police had made an effort to circulate the list of the stolen Smorgon artworks to prominent galleries and art dealers given to them by Victoria Police, then the paintings might have been discovered at this point, but the list had not been circulated.

While Farquhar was making all this effort to get the paintings authenticated, he didn't seem at all interested in questioning why none of the art came with any provenance other than the name of the mysterious 'Edward Morgan', who was unknown as an art collector. Farquhar later told the jury that he saw 'absolutely nothing unusual' in the paintings' sale.

Paying $58,000 in cash for anything is unusual; $58,000 is a lot of cash to raise. Nevertheless, a Sydney chemist, Robert Pavan, agreed to loan Farquhar $50,000 for a month plus a 10 per cent bonus, no questions asked. Pavan contacted Anthony Gerace, a fruit broker who delivered it in $100 bills in a brown paper bag. Farquhar told Pavan, "I wish not to disclose what the money is for." When Pavan phoned about the money a month later, Farquhar told him there were "a few minor problems".

Farquhar didn't want to hang the paintings on the walls of his flat; he was more interested in selling them than anything else. On May 26, Farquhar left the Fairweather painting at Christie's Auctions and the Buvelot painting with Woollahra art dealer Trevor Bussell. Neither Christie's nor Bussell had heard of the Smorgon theft because NSW Police had not distributed the list of stolen paintings. Unlike when he introduced himself to Silver, Farquhar did give his correct name and address when he left paintings at Christie's and with Bussell.

Although Farquhar admitted to the jury that he harboured "frightening suspicion" that the paintings were stolen after Silver showed him the *Australia's Most Wanted* promo on video, he did not go to the police because he wanted to see a complete list of stolen works.

The story of the random, unidentifiable man in a pub is a classic excuse for possessing stolen property. And Farquhar, with his decades of experience in court and associating with underworld figures, would have heard it before. In his summing up, Judge Ducker asked the jury if they considered Farquhar the "victim of a confidence trick" or "a person who knew all the ins and outs of criminal law".

The jury deliberated for five hours on Friday before the foreman told Judge Ducker that they were, "running around in circles". On Monday, the jury continued and, after nearly thirteen hours, acquitted Murray Farquhar of all charges. Judge Ducker announced his surprise at the jury's verdict and confessed he found it difficult to "keep a straight face" during some of Farquhar's testimony. He refused Farquhar's application to have his legal costs for the trial paid.

Farquhar maintained that publicity surrounding his arrest scared off 'Edward Morgan' and 'Michael'. The NSW police maintain they never existed, but private investigator Duncan McNab believes that 'Michael' did. Mc Nab was a former police detective working for North Sydney insurance investigators JEB Investigations (he is now a true-crime author). In September 1988, a regular source had told McNab that knew someone with the Smorgon paintings.

McNab talked to a man with a Yugoslav accent on the phone who called himself 'Peter'. 'Peter' said he had information about the stolen Smorgon paintings. McNab replied, "This is all very fascinating, but we need photographs." 'Peter' provided proof by putting several Polaroid photographs of some of the stolen paintings in Mc-Nab's letterbox in early December. Each photo was imprinted with the electronically recorded date of '2.12.88'.

JEB Investigations sought a QC's advice on how to proceed and then dropped the matter because it was too legally murky for them to pursue. They didn't want to be involved in dealing with a ransom.

After talking with Farquhar, McNab believed that 'Peter' and 'Michael' were the same. "He had the same thick European accent, the same speech mannerisms, the way he punctuated everything with a swear word." Later another man was charged with possessing another two of Sam Smorgon's paintings, and this man gave the police the same description of 'Michael'.

Murray Farquhar died from a heart attack in 1993 while on trial for conspiracy to obtain stolen passports. The three men and one woman who robbed the Smorgon house were never caught, and half of the stolen paintings were never recovered. Paintings by Arthur Boyd, Charles Conder, S.T. Gill, Kate O'Connor, John Perceval, Eric Thake, Camille Pissarro, Celso Lager, Marc Chagall and Armand Guillaumin are still amongst Australia's most wanted.

Hot Tucker

Bert looked at the two sets of photographs again. Was he losing his marbles? He was getting old; there was no denying that. It was July 1994 and he was eighty years old. He walked with a cane and had a hearing aid, but he sure as hell still had his faculties.

He had photographic proof of that; the painting was in the first photograph, missing in the second one. Bert took the second set of photographs because he wasn't happy with the first set, as the camera's lens hood was visible on the picture's edge. Looking at the two sets of photos, he began noticing the differences. What was going on?

In the first set, he could see Danila Vassilieff's abstract painting leaning against the wall near the kitchen door behind a Sidney Nolan painting of a crouching woman. In the second set, the painting was missing. Bert searched his house again, but there was no sign of the painting by his Russian friend, Vassilieff.

Now that Bert had started looking around his big old house on Blessington Street in the Melbourne bayside suburb of St Kilda, he was sure there were other paintings missing too. A self-portrait had disappeared, along with some books and some rare magazines. It was hard to be sure after a lifetime of acquiring things.

His plan was to donate the house and his art to the National Trust to be preserved as an artist's house museum open to the public after his death. He was confident that the public would want to see the great Australian modernist painter Albert Tucker's home and art collection. The photographs were intended to show the National Trust what the house looked like when he lived there.

Born in 1914, Albert Tucker lived through many of the twentieth century's significant events, including two World Wars. He started out in Melbourne's working-class suburb of Footscray with a basic education and no formal art training. But, determined to become an artist, he attended life drawing classes at the Victorian Artists' Society (aka VAS) for three nights a week for seven years. And fell in love with Joy Hester, a 17-year-old suburban Elsternwick beach girl and National Gallery art school student.

They joined a small circle of modern artists in Melbourne, including Arthur Boyd, Sidney Nolan and John Perceval. It was a tiny circle; all the modern artists in Melbourne could fit into one lounge room, and they did at John and Sunday Reed's house, 'Heide', at Bulleen, now the Heide Museum of Modern Art.

After WWII, Joy left Bert to go to Sydney with her lover, leaving behind her son, Sweeney, who was adopted by John and Sunday Reed. Bert left Australia. 'A refugee from Australian culture,' as he described himself. He struggled to survive as an artist in England and the United States until his paintings began to sell, including to the New York's Museum of Modern Art and the Guggenheim Museum.

Bert returned to Melbourne in 1960, at the height of his fame. Melbourne had changed, but Bert had changed more. No longer a poor, struggling artist. Along with Sidney Nolan, he had become one of the most famous living modern Australian artists. He was a bit of a dandy with his neatly clipped moustache and a goatee beard. In 1964 he married his second wife, Barbara Anne Bilcock.

Tucker's paintings tell the history of Australia: distorting to emphasise the discomfort he felt. Victory girls in wartime Melbourne –

all teeth, tits and red lips, being groped by piggish American soldiers in green uniforms. European explorers with rigid profiles, as if cut from corrugated iron, crossing a yellow muddy river.

Bert had an enormous art collection in his house. It wasn't just his own art; there were works by other artists. Joy Hester had left behind about 200 works of her art when she left him. In addition, he had art by other members of the Heide circle: Arthur Boyd and Sidney Nolan. He also had a collection of art by European modernists: Raoul Viard, Pierre Bonnard and Eric Gill.

With all this valuable art, Bert was serious about security. No one was allowed unsupervised access to his house. He had a purpose-built security room for storing part of his collection. He kept his studio and other rooms locked, unlocking and locking them to show visitors, including James Mollison, former director of the National Gallery of Victoria, and Lauraine Diggins, his art dealer since 1988. Even his wife did not have keys to the studio or the secure storage room.

In 1994, eighty-year-old Bert was unlocking and locking doors with his big ring of keys when Max Joffe first visited his house.

Max Michael Joffe and Lorraine Finlay were an attractive couple of baby boomers. Max was born in 1948, his parents having just emigrated to Australia the year before after surviving the Vilna Ghetto and concentration camps. Max's father ran various businesses in Melbourne, and his mother worked in the jewellery department at Myer. Max had started as an art teacher at Box Hill Technical School in the early 1980s before becoming one of eight teachers or 'education officers' at the NGV until budget cuts threatened their positions. He became the head of the art department at Moorabbin TAFE in Melbourne's south-eastern suburbs. However, he and the rest of the staff did not get along; one of the other art teachers sued him for defamation, and it was settled out of court for damages and an apology. Max resigned from teaching TAFE in 1994.

Lorraine Finlay had been George Mora's assistant at Tolarno Galleries in South Yarra. Max and Lorraine then set up and ran Melbourne Contemporary Arts Gallery (aka MCA) in the early 1980s. MCA was a commercial art gallery on Gertrude Street, Fitzroy, a pioneer in a street that would later become a prime location for art galleries. MCA started out above a Turkish takeaway on the corner of George Street. Then in 1990, Max and Lorraine refurbished a two-storey Victorian building at 163 Gertrude Street. I remember going to an exhibition opening upstairs at MCA in the late 1980s; it was a typical gallery space with white walls and bare floorboards exhibiting mid-career Australian artists.

Although the MCA was a commercial gallery, it wasn't making any money. With Max out of work, they could no longer afford to keep it open. Max might have been desperate, but he didn't show it. He always appeared to have more money than an art teacher would earn; he drove a Mercedes, often travelled overseas, and had an art collection. Was it all on credit? Did he still owe money to George Mora for the art on the walls of his house?

Albert Tucker had met Max at the MCA. Bert was always a loner; the angry young man had matured into a grumpy old man. After Joy left him, he had no circle of close friends. His manner often alienated people; he had no time for small talk. But Bert got on well with Max; Max knew and admired Bert and the other artists in the Heide circle.

Max offered Bert some secondhand picture frames and mount boards he had used at the MCA. Max knew that Bert needed frames for his art collection. Bert agreed, and Max brought over another stack of frames. At first, Max came to Bert's house to mount and frame art. For this, Bert gave him a watercolour painting from his series, *Images of modern evil, clown's head*, a $1300 ($2500 today) suit, and $650 ($1245 today) in cash. Bert also sold him another larger watercolour, *Woman lying on the floor*, for $500, about one-sixth of its actual value.

Max was 34 years younger than Bert and worked hard to build his friendship with Bert. He would send cards to Bert and buy him small gifts when he was overseas. He mowed the couple's lawn and went shopping with them, helping Barbara buy a secondhand Mercedes and Bert a new suit. It was a little bit embarrassing for Barbara and Bert.

In 1994 Bert was about to turn eighty, and his collection was in a chaotic mess. He was in a personal crisis; he had always been a lousy ledger keeper. What if he died and someone else who didn't know had to sort through all of this? So in early 1994, Max started to catalogue Bert's collection. Bert wanted to get his art collection documented and his affairs in order before he passed away. He didn't want to leave it to Barbara to deal with it. Max was paid for this with a combination of money and two paintings by Joy Hester.

After so many visits, Bert started to trust Max enough to leave him unsupervised with his collection. Bert would go for lunch or to answer the telephone and leave Max working alone. Max was to help prepare the collection for a public bequest. Bert appointed Max a trustee of his trust foundation for the proposed house museum.

There were so many valuable works of Australian art in Bert's collection, works by artists that Max had spent years studying and admiring. The temptation was too much; he had been shown his ultimate treasure trove worth millions of dollars, and the door had been left unlocked.

Unlike many people who steal art, Max Joffe knew how much an Albert Tucker painting was worth, where and how to sell it. Max sold four works by Albert Tucker to Julie Thomas, a bank manager who had known Max socially for fifteen years. Max told Julie that she could get them at a bargain price of $74,000 ($136,700 today) by avoiding auction house fees and emphasised discretion because the deal was outside Tucker's arrangement with his art dealer. Julie took out a bank loan to pay for the paintings.

Joffe put two works by Tucker up for auction at Sotheby's in Melbourne. However, unusually for a seller putting paintings up for sale, Joffe refused to have photographs of the works included in the catalogue, even though there was no additional charge to add photos. He then withdrew the paintings from sale before the auction.

When Bert confronted Max about the missing Sidney Nolan book, *Paradise Garden*, and a complete set of the infamous avant-garde journals, *Angry Penguins*, Max miraculously found them. Bert decided that it was time he had the locks changed. He phoned and asked Max and Lorraine to come over to his house on Sunday, December 4, 1994.

Max was frightened, too frightened to go through with the auction. And his fear developed into a panic. Did he expect a sudden police raid? Had he, in his desperation, ripped up two drawings by Tucker, *Cinema* and *Soldier and girl*, throwing them in a rubbish bin in the street? Each was valued at $10,000 ($18,500 today). Later, Max claimed he was shocked to find that he had accidentally torn two works as he threw some rubbish away. He then didn't know how to approach Tucker about the matter. Lorraine was outraged. She yelled at Max, "Why did you tear them up? How could you?" She then recovered the pieces from the rubbish bin to return them to Bert.

That Sunday, Barbara Tucker went to their beach house in Blairgowrie; she had a feeling about what would happen and didn't want to witness the scene. Max denies much of Bert's version of the day's events. Max and Lorraine brought a parcel of eleven missing paintings and a rare copy of Robert Hughes' book *Art in Australia* back to Bert. Max admitted tearing the two watercolours and placing four paintings up for auction.

Bert yelled at Max, painting a picture in colourful, expressionist language of 'a moral black hole'. The worst thing for any criminal is getting caught; no punishment compares to it. At first, Max tried to negotiate. Both Max and Bert agree that Max insisted Tucker choose any works he wanted from Joffe's collection to compensate him for the damaged drawings. Tucker wanted to believe Joffe and reluctantly agreed. Max begged for forgiveness from Tucker and threatened to kill himself. Bert asked if there were any more missing artworks. Max slumped onto the couch and claimed that was all.

But that wasn't all. In February 1995, Claire Jager was filming at Bert's house for her documentary, *The Good Looker – Joy Hester*. Bert couldn't find some works by Hester and had no doubts that Max was responsible. With his art dealer Lauraine Diggins, Bert conducted an audit of his art collection and discovered that about eighty works of art were missing. He was not going to shout at Max this time; he called the police.

Major fraud squad detectives Detective-Sergeant Greg Sevior and Senior Constable Grant Robinson headed 'Operation Arato'. Neither detective knew anything about art or anyone in the art world, but that didn't put them off. In March 1995, the police recovered thirteen pieces of Tucker's art from Joffe's home in Myrtle Street, Ripponlea; works from the 1940s by Tucker, Arthur Boyd, Vassilieff and Hester. Max Joffe was charged with theft and accepting $75,000 in cash from Julie Thomas to purchase the four Tucker paintings. Six more paintings were recovered from the Christie's, Sotheby's and Lawson's auction houses. A total of thirty Tuckers were recovered, but forty-two paintings remained missing, including Tucker's *Self portrait* and *Sunday Reed at Heide*. Detective Robinson wrote to about 500 galleries asking if they had sold any Tuckers since 1990 and attempted to track the missing works.

On July 14, 1995, when news of the stolen art was reported to the public, the police, who had bugged Joffe's home, heard Max and

Lorraine arguing. Max maintained that this conversation was not about Bert's paintings but about works placed on consignment with him by the Israeli painter Yosl Bergner, who had lived in Australia between 1937 and 1948 and was part of the Heide circle.

"What are you doing to our families, Max? It's going to put you in jail. Tell me the truth, Max. Are there any more?"

"No, there aren't any more."

"But that's what you said last time and the police came here and they found that folio."

"You've got to believe what I say."

On Monday, May 6, 1996, Max Joffe appeared in the Prahran Magistrates Court on eighty-nine charges of theft. His mother stood surety for his bail, but it wasn't just his mother who stood behind him; many people believed he was innocent. How could such a charming, friendly man be guilty? How could a man who had done so much to help artists steal from Albert Tucker?

On Thursday, May 28, 1998, the trial began in the County Court before Judge Leslie Ross. Max Joffe denied he had stolen anything and pleaded not guilty to eight-one counts of theft of artworks worth between $2 million and $3.8 million. His defence was that Bert had given him the artwork in lieu of payment.

On one occasion, Bert had given him two works on paper in exchange for two preparatory drawings from the 1940s by Tucker that Max had bought at auction. These preparatory drawings were used to make an underpainting and are known as 'cartoons'. Bert was horrified that they were still in circulation as he did not consider them complete works of art. Max claimed to have bought other works from galleries. Max also claimed that Bert was desperate for cash and sold him works. Max's defence lawyer, Michael Rush, cross-examined Bert, going over all the details for two days. It was painful for Bert, who was also suffering from painful shingles threatening the sight in his left eye.

The jury spent five days deliberating before finding Joffe guilty on twenty-four counts of theft and one count of obtaining property by deception and not guilty for the other fifty-seven counts of theft. Max Joffe was sentenced to three years. He appealed the conviction but was unsuccessful and spent eighteen months in prison.

The whole experience was exhausting and demoralising for Bert. He was also annoyed at how much of his remaining time it had taken up. Instead of donating his house in St Kilda to the National Trust, he sold it. He donated over 200 works, worth an estimated $15 million ($25 million today), to Heide Museum of Modern Art. Albert Tucker died the following year on 23 October 1999; he never recovered from Max Joffe's betrayal of trust.

The Cleaner

Ethel Carrick (aka Ethel Carrick-Fox) was an impressionist painter and later a post-impressionist who travelled the world painting beautiful places in increasingly broad brushstrokes. She painted outdoors, depicting everyday scenes as she travelled around the Mediterranean, the Middle East, Asia and the Pacific – market scenes, flower gardens and beach scenes – and exhibited them in Britain, France and Australia.

Born in England in 1872 and educated at the Slade School of Fine Art, Ethel Carrick was an accidental Australian due to her marriage in 1905 to Melbourne-born impressionist painter Emanuel Phillips Fox. Unfortunately, they were only married for ten years before her husband died. Ethel Carrick only lived in Australia for about a decade.

Carrick is hardly a household name, but in 1996 she held the highest price for a painting by an Australian woman when one of her paintings of a French flower market sold for $105,500. Given that record price, the National Gallery of Australia (aka NGA) was pleased that it had bought another of Carrick's paintings of a French flower market, *In the Nice flower market,* for $25,000 in 1972.

In the Nice flower market is an oil on canvas, about 60 centimetres high and 80 centimetres wide, depicting an outdoor flower market in Nice, in the south of France. It is signed, 'Carrick-Fox', in the lower left-hand corner. It doesn't have a date on it, but it is believed to have been painted around 1926.

The NGA provides the art for federal government offices (and state galleries give the same service for state government offices). In 1981 it loaned *In the Nice flower market* to the offices of the Governor-General in Treasury Place, Melbourne. There it hung on the wall as three different men occupied the office until it was reported missing on November 25, 1994.

George Kourounis (not the celebrity Canadian adventurer and storm chaser, but the middle-aged director of a Melbourne cleaning company) pleaded guilty to possessing the stolen painting. His cleaning company was responsible for cleaning the Governor-General's office and had keys to the offices where it was hung.

He knew what he was stealing. Since the early 1980s, Kourounis had been passionately interested in art and had an impressive collection. In 2011 the University of Queensland Art Museum borrowed Belle Bassin's *Disruptive peach* 2010, a 2.5×3.5 metre watercolour on paper from Kourounis's'collection, for their exhibition, New Psychedelia.

Only Kourounis did not steal *In the Nice flower market* for a secret art collection to gloat over. He only had it for a few months before selling it for $35,000 ($65,000 today). Explaining away the lack of provenance, Kourounis said that it had been bought overseas. The painting ended up on sale at Deutscher Fine Art in Malvern Road, Malvern, before the Australian Federal Police recovered it.

One would think that stealing from the office of the Governor-General would be unforgivable, that it would be the end of any chances of getting government contracts. Still, fortunately for George Kourounis, he had some very forgiving and well-connected friends, and he soon had another government cleaning contract.

Copper-belly

Virginia Trioli claimed to have abducted *Larry La Trobe* in 1995 when she was the art critic for *The Age*. Someone did steal the bronze dog from Melbourne's City Square, but it wasn't Virginia. She had never liked Larry, but her story about unscrewing his 30-centimetre bolts one freezing winter night before throwing him into the Yarra River is more Hunter S. Thompson-esque journalism than a confession. Her public declaration in her newspaper column that she did it in defence of good taste is an unlikely story.

At first, *Larry*'s sculptor, the Melbourne-based artist Pamela Irving, thought it was a prank and that *Larry* would be returned. The police questioned her because they also thought it was a prank.

Larry is a heavy dog and weighs about 75 kilograms. This would have made him worth, in 1995 terms, when scrap copper was around $4 a kilo, a bit more than $200 (approximately $340 today value).

The current *Larry La Trobe* is another edition of the sculpture courtesy of Peter Kolliner, the owner of the foundry Artworks in Bronze, where the original was cast. Many people were pleased to see *Larry* again when he was reinstalled in September 1996 but not Virginia Trioli.

Larry's theft was at the start of a spate of bronze public sculptures being stolen that came about due to three factors: the increase in public sculptures, their accessible, ground-level locations, and the price of copper.

In 2004 the price of pure copper climbed from $3000 a metric ton to $4000. Then, in 2005, it shot up to over $10,000 a metric ton. This boom in copper prices was caused by increased demand from the BRICs nations: Brazil, Russia, India and China, especially China, where copper wire was needed for its construction boom. In 2009 the price dropped to just above $4000, but by 2010 the price had rebounded to above $9000. Since then, copper has stabilised at between $7000 and $8000 per metric ton.

Bronze is an alloy made from about 88 per cent copper with 12 per cent tin, and although the price for scrap copper is less than pure copper, it does keep track with the price. When prices for raw materials rise like that, the temptation to steal them increases by equal measure. So around the world, anything with any copper was now a target: electrical wire, wire from the signals at railway stations, and bronze public sculptures.

The philistines who steal public sculpture know the price of copper but the value of nothing. They don't see sculptures as anything more than metal they can sell. Nothing is sacred to such people; they would cut the arms off a statue of Christ if they could make money from it. Someone did just that to a one-metre-tall bronze statue of Christ outside Templestowe's Holy Cross Church in 2009. It was easier to cut through the arms than remove the large nails holding them to the cross. Copper prices peaked at above $9000 per metric ton that year.

It is a relatively safe crime for thieves as no one has been charged with or convicted of stealing a bronze public sculpture. Even when parts of Ayad Alqaragholli's two-hundred-kilogram bronze sculpture of two figures about to embrace, *Hyatti* ('*You are my all, my everything*'), taken from a park in 2018, were discovered in a Perth scrapyard the following year.

Alqaragholli's sculpture has since been replaced with another edition. The only good news is that some of these sculptures can be replaced because their mould is still around at a local foundry.

And there are many substantial and heavier temptations just sitting by the side of the road. The signature move of scrap metal thieves is to use a chain and a car to snap the statues off along the weld seam at the ankles.

A seven-hundred-kilogram bronze sculpture of a dugong was mounted at the entrance of a gated community in Port Hinchin-brook in Queensland. It was first taken in February 2014 and was found by a hiker hidden in bushland just a few days later. The determined thieves returned in April of the following year to finish the job.

The most valuable public sculpture to be stolen in Melbourne was a $50,000 bronze sculpture and fountain, *Boy and urn*. The neoclassical sculpture was installed in the gardens as part of a rockery around 1900. It was poached from Fitzroy Gardens in March 2016. The $50,000 price tag was the insurance value of what it would cost to replace the antique sculpture; the value of the bronze as scrap metal is far, far less.

The most artistically significant public sculptures stolen were two bronze figures by the acclaimed British artist Anthony Gormley. Gormley likes to place his figurative sculptures in unusual locations, on the ceiling, on top of buildings, or in this case, in the middle of Lake Ballard, a dry salt lake in the Goldfields-Esperance area of Western Australia. Gormley's *Inside Australia* was installed for the Perth International Arts Festival in 2003. It consisted of fifty-one figures dotted ten kilometres around the wavering heat mirage-filled horizon of the salt lake. Now there are only forty-nine figures because, in 2015, two were ripped off.

West Australia is a hot spot for the theft, ransom and vandalism of sculptures. So many sculptures are taken that West Australian sculptor Greg James has had four stolen in two years. Bronze sculptures will continue to be stolen year after year while the price of copper remains high.

The Australia Day art heist

According to Mark Cyril-Stanley, he was distracted by the television on Australia Day 1998. And the first he knew about the robbery was when he saw a man in a balaclava pointing a handgun at him. It was ten o'clock in the evening, and he was no longer alone in his bedroom. There were two or three men wearing balaclavas in his house. They tied him up and blindfolded him.

Until now, life had been kind to the 36-year-old property developer. He had started selling cars, moved into finance and then property. Now his South Yarra mansion had a blue-chip investment collection of paintings by prestigious Australian artists.

The robbers cut Rupert Bunny's *Woman with rose*, circa 1903, out of its frame and rolled up the canvas, further reducing the value of what they were stealing. It was valued at $300,000 before it was cut but a lot less after the damage. They ignored a work by John Brack as they headed out the door with nine paintings, leaving the most valuable one behind, Arthur Streeton's *Storm over Macedon*. The Streeton was worth almost half as much as all the other paintings they stole.

They left in Cyril-Stanley's Range Rover with nine paintings, including two Frederick McCubbins – *Hanging rails for fence* and *Mount Macedon*; William Dobell's *London boy*; Tom Roberts'

England winter; Lloyd Rees' *Red roof*; Louis Rigall's *Returning home;* a painting by John McArthur, and *Picking wattles in Ballarat* by an unknown artist.

Two hours later he Houdinied himself free of his bonds enough to call the police. The robbers had locked the house on their way out, and the police had to break in to free him. There was no sign of a forced entry. The robbers were never caught, but the stolen paintings were recovered, abandoned in a hotel room.

There are so many unanswered questions about this unsolved crime. How did the robbers gain access to the house? How did they know that Cyril-Stanley had a valuable art collection? Why cut the Rupert Bunny *Woman with rose*? Why did they only take art when they didn't know how to fence it? Why did they abandon them so quickly? Why didn't they think to ask for a ransom?

Ten years later, in 2008, the now-bankrupt Mark Cyril-Stanley pleaded guilty to two charges of theft, one of dishonest conduct as a company director, one of aiding a company to engage in dishonest conduct and one of defrauding the Commonwealth government. He claimed the stress from the robbery's terrifying ordeal had changed him and he had started to use considerable quantities of cocaine and alcohol. To pay for his four-gram-a-week cocaine habit, he had defrauded investors and the Commonwealth of millions of dollars.

The Gloaters

Near Numurkah, a small town north of Shepparton, the Goulburn Valley Highway runs through flat open country, just a line of trees beside the road running parallel with the railway line. In February 2000, two men were in a car driving north on the highway when they saw the flashing blue lights of a police car in the Shepparton Traffic Operations Group (TOG) behind them.

The driver was Richard George Sissons, a 61-year-old pensioner living in Crib Point on Western Port Bay in Victoria. Apart from one drink-driving conviction, he had never been in trouble with the law. He pulled the car over, hoping that this would just be a routine traffic stop.

But this was no routine traffic stop or random breath test. The police knew exactly what they were looking for: Albert Tucker's *Flying ibis* was on Sissons' car's back seat.

On his return to Australia in the 1960s, Tucker painted dozens of oils depicting ibis on composition board. The black curve of an ibis's bill and neck with white brushstrokes wings flying against the dark bush background of trees and foliage.

Now that he was successful in England and the US, Australians were also buying his paintings. The original owner of *Flying ibis* had bought it for £500 ($12,200 today). In April 1986, it was stolen from Saville Gallery in Sydney. The painting was insured against theft, and the owner was paid $18,000 by the insurance company.

Sissons was what is known in the trade as a 'gloater', an art collector who knowingly purchases stolen art to gloat over it in secret. Most owners of Tucker's paintings like to display them where they can be seen and admired by visitors, but not Sissons. Sissons had acquired his Tucker from a man who owed him $10,000. He occasionally hung it in his home or office, and when he did, he was careful about who saw it. Otherwise, he had kept it in his cellar for the past fourteen years.

In 2000, Sissons was tired of gloating and was ready to sell the stolen painting. It was the year after Albert Tucker's death, and Sissons was wondering how to cash in. He wasn't sure how much it was worth, but he figured it must be much more after Tucker's death.

Another thing Sissons wasn't sure about was how to sell a hot painting. Who do you contact when you want to sell art on the black market? Sissons put out some feelers.

His enquiries brought back a man who told him: 'I know someone in Queensland who would pay $25,000 ($38,500 today) for it in opals.' The *Flying ibis* was actually worth a lot more; at the time, Tucker's dealer, Lauraine Diggins, estimated that the painting was worth between $70,000 and $75,000. Sissons agreed to the deal and was driving with the middleman to make the exchange when he was pulled over near Numurkah.

Sissons was charged with two counts of handling stolen goods. In 2002 he pleaded not guilty in the County Court. His lawyer suggested that the painting might have been acquired before the break-in at Saville Gallery or that it could be a forgery. Diggins disagreed; in her opinion, *Flying ibis* was genuine.

The jury found Sissons guilty. In sentencing Sissons, Judge Elizabeth Curtain told him that "there would be fewer thieves if there were fewer handlers" and that he "deprived the painting's owners and the Australian national estate of the pleasure of Tucker's *Flying ibis.*" Sissons was sentenced to three years, but the whole sentence was suspended due to his age and ill health.

The other man in the car with Sissons was not charged because he was a police informer.

Another kind of gloater is an art thief that steals for themselves because they love the art. They are rarely caught, but there was one good thief in Melbourne who gave the art back. The stolen painting by a famous American artist hung in his home for almost thirty years. An outline in green paint of a crawling baby with lines radiating from it painted on a small wooden door, 65.2 × 71.7 cm. Underneath the radiant child in big block letters was the name "K. Haring".

Keith Haring developed his style and images drawing in white chalk on the black paper covering vacant advertising spaces in New York's subway. The skinny white kid from Klutzville, Pennsylvania, with thinning blond hair and big round glasses, became the first internationally known street artist.

His technique was simple line drawings. His genius was in the iconic figures that populated his images, dancing figures and, most famously, his signature image, the radiant baby. His lines could fill any space: a wall, a T-shirt or Grace Jones' naked body. His art was the opposite of the minimalist and conceptual art of the time. It appealed to a younger crowd, the kind of people who danced at nightclubs.

Haring was in Australia from February 18 to March 8, 1984. He had a full schedule, painting the NGV's front entrance's water-wall in public, only for a vandal with a slingshot to destroy it a couple of days later. Next, Haring painted walls in the Art Gallery of NSW and a Haring-themed float for the Sydney Gay & Lesbian Mardi Gras. Back in Melbourne, he painted on walls in Collingwood, in clubs, anywhere anyone let him put a brush or marker pen.

Before Haring flew out of the country, he donated a day to paint "for the kids" at the Collingwood Education Centre (aka Collingwood Technical School, CTS). The inner-city school wasn't as impoverished as some places in the US where he had painted, but it wasn't affluent. The two-storey high brick wall on the side of the building facing the car park had been painted yellow the Saturday before by student volunteers led by CTS teacher Ray Collier.

On Tuesday, March 6, as hip-hop music played on his Kenny Scharf decorated boombox, Haring painted from 9am to 6pm. He was back the following day to give a slide show at the school assembly and do more work on the mural. He finished it on Thursday, flying back to the US that day.

Haring painted the mural without any preliminary drawings, apart from a demo chalk demonstration drawing of the centipede. He started working with a large marker pen and then went over the lines with a paintbrush in ordinary house paint. It was the first time he used a scissor lift, and he found it a liberating experience.

Haring's mural shows humanity under threat from computer technology – in 1984, the personal computer was Time Magazine's "person of the year". At the top was the tyranny of the computer-headed centipede ridden by a couple of individuals with power-wands, contrasted with the freedom of the mass of dancing humans on the lower half.

Years passed: Keith Haring died of AIDS-related complications in 1990; he was only thirty-one. The Collingwood Education Centre was closed and abandoned. In 2000 after a gig at the Tote Hotel, Melbourne's grungiest pub music venue, the thief went to the old Education Centre next door. Equipped with a screwdriver, he removed the small wooden door covering a utility space on the wall. And brought it home in his car's boot.

The paint weathered as the decades went by, and the colours slowly faded on the mural. Red lines were particularly faded. If anyone had suggested to the thief that he return the door, he would have laughed. In his mind, he hadn't stolen it but "rescued" it. He was taking care of it when its legal owners didn't care.

The art world has a long memory, and a community campaign grew with calls to look after the old mural. From 2010 to 2012, there was a debate about how this should be done. Should it be restored with a fresh coat of paint, or should it be conserved?

A restoration would make it look like new again, but Haring's original brush marks would be lost under the fresh coat of paint. And it is the line, the quality of Haring's hand movement, the way he draws that is central to his work. Whereas if the mural were conserved, it would be cleaned, repaired, and further decay arrested. As it is one of the few surviving exterior murals by Haring in its original form, it was decided to conserve it.

In preparation for the mural's conservation, Jessica Hochberg, an Arts Victoria project officer, researched the Collingwood site's history. She wanted to find the missing part of the mural. She asked around about the door, promising not to turn the thief in to the police.

Through his social network, the thief heard Hochberg's plea for the return of the door and her promise of indemnity. He took Haring's radiant baby down from his wall and wrapped it in thick black plastic. He wrote "Jessica Hochberg" in purple texta on the plastic and dropped the package off at Arts Victoria.

The thief actually did the mural's conservators a favour. As it had hung inside, it was not exposed to direct sunlight. Consequently, the bright turquoise paint colour was better preserved and could be used by the conservators as a reference.

The conservation returned the mural closer to its original appearance. The wall's rough surface was cleaned using artists' gum pencil erasers; this removed material on the wall that had built up, obscuring the paint. And a transparent red glaze over the red lines meant that you can still see the original brush strokes while reinforcing the colour.

After 29 years, the missing radiant baby was returned to the public. A replica door was installed on the wall, and the original door was donated to the NGV. Scientific tests confirmed that the painting on the door was the work of Keith Haring and the Keith Haring Foundation authenticated it. The old Collingwood College is now an arts centre, and Haring's mural is open to the public.

The worst art thief in Australia

With his long grey hair and colourful clothes, artist, guitarist and eccentric John Opit is a bit of local legend around Limpinwood, near the Queensland border in north-eastern New South Wales. In 1992 the Tweed River Shire Council bought one of his paintings, *Tyalgum Teamster*, a portrait of a local bullock driver, as a sesquicentennial gift for the City of Sydney.

Imagination is a wonderful thing; without it, we would not have art. Opit likes to imagine that an old canvas is a painting by the late-nineteenth-century French painter Paul Cezanne. That it depicts Cezanne's only child, Paul junior, seated in a high chair, the initials 'PC' in the corner support his attribution and that it is worth $50 million. He imagines that he is an art restorer, one without any clients, insurance or qualifications, who has only worked on one painting, his 'Cezanne'. And who am I to tell him otherwise and deprive him of the pleasure his imaginative attribution brings him?

Cezanne's only son was born in January 1872. At the time, Cezanne was painting impressionist landscapes with fellow painter Camille Pissarro in Auvers-sur-Oise on Paris's north-western outskirts. Cezanne did a couple of sketches of the young boy's face but no paintings. If he had done one, it is unlikely that it would have been sold but kept in the family; the son of a banker, Cezanne, was never short of a franc.

Opit bought the painting from a Lismore antique shop for $20, or maybe, he inherited it from his grandparents or found it at the back of a rumpus room cupboard of his father's home in the 1970s. His story kept changing.

Unfortunately for Opit, his painting is not listed in any of the published *catalogue raisonnés* of Cezanne's art. A *catalogue raisonnés* is the definitive list of an artist's work assembled over many years by a team of researchers. Cezanne's art dealer started to gather the information two years before Cezanne's death from pneumonia in 1906, but a bonafide catalogue was not completed until 1936.

Opit is right that a painting by Cezanne would be worth an eight-figure sum. In 1999 a still life by Cezanne was sold at auction for $60.5 million. At the time, it was the fourth-highest price ever paid for a painting. More likely, dreams of wealth than Cezanne's characteristic brushwork and rejection of a single-point perspective inspired Opit's attribution.

Brett Michael Williams heard about Opit and his fantastic art collection. He didn't know about Cezanne and post-Impressionism, but, like Opit, he imagined it could be worth millions. If only he had a better imagination, he might have thought about it and not made as many mistakes. Unfortunately, Williams was a bad burglar. He was so terrible at it that he already had several burglary convictions. This time he made three big mistakes and became the worst art thief in Australia.

His first mistake was believing that Opit had a valuable art collection. His second was breaking into Opit's house. Williams had heard that Opit would be out of town and that his remote Mullumbimby home would be empty. Sometime between February 21 and 26, 2004, he disabled the security system and smashed in the front door.

He stole eighteen works of art that Opit extravagantly attributed to Paul Cezanne, Winslow Homer, Arthur Streeton, John Peter Russell, John Glover and Norman Lindsay. As well as a Matchbox car collection, a laptop computer and an electric guitar. The electric guitar and laptop were probably the most valuable items pinched and the easiest to fence.

Williams's third and final mistake was not knowing where to sell stolen art. He decided to stash the stolen painting while he worked that out. Again, William's imagination failed him when he chose to hide the stolen art in the garage of an elderly female relative living in a duplex in Robina on the Gold Coast. Even though she rarely went into it, it was not a wise move.

The story of a Cezanne worth millions stolen from an art restorer's rural property made national and even international news. Photographs of the 'Cezanne' painting of the child in the high chair were in the newspaper and on television. So even though William's elderly female relative was not an art expert, and it was three months later when she looked in her garage. She remembered the stolen painting from the news. We can only imagine how she felt when she called the police.

Williams was found guilty, and Opit got the 'Cezanne' of his imagination back.

Five-Finger Discounts

Small works of art are especially vulnerable to being carried out the door for a five-finger discount. Who knows how many works of art are stolen each year from art galleries and exhibitions, but there are regular reports of it happening.

The most valuable of these was Frans Van Mieris's *A Cavalier*. Painted around 1657-1659 on an oak panel by Frans Van Mieris the Elder, the patriarch of a family of Dutch painters from Leiden. It depicts a well-dressed young man with frizzy auburn hair under a wide-brimmed black hat decorated with feathers. He rests his arm on a table, displaying the fabulous yellow and black sleeve of his jacket, fashionably slashed to ribbons, revealing the crinkly folds of his white silk shirt. It is a small painting, 20x16 centimetres, but it is valued at over one and a half million dollars.

It was hanging on the wall of the Fairfax Gallery when the Art Gallery of New South Wales (aka AGNSW) opened on Sunday morning at 10am on June 10, 2007. It had hung in a nook to one side of one of the older rooms in the art gallery since 1993. Attached to the wall with two keyhole plates and Phillips head screws. Sometime that morning, someone unscrewed it from the wall.

The nook was not covered by the CCTV nor under continuous observation by gallery attendants. Even more negligent, the NSW government had ignored the gallery director, Edmund Capon's warnings about the inadequate security.

Small works of art had been walking off the AGNSW's walls for decades. In 1955, William Dobell's oil painting *The Milliner* was prised from its frame at the Art Gallery of NSW. The portrait of a woman in a black dress was just fifteen by twenty centimetres and easily concealed. Fortunately, it was returned four days later, undamaged by parcel post. In 1984, another small painting by Dobell, *Souvenir*, was unscrewed from the gallery wall and removed from the gallery. Again, it was returned after the vaguest of telephone tip-offs to look for it in 'the library'; staff at the Mitchell Library in Sydney found it.

At 12:30pm, *A Cavalier* was reported missing. However, the gallery did not immediately call the police, and it was three days before Customs was notified to be on the lookout for a stolen painting.

Unfortunately, this was not a repeat of Dobell paintings, nor the abstraction in colonial Adelaide intended to demonstrate the gallery's security inadequacies. *A Cavalier* has not been seen again. It has been heard of since; the British art crime blogger Turbo Hendry (aka Paul Hendry) claims it has been offered for sale on the black market in the United States. It might be traded on the black market, used for criminal transactions instead of bulky cash, or stored for use as a plea-bargaining chip. Although NSW police suspended their investigation in 2008, the FBI's art crime team is still pursuing the painting. The theft of Van Mieris's *A Cavalier* remains in their top ten art crimes.

The Stolen Gods

In August 2008, the village of Sripuranthan in Tamil Nadu State in India was about to install a new folding iron gate on its temple. A nine-hundred-year-old stone Sivan temple was constructed when the Chola dynasty ruled an empire centred on what is now Tamil Nadu in southern India – one of thousands of such small village temples erected at the time. This temple had been unused for the last decade due to insufficient funds for maintenance. Its only security was a rusty, iron-grilled gate at the entrance, locked with a chain and padlock.

The village had been warned about the safety of the ancient bronze idols inside their temple. The Tamil Nadu Hindu Religious and Charities Endowment Department offered to take the nine-hundred-year-old idols for safekeeping, but the local people objected. The gods belonged in their temple; they were part of the village's identity. Removing them from their original context would reduce their meaning and significance.

As a compromise, the villagers had agreed to install new security gates at the temple. They then discovered they were locking the temple door after it had been looted. The padlock on the old gate had been glued together by thieves to appear intact. Inside the temple, the ancient idols had already been stolen.

The largest was the *Sripuranthan Nataraja* (aka Shiva Nataraja, The dancing Shiva, The Lord of the Dance), an elegant one-metre-high bronze statue depicting the god Shiva dancing. Two of his four arms are extended to each side, and two are held in front. His long hair is flying out; amongst the strands of hair is a skull, a flower, a crescent moon and the river goddess, Ganga. His left leg is raised, and under his right foot is a dwarf demon representing ignorance. He is ringed by fire representing the dynamic cosmos. Dancing the universe into existence, dancing to sustain it and dancing its destruction.

Along with the Shiva Nataraja were smaller statues. Shiva's wife, Parvati, their son, the elephant-headed god Vinayagar (aka Ganesha), the divine mother Thani Amman, another aspect of the goddess Shivagami Amman, a Chandrasekar (another form of Shiva as the husband of Parvati), and two Tamil poet-saints, Manikkavasagar and the dancing Sambandar.

By the time the theft had been reported and information on the bronze statues uploaded to the Tamil Nadu Police website, the village's stolen god was on exhibition in the National Gallery of Australia (aka NGA), and $5.6 million had changed hands.

Ron Radford, the director of the NGA, wanted to expand the gallery's Indian art collection. In 2007 he flew to New York to personally negotiate its purchase, along with a money-back guarantee. The acquisition was funded by Roslyn Packer, the widow of Kerry Packer, who died the wealthiest man in Australia.

The *Sripuranthan Nataraja* was for sale at Art of the Past Gallery on Madison Avenue at 89th Street. As their address would suggest, Art of the Past sold high-quality antiquities to major art institutions and collectors in the US, Canada, Germany and Singapore. The NGA had done business there before; they were repeat customers, but they didn't get any discounts. Including the $5.6 million for the *Sripuranthan Nataraja*, the NGA spent $10.7 million on 22 works between 2002 and 2011.

Art of the Past was run by Subhash Chandra Kapoor. Kapoor was born in India in 1949 into a family of antique dealers. His father, Parshotam Ram Kapoor, had been tried for art theft and smuggling. And when a child, Subhash was kidnapped. During that ordeal, part of his right ear was bitten off by one of the kidnappers. It was that kind of family business.

The man with a bite out of his ear made a reputation in New York City as a connoisseur of Indian art. Kapoor networked, schmoozing at Manhattan parties and gallery openings, cultivating clients amongst major museums and often donating antiques to the museums.

Before he went shopping for Indian antiquities, Radford had been warned that India is on the International Council of Museums' Red List of countries with cultural heritage vulnerable to destruction or looting. India's Antiquities and Art Treasures Act prohibits the export of any object over a century old. Any purchase of Indian antiquities should have been treated as suspect.

The NGA conducted checks on the provenance of the *Nataraja*. However, instead of intense scrutiny of the details, given the vulnerability of Indian antiquities and the legal issues regarding their export, a kind of optical due diligence was performed to create the right look. This is not uncommon, and many other international museums also lack rigorous provenance-checking procedures. If there is such a thing as the world's best practice for provenance checking, it isn't effective at stopping illegally acquired artefacts.

Determining if an antiquity has been legally obtained is not always easy when criminals work hard to deceive. Unscrupulous dealers are aware of how the provenance they supply would be checked. However, questions need to be asked when so many stolen artefacts end up in state collections.

The glaring error in checking the *Nataraja*'s provenance was that there was only one source – Kapoor. According to the photocopied statements, the *Nataraja* had previously been owned by a now-deceased Sudanese diplomat, Abdulla Mehgoub. It claimed that Mehgoub had purchased it from the Fine Art Museum (a shop that never existed) in the Red Fort Arcade in Delhi in 1970 when he was on a diplomatic posting from 1968 to 1971 and that it had been out of India since 1971, the cutoff date for the legal export of Indian antiquities.

A second photocopy, "letter of provenance", from Mehgoub's widow, Raj Mehgoub, stated that she had inherited the *Nataraja* from her husband. There was also a copy of Art of the Past's fake purchase invoice of the *Nataraja* from Raj Mehgoub on October 18, 2004. The NGA didn't confirm this information with the widow; instead, they checked her American addresses with the White Pages and Google Earth. There was a Sudanese diplomat called Abdulla Mehgoub, but it is not known if he had an art collection and why a Sudanese Muslim was collecting ancient Hindu idols.

If these documents' veracity had been investigated, the NGA would have discovered a fiction created by an art history graduate of Rutgers University, Kapoor's office manager, Aaron M. Freedman.

The Idol Wing, the antiquities theft squad of the Tamil Nadu Police's Economics Offences wing, is needed because of the frequency of theft of idols and other antiques since 1980. Hundreds of thefts from temples in the state, and only about 10 per cent see any progress. So it is remarkable that seven months after the theft of the *Sripuranthan Nataraja* was reported, the Idol Wing made six arrests. In early 2009 they arrested six locals for stealing the idols from the Sivan temple in Sripuranthan village. The locals were looking at two years in prison for stealing from a temple; they would be facing seven for housebreaking. Their statements added to the chain of evidence in the form of shipping bills, courier receipts and bank documents the Idol Wing collected.

The Idol Wing also collects intelligence on, what it describes, as the "nefarious activities of antique dealers and art collectors". Two nefarious antique dealers had met in September 2005 at the five-star Taj Connemara Hotel in Chennai (aka Madras), capital of Tamil Nadu – Subhash Kapoor and Sanjivi Asokan (aka Sanjeevi Ashokan, aka Sanjeeve Asokan).

Asokan knew the ancient temples in the region and the people who robbed them. He drove Kapoor around to show him temples. And Kapoor paid an advance to Asokan to steal Chola-era idols from the Sivan temple at Sripuranthan. Ultimately, Asokan was paid $US12,000 from Kapoor's HSBC bank account.

The thefts from the temple started one night in January 2006. The thieves broke the padlock that locked the door and stole some of the idols from the temple. They glued the padlock back in place and took their loot to Asokan.

Three times the thieves raided the temple. The *Nataraja* was the last of the idols to be abducted because it was so large that a rented truck was needed to transport it. The thieves skirted the village, driving along a dried-up river bed, where they parked out of sight. Soon after, a photograph of the *Sripuranthan Nataraja* in an unknown room somewhere in India was sent to Kapoor.

One of Asokan's assistants ran a front organisation, Ever Star International Services Inc., to export the antiquities. The authentic antiquities were hidden amongst replica bronze idols. Forged documents, along with bribes to customs officials, obtained the required certificates for export.

The *Sripuranthan Nataraja* was exported on November 25, 2006 from Chennai harbour. It was first shipped to Hong Kong and then to London art restorer Neil Perry Smith who cleaned the statue up for sale.

Tracking the export's paperwork led to Nimbus Import Inc., a cloudy cover company in New York owned by Kapoor. There was enough evidence for the Idol Wing to ask Interpol to put a Red Corner Notice for Kapoor's arrest. He was arrested five days later, on October 30, 2011, at Frankfurt International Airport.

While awaiting extradition to India in a German high-security detention centre, Kapoor smuggled out two handwritten notes. They were to his sister, Sushma Sareen, in New York, who ran the business after her brother's arrest, and made a cryptic reference to four idols.

Sareen didn't run her brother's business for long. The Idol Wing's more illustrious and better-funded colleagues in the FBI's art crime team had also investigated Kapoor. They had a wiretap in Kapoor's New York office since 2005. But it was only in 2012, when they intercepted a shipment with a stolen statue, that US authorities could build a case against him.

On January 5, 2012, the United States Homeland Security Investigations raided Art of the Past Gallery and storage facilities connected with Kapoor. Operation Hidden Idol found millions of dollars worth of looted Indian antiquities, including the Amman and Shivagami statues, from the temple at Sri Puranthan village.

More searches followed, and in 2013 Sushma Sareen was charged with four counts of first-degree criminal possession of stolen property for hiding four bronze statues of Hindu deities worth a total of $US14.5 million. These were the four idols Kapoor mentioned in his note smuggled out of detention in Germany. Thanks to Kapoor's warning, Sushma had arranged to move them to another location before the initial raids on Kapoor's storage units.

The Sripuranthan temple was not the only one the thieves robbed, nor were these the only antiquities smuggled from India to Kapoor. In one of the biggest antiquities smuggling rackets the world has seen, Kapoor smuggled antiquities from Afghanistan,

Cambodia, India, Nepal, Pakistan and Thailand. Over thirty years, Kapoor sold about $US145 million in stolen property.

In late 2013 Kapoor's office manager, Aaron M. Freedman, pleaded guilty to one count of criminal conspiracy and five counts of possession of stolen property. One of those counts was for the *Sripuranthan Nataraja,* where he admitted using the Mehgoub name and details to falsify the provenance of the *Nataraja.* His guilty plea was part of a plea deal in exchange for cooperating with investigators to help prosecutors go after his boss.

Another gallery associate and one-time girlfriend of Kapoor, Selina Mohamed (aka Salina Mohamed), also pleaded guilty to a misdemeanour charge of conspiracy and was given a one-year conditional release. She wrote false provenance letters for three items sold to the NGA that stated her parents had bought the *Goddess Pratyangira,* a pair of door guardians [dvarapala], and *The divine couple Lakshmi and Vishnu* from various Indian antiques dealers, including Kapoor's father.

Of the eight idols at the Sri Puranthan temple, six had been in Kapoor's possession. The *Nataraja* was sold to the NGA, the *Ganesha* (aka Vinayagar) was purchased by the Toledo Museum, *Parvati* (aka Uma Parameshvari, the Great Goddess) went to the Asian Civilizations Museums in Singapore, the bronze of the poet-saint *Mannikkavasagar* was purchased by a private collector, and the *Amman* and *Shivagami* statues were found in Kapoor's storage.

In March 2014 Indian government formally requested the return of the *Sripuranthan Nataraja* in thirty days. The embarrassment of the village from having their idols stolen was not matched in Australia. Australian taxpayers were relaxed and comfortable about buying stolen property. Unlike other times when art is connected to a crime, there was no hurricane of media outrage.

As the criminal investigations revealed more and the international scandal grew, Radford said nothing. He did not want to believe that the *Nataraja* was hot property. He was still in denial even as the Australian government started legal action to sue Kapoor to return the money it paid. The money-back-guarantee he had negotiated with Kapoor was worthless now as Art of the Past was closed.

The *Sripuranthan Nataraja* was not the only one that Radford had bought. Before his appointment to the NGA, when he was the director of the Art Gallery of South Australia, he purchased another stolen Nataraja from an art dealer in London. Looted from a temple in the city of Nellai in Tamil Nadu sometime before 1982, it was returned to India in September 2019. The old saying goes: "Fool me once, shame on you; fool me twice, shame on me."

After a decade in the position, Radford's term as the NGA's director expired in September 2014. That month, Australian Prime Minister Tony Abbott officially returned the *Sripuranthan Nataraja* to India. He also returned a stone statue of *Ardhanariswara* that the Art Gallery of NSW had purchased in 2004 for $300,000 from Kapoor. It was not the only antiquity that they had bought from Kapoor. Five of the six items had no provenance and no paperwork except for receipts from Art of the Past. The *Ardhanariswara* had fraudulent documentation that said it had been in Selina Mohamed's collection since 1990.

It was only the first in a series of stolen art returning to India. In 2016 three more antiquities were repatriated. Two had been purchased from Kapoor: an 1800-year-old limestone Buddhist carving and a thousand-year-old stone goddess Pratyangira (aka Lion Lady). In 2019, the NGA returned three more stone statues. In 2021 it announced that it would be returning a further 14 objects worth $3 million acquired from Kapoor and that another 12 objects in its Asian collection were still under investigation.

Australia was not the only country returning stolen sculptures that Kapoor had fenced. US Attorney General Loretta Lynch returned 200 looted antiquities. Many of these had been seized from Kapoor or his clients, including the Ganesha and the Manikkavasagar from the Sri Puranthan temple. Asian Civilisations Museum in Singapore agreed to return the looted statue of Parvati from the Sri Puranthan temple. Several museums are still examining the provenance of the items in their collection and reviewing what to do with the antiquities Kapoor donated.

Kapoor was not the only antiques dealer operating an international criminal enterprise. In the last decade, thousands of misappropriated artefacts have been returned to their country of origin. The restitution of illegally acquired art and antiquities will be an ongoing issue for many art museums. Without proper provenance, they are meaningless without context and unable to be sold.

Why does the NGA need a multi-million-dollar collection of Indian antiquities? In part, they want to emulate colonial institutions like the Louvre and British Museum and have an 'encyclopaedic' collection with items from every culture and period of history. Another way of looking at it is as a dragon with a horde of looted treasure from palaces and temples, like the Benin bronzes and the Acropolis marbles in the British Museum. There are no gloaters as blatant with stolen art collections as state and national galleries.

Their gods had returned. On its return to Sripuranthan village, the *Nataraja* was decked with garlands of yellow and red flowers. Six of the eight bronze idols from the temple are back in India. They are still used in an annual village festival. At other times they are displayed in the security of the Government Museum in the town of Kumbakonam.

Indian justice is slow, especially when Kapoor kept its courts busy with applications and a petition to the Madras High Court. He spent over a decade on remand in Trichy Central Prison in

Tiruchirapalli, Tamil Nadu, only to be sentenced to ten years in November 2022 for receiving stolen property, concealing stolen property and criminal conspiracy. However, Kapoor won't be free with time already served while on remand; other jurisdictions in India, Germany and the US have brought further charges against him.

In 2019 New York District Attorney's Office charged him with 86 felony counts along with six other co-conspirators. More charges against further co-defendants followed, including the extradition of British art restorer Neil Perry Smith. Smith was charged with possessing and restoring twenty-two stolen pieces, including the *Sripuranthan Nataraja*.

"Without restorers to disguise stolen relics, there would be no laundered items for antiquities traffickers to sell," said District Attorney Cyrus Vance. "The arraignment of Neil Perry Smith serves as a reminder that behind every antiquities trafficking ring preying upon cultural heritage for profit, there is someone reassembling and restoring these looted pieces to lend the criminal enterprise a veneer of legitimacy. Thanks to our Antiquities Trafficking Unit and our partners at US Homeland Security Investigations, Smith will now face justice on US soil, and we look forward to seeing alleged ringleader Subhash Kapoor inside of a Manhattan courtroom in the near future. In the meantime, we will continue to pursue these cases vigorously and return these stolen items to the countries from which they were stolen."

Bullshit Artists

False Representations

Captain James Cook's voyage on the *Endeavour* along the east coast of Australia; the first governor of New South Wales, Arthur Phillip; and the first fleet's arrival in Botany Bay. These icons of a British Empire version of Australian history were established before the new Australian federal parliament. And the desire to feel connected to this history was already being exploited by art fakers.

Miniatures are portable portraits painted on thin sheets of ivory with tiny dots of watercolour and opaque white from the tip of a very fine brush. They could be worn as jewellery or held in the palm of a hand. On the afternoon of Tuesday, October 23, 1906, a miniature of Captain Cook was in Frederick George Waley's wrinkled hands.

This particular miniature was of Cook dressed in his naval uniform, was set in an oval frame and looked as if it had been passed through many hands. There were the initials M.A.S. on the tiny painting. Did they mean it was the work of Sir Martin Archer Shee, the famous Irish portrait painter who was elected to the Royal Academy of Arts in 1800 and eventually became its president?

Waley was not impressed with the silver tankard and considered that £10 was too much for it. Although it was well painted, he had doubts about the miniature. He thought that the dates didn't match. He was right; Sir Martin Archer Shee was born in 1769 and would have been ten when Cook was killed in Hawaii in 1779.

Perhaps he, as a member of the Royal Sydney Yacht Squadron, was too keen to own Cook memorabilia or was persuaded by David Andrews's story.

Andrews had told him a story about obtaining the miniature from a man in a grand Melbourne family. He didn't inform him that he had it on approval from Lovell and Co., an antique shop on George Street in Sydney.

When Waley tried to remove the painting from its oval frame, he had the misfortune of breaking it. He discovered a piece of paper underneath the miniature: "Captain Jas. Cook miniature in ivory, painted by Sir Martin Shee R.A. Royal Scottish Academy. Came to London, 1788: entered acc. 1790."

Later that month, Andrews showed Waley two miniatures of Joseph Banks and Arthur Phillips, but Waley wasn't interested after his experience with the one of Cook.

The elderly antique dealer next attempted to sell the two miniatures to the Mitchell Library, the lending branch of the State Library of NSW. He hadn't done business with the library before and, on November 2, approached Hugh Wright, the assistant librarian. Andrews told Wright that the two miniatures were by Henry Raeburn R.A. (Royal Academy), a famous portrait painter.

"Are you sure?"

"Oh yes, there are the initials." He replied helpfully, pointing out the tiny letters.

The eighteenth-century Scottish artist Sir Henry Raeburn R.A. had painted some miniatures as a teenager but soon moved to oil painting and, much later, became the president of the Scottish Academy.

Frank Murcott Bladen, the head of the Mitchell Library, was a heavy drinker and a slip-shod administrator, but he was wise enough to be suspicious of the two miniatures. The backs of the ivory sheets on both looked new. He questioned Andrews about them and thought that although Andrews was initially confident, he became shaky about their authenticity.

Andrews told him a story fit for a tabloid newspaper involving royalty and sex workers. He had known that the miniatures were in the possession of a pawnbroker in Melbourne for several years. And that the pawnbroker had received them from some ladies. The ladies had acquired them from the Duke of Edinburgh, George, the second son of Queen Victoria, on one of his visits to Australia. This was after a dance at Government House where "he visited a place where he either lost them or they were taken from him."

Andrews wanted 50 guineas for the two miniatures. Bladen asked Andrews to leave the miniatures for his consideration. The librarian then did his research; he looked up Michael Bryan's five-volume *Dictionary of Painters and Engravers*; Raeburn did not appear on the list of miniature painters. Next, he consulted with an expert, artist, architect, secretary and the superintendent of the Art Gallery of NSW, Gother Victor Fryers Mann. Mann was confident that they were forgeries and called the police.

When Andrews returned to Bladen's office at the library, just after noon on November 20, Mann, Bladen and Detective Bradley of the NSW police were waiting for him. Bladen soberly told him that they were unquestionable frauds and that he had handed them over to the police. Detective Bradley then arrested Andrews.

Many more professional miniature painters were working in Australia at the start of the twentieth century than there are now. So it is remarkable that Detective Bradley managed to find the two people who had painted the miniatures that Andrews had sold.

Recently arrived in Australia, Constantin Celli trained in painting miniatures in Florence. In 1904 John George Cousins asked him to paint a miniature of Cook. The Italian artist was proud of his work, later telling the court that he considered his painting better than the image from a book Cousins instructed him to copy. He did not sign or put his or anyone else's initials on the miniature; the "M.A.S." was added by someone else.

Cousins was a partner in the antique shop Lovell and Co. with John Lovell; together, they had over eighty years' experience as antique furniture and art dealers. When Celli first showed his Captain Cook to Cousins, he was told that it looked too new and to "put it in a little box, make a little hole in it, and when you smoke, blow some smoke in." He did that and was paid £1 ($147 today) by John Lovell for the newly 'aged' work. It was a low price for such high-quality work, but Celli hoped to get more commissions from it.

Gladys Laycock (aka Glady Daphne Osborne) of Arthur Street, North Sydney, charged more than Celli for her miniatures: £2 and 6 shillings each. Born in Newtown, Sydney, Laycock had studied in London at the Heatherly Art School and in Paris. In 1905 she had set up a studio shop in the retail grandeur of the Strand Arcade in Sydney's central business district with its cast-iron balusters and glass ceiling. Lovell and Cousins met her there in 1907. She made twenty miniatures for them, all copies, and amongst them were Governor Phillip and Joseph Banks. She did not age them, nor was she instructed to, but she did add the initials H.R. on Lovell's instructions. What happened to 18 other miniatures she painted for Lovell and Co. is unknown.

Had Andrews, Cousins and Lovell, in the words of the elderly prosecutor, Mr William Hall Mant of the Crown Law Office, "willfully and wickedly conspired" to defraud Frederick Waley and the State Library? Although the case was strong enough to go to trial without any inside knowledge of the conspiracy, it would be difficult to prove.

On February 14, 1908, all three pleaded not guilty at the Darlinghurst Sessions Court. The three old accused men were allowed to sit with their lawyers outside the dock.

The prosecution did not expect the three accused to turn on each other, as each made sworn statements to the jury.

Andrews claimed that Waley was not correct in how he divided up his sale: the genuine silver tankard was £25, and the miniature £20. He denied that he represented the two miniatures as authentic to Bladen, and only told Waley what Cousins had told him. He maintained the purpose of telling Bladen the story about the Duke of Edinburgh was only an excuse to avoid divulging the names of "principals", and he still believed what he sold was genuine.

Cousins denied giving Andrews the miniature on approval for £15, claiming that he had sold them to him outright. While he might have said the tankard was eighteenth-century, he did not say that miniatures were by any notable artists.

Likewise, Lovell claimed that Captain Cook's miniature had never been represented as genuine but was easily worth £15. He had no idea how the piece of paper stating that it was painted by Sir Martin Shee arrived behind the painted ivory. Furthermore, he denied telling Andrews the stories about the other miniatures belonging to the Duke of Edinburgh.

The three accused were implicating each other of fraud. Was Andrews a freelance conman using Lovell and Cousins's stock, or was he an ignorant dupe used as a front to peddle their fakes? Cousin's barrister, James Conley Gannon, wanted a ruling from the judge on whether Andrews's evidence should be considered evidence against Cousins and Lovell; if it was, then a new defence would have to be presented. Judge Ernest Brougham Docker replied in his usual forthright manner, "You will be entitled to do that not only in cross-examination, but you are entitled to contradict by your own evidence. The jury would be told to consider the whole evidence."

Gannon then proceeded to cross-examine Andrews about what he had told Bladen. During this cross-examination, Andrews collapsed, and the court adjourned to give him a brief rest. After

Andrews recovered, Gannon continued his cross-examination: "Did you tell Mr Bladen that Raeburn was the president of the Scottish Royal Academy?"

Andrews collapsed again. When he recovered, he revealed to the court: "I did not know that there was such an academy."

With the case concluding on a Friday, you might imagine the jury would quickly reach a verdict. On Saturday morning, after being locked up for the night, the jury's foreman told Judge Docker that they could not reach a verdict.

Docker: Is there any chance of your being able to agree if we were to wait a little longer?

Foreman: I don't think so, Your Honour. We have considered the matter fully, and there is no prospect of our coming to an agreement.

Docker: In that case, I will now discharge you.

Nugent Robertson, the barrister appearing for Andrews: May I say, your Honour, that it is possible that the jury may have agreed with regard to one of the accused?

Docker: Have you agreed with regard to one of the accused?

Foreman: We think that fraud has been committed in a general way.

Docker: I only want to know if you have been unanimous with regard to any one of the accused?

Foreman: We are not unanimous on any point with respect to any particular one of the accused.

A week later, the re-trial began, but its jury failed again to agree on a verdict. After the two failed attempts to obtain a conviction, the prosecution of the three old antique dealers was abandoned. The fake miniatures continue circulating in the antique market, and the difference between the manufacture and the sale continues complicating art forgery trials.

Pro art forgers

In Adelaide, in the lead-up to Christmas 1950, thirty to forty people purchased watercolours purportedly by famous Western Arrarnta artist Albert Namatjira (aka Elea Namatjira). They were forgeries. The police investigated, but no arrests were made.

Namatjira was the first internationally known Indigenous artist, and his European-style watercolours were in high demand. His paintings captured the blue shadows on ghost gums and the ancient iron oxide red rocks around the MacDonnell Ranges in Central Australia. In 1938 his first two exhibitions in Sydney and Melbourne sold out, and the demand for his art did not diminish during his lifetime. In his 25 years of working as an artist, Namatjira painted one or two paintings a week, adding up to thousands of landscapes of his country.

However, fakes of Namatjira are also common. In 1952 Victoria and SA police investigated more fakes. They were trying to find the source of the forgeries of Namatjira's signatures found in Melbourne and Adelaide. And again, no arrests were made.

It is not illegal to make art that looks like another artist's work; artists have been doing that forever, and copying is a legitimate part of many artists' education. To further complicate things, numerous watercolours of Central Australian landscapes look like Namatjira's paintings.

Some of these are by his relatives. Albert Namatjira was the first and most talented of the 'Hermannsburg School', but he was not the only Arrernte artist from Ntaria (aka Hermannsburg) painting watercolour landscapes of the same country. Although never intended to be forgeries, watercolours by people in the Hermannsburg School can become instantly more valuable by replacing the artist's signature with a forged one.

'Authentic' is at one end of a scale, which goes from originals, replicas, versions, revivals, copies, reproductions, and mistaken attributions to outright fraudulent misrepresentations at the other end. It only becomes illegal when fake art is used to obtain money by pretending they are genuine.

How much of the art in the secondary art market are fakes and forgeries is a matter of conjecture. Every time a forgery is discovered, art dealers contend that the police and public are unaware of the severity of art fraud. For when one forgery is found, it means that others haven't been. Consider the incidence of people in the 1970s forging another painter from outback Australia, Pro Hart (aka Kevin Charles Hart).

The Broken Hill brushman's art wasn't cheap but wasn't unaffordable, either. Pro Hart's loose brushwork, arty inventiveness and vibrant colours are very recognisable and, in the 1970s, were desirable. His style was enjoyed by the general public, and he was the star of carpet advertisements on TV. In the advert, Hart would paint his signature dragonfly with spilled drinks and food across a white carpet, only to be cleaned away thanks to an ethnic stereotype and the carpet's stain-resistant powers.

In January 1975, three forged paintings attributed to Pro Hart were discovered in Adelaide. Hart described them as "pathetic copies" but complimented the quality of the forged signature. All came from the same source; a young man was selling them in November

1974. People had paid up to $900 (equivalent value of $6100 today) for the larger paintings. Forty-nine more forgeries were uncovered, but nobody knew how many more were out there. After that, Hart assured reporters that he would be keeping better records.

Newspaper reports of the Pro Hart forgeries were published across the continent. At the time, one art dealer told the *Sydney Morning Herald* that he was worried that forged Nolans, Drysdales and Boyds were being mass-produced by a cottage industry involving hundreds of people in Holland and Belgium. I doubt there were so many people or that they were so far away. One hardworking art faker, determined to produce mediocre imitations, can paint a lot of pastiches. (And later in this book, you will encounter a very hardworking and determined art faker from Sydney. A one-man factory that produced thousands of paintings.)

Dr George Robert Cockburn turned a suspicious eye towards the two paintings hanging on the wall in his home on Whale Beach. He had read the newspaper reports about Pro Hart forgeries. He had bought the two paintings from Jan Pieter Damsleeg, who claimed they were by Pro Hart, but who really painted *Waterhole* and *The Fencer*?

Cockburn had paid $700 for the larger, *Waterhole,* and $290 for *The Fencer*. And Damsleeg had given him certificates of authenticity for the paintings from a Sydney art gallery. He had to know whether Damsleeg had deceived and ripped him off for almost $1000 (worth about $7000 today). So Dr Cockburn drove the 1200km to Broken Hill to show Pro Hart the two paintings.

Hart described them as "generally rough and a crook painting" and "pretty amateurish". After that, Dr Cockburn contacted the police, who charged Damsleeg with two counts of obtaining money by deception.

Damsleeg claimed he had bought the paintings from a man in Melbourne. The man told him that he had them authenticated by a Sydney art gallery and had certificates of authenticity to back him up. If they were forgeries, then they had fooled him.

Had Damsleeg painted these works himself? He was an amateur painter and had given two paintings to Dr Cockburn's daughter Suzanne. Pro Hart testified at trial that he thought that Damsleeg's paintings were similar and that it was his opinion that they were all painted by the same person. (At this point, my head explodes with possible motivations.)

However, there was no evidence that Damsleeg knew the paintings were forgeries. Perhaps he did buy them from a man in Melbourne. Maybe he, too, had been fooled. With this reasonable doubt, a jury found him not guilty in 1977.

Both Pro Hart and Albert Namatjira were popular artists with a clearly defined style, and, at the time, their work was in high demand. And when the art market heats up, need, speed and greed allow attribution to slip. However, this is not to condemn their buyers; people sometimes dismiss forgery as a result of art collectors motivated by greed and not a love of art.

What we love is individual and not interchangeable: love is about a particular individual, not their identical twin. Loving a person – or a work of art – is not just about loving that individual's qualities.

Art forgery is like identity theft because it abuses personal identity and history; it hurts many more than just those who lose money. Artists feel sickened by the 'abuse of their name' because forgeries don't aspire to be great works of art; the forger aims to produce an imitation of the artist's less-than-average work that will still sell. If forgeries are accepted as genuine, they dilute the total quality of the artist's work.

For that reason, Pro Hart spent $8000 (about $23,000 today) in the late 1970s buying fakes of his work to get them off the market. Still plagued by forgeries, Hart took advantage of new technology and started to label his work with his own DNA. As the cleaning lady from the *Stainmaster* advertisements would say: 'Oh, Mr Hart! What a mess!'

A dealer in 'Drysdales'

Peter Cornelius Sparnaay could always spin a yarn. The naturalised Dutch immigrant had been telling them socially and professionally for many years, as a husband, as a washing machine repairman and as an art dealer.

Sparnaay persuaded John Galvin, a solicitor living in Malvern, to pay $485 ($3700 today) for a drawing of a nude in March 1974. He told him it was by the great Australian modernist painter of dry gullies, elongated people and streets of weatherboard houses in the iron-oxide reds and browns of outback droughts – Russell Drysdale (aka Tass Drysdale). After all, 'Russell Drysdale' was written under the drawing.

Sparnaay explained to Galvin that Drysdale's eyesight was failing and that this drawing would be amongst his last. Sparnaay was right about one thing, Drysdale's eyesight was failing; it had been most of his life due to a detached retina he suffered when he was 17. But nothing else Sparnaay said was true, and he knew it.

Sparnaay had bought about seventy drawings for $11,000 ($73,000 today) from Barry Simpson between 1974 and 1975. Simpson had purchased them from an estate because he believed they were original Drysdales. Simpson sent four of the drawings to Leonard Joel auctions, where Paul Dwyer looked at them and concluded they were fakes.

Dwyer knew what was and wasn't a Drysdale drawing. He had grown up looking at Australian art. Unlike Sparnaay, Dwyer hadn't just started selling art a couple of years ago. Dwyer was the second generation of his family to sell art as a business, and he had been looking at Drysdales all his life.

Simpson phoned Sparnaay to report the bad news.

"OK, as long as I get my money back," Sparnaay replied.

Simpson wasn't going to give Sparnaay a refund. He'd never claimed the drawings were by Drysdale – he just thought they were. So Sparnaay continued selling them at his Upstairs Gallery amongst the antique dealers and boutiques of Armadale. He priced them between $600 and $2295 and was careful to only put a few out at a time so as not to arouse suspicion or to flood the market. Sparnaay didn't make his money back before he was arrested. He sold a total of $2915 ($24,175 today) to six buyers. Two of the buyers were 'art dealers', whose professionalism appears to be on Sparnaay's level.

It is unlikely this was the first time Sparnaay had lied to make an art sale. Sparnaay was a very dodgy dealer with four previous convictions, all involving deceit.

One June morning in 1963, Sparnaay was in bed with Nola Joy Milthorpe when three "licensed inquiry agents" (aka private detectives) entered the house in Toorak. Kenneth Osmond, George Hooking and his wife Colleen Hooking shone flashlights in Sparnaay's face and took a photograph. Sparnaay jumped out of bed, punched Osmond in the face, hit Colleen with the wine bottle and went at George Hooking with the broken bottleneck before Colleen hit him with her torch. Before no-fault divorces, it was necessary to prove adultery, desertion or other faults, and the three private detectives were employed by Mrs Sparnaay. The magistrate was sympathetic to Sparnaay's rude awakening and fined him £38 ($1020 today). Mrs Sparnaay was not and divorced him.

In 1967 he was convicted and sentenced to three years for being the mastermind in a conspiracy defrauding people over repairs to refrigerators and washing machines. In sentencing him, Justice Starke told Sparnaay, "You preyed basically on housewives, were prepared to obtain their appliances by hook or by crook, do as little as possible in the way of repairs, if at all, and charge excessive prices."

In 1977 Sparnaay was in the County Court again; this time, he was pleading not guilty to six deception charges and one charge of attempted deception. It was art fraud rather than art forgery because the artist may not have intended to deceive anyone – they drew something that looked vaguely similar to Drysdale's work. Who had written the name Russell Drysdale on them and why is another question.

Art forgery and fraud are not easy crimes for law enforcement. Two more charges of deception against Sparnaay were dropped due to insufficient evidence. The chief difficulty is obtaining proof of the intent to deceive. It is often easier to sue the seller of a fake in civil law than to prosecute in criminal law. Most disputes about the authenticity of art are settled out of court. The buyer is refunded, and the fake art is returned to the dealer for another attempt at a sale.

If Galvin's testimony wasn't enough to prove that Sparnaay had intended to deceive them the prosecution also had Barry Simpson, who had told Sparnaay of Dwyer's opinion that the drawings were fakes. This made it clear that Sparnaay had not been duped into selling fakes.

And to allay any doubts that the drawings weren't really by Drysdale, the sixty-five-year-old artist came from Gosford to give evidence. When Drysdale was in the witness box, he was shown thirty-four pen and ink drawings of nude women. "None of these are by me. I haven't drawn nudes like these for a long time. These were drawn from life class models, and I haven't drawn from nude models for a long period."

Drysdale was telling the truth; he hadn't drawn from a nude model in decades. The Art Gallery of NSW has a pencil and water-colour drawing of a female nude by Drysdale from 1937 when he was still a student. After the 1940s, he focused on images of drought-ravaged landscapes populated by thin people in shapeless clothes.

Sparnaay's defence team had one more stab at establishing his ignorance that the drawings were not by Drysdale. They argued that a guilty man would not have openly displayed the fakes while the artist was still alive and able to identify them as fakes. It didn't convince anyone. In was the first successful prosecution for art fraud in Victoria. Sparnaay was found guilty of five of the six counts of dishonestly obtaining money and sentenced to two and a half years.

The fake dripper

"There has been nothing like this since 'Blue Poles' Jackson Pollock Exhibition in Australia". On April 19, 1978, *The Australian Woman's Weekly* ran this headline with a full-colour spread on pages 2 and 3 of images of drip paintings purported to be by the famous abstract expressionist. Long dripping trails of bright red, yellow, white and blue paint obscured areas that had been painted with a brush.

Only the paintings were not by Jackson Pollock; the entire exhibition was fake. This is not about expertise, talent or detection but selling a con.

The name of the influential American Abstract-Expressionist painter, Jackson Pollock, was familiar to many Australians in 1978. The avant-garde artist appeared in mainstream magazines. In 1949 *Life* magazine asked, "Is he the greatest living painter in the United States?" In 1958 *Time* magazine dubbed him "Jack the dripper". And by the 1970s, Pollock's place in art history was assured, including in high-school textbooks.

In 1973 the National Gallery of Australia purchased Pollock's 'Blue Poles' (aka *Number 11* 1952) for $1.3 million. The subsequent media and political controversy over the price for a drip painting had made Pollock a household name across Australia. However, far fewer people in Australia had actually seen 'Blue Poles'. It had yet to go on exhibition because the National Gallery of Australia was still under construction.

Australia needed an American abstract-expressionist painting in its national collection to tell the story of post-war art, at least the version of loyalty to the US. It is a Cold-War story; the lone, anxious, rebel, genius American painting of inarticulate abstracts contrasting with socialist realists. The vague spiritual nature of the abstract contrasted with the propaganda value of images of Soviet realism. Even if you didn't like Pollock's art, you had to admit he had freedom of expression.

The Pollock exhibition was at Bohdan Ledwij's Fine Art Galleries, at 252 Adelaide Terrace in central Perth. Its thirty-two-year-old director knew how to get a story published (give inducements to the editor), but he outdid himself this time. *The Australian Woman's Weekly* had a gigantic circulation but was better known for its recipes than its arts coverage.

Bohdan Ledwij (aka Bob) claimed to be an entrepreneur and art dealer who had amassed a collection of Pollock paintings allegedly insured for $4.1 million. He told the *Woman's Weekly* that the Pollocks had been acquired from probate cases and divorces. A strange kind of art dealer who talked down his collection while playing to popular prejudices. "So many of his paintings look alike – grotesque trails and splurges of thick paint usually flung at the canvas when Pollock was in a drunken stupor."

The exhibition consisted of nine handsomely framed paintings, including four small studies for 'Blue Poles': *Blue Polls, Autumn Song, Arabesque* and *Vacant Spaces*. The works were all paper mounted on board. Looking at the paintings reproduced in *The Woman's Weekly* with their garish paint drips of primary colours, it is hard to comprehend how people were deceived.

A genuine Pollock has a dense network of often delicate lines of dripped paint, emphasising the flat canvas and the end of illusionary space. Painted with the canvas flat on the floor of his studio, Pollock worked on all sides spreading the drips evenly across a large canvas.

So where were the experts who knew what Pollock's paintings looked like – that they are on canvas and not paper? That he eschewed paint brushes, didn't do studies and numbered, not named his paintings? Not in Perth, the capital city furthermost from the rest of the world, the last state in Australia to see modern art. Maybe some of the people at the exhibition could have known better. Four years earlier, there had been an exhibition of American Abstract-Expressionist paintings at the old Art Gallery of Western Australia (aka AGWA). And the American art critic, and expert on Pollock, Clement Greenberg, travelled to Perth and gave a talk at the exhibition. However, this is not about people paying attention and remembering exhibition floor talks four years later. People don't go to art galleries to doubt the work's authenticity; they go to see art and socialise.

I wonder who paid for Elwyn Augustus Lynn (aka Jack Lynn), the then curator of the Power Gallery of Contemporary Art at Sydney University and an art critic for *The Australian*, to fly across the continent to open the exhibition. Although Lynn was well read, he was hardly an expert on Pollock or abstract expressionism. Andrew Saw, *The Australian's* young art critic in Perth, had less experience and gave the show a gushing review.

Not everyone who came to Ledwij's "Paintings by Jackson Pollock" was convinced by what was on show. Perth artist Bill Elwyn Hawthorn remembers seeing it and described the paintings as uniform, very clean, underworked pastiches. When he asked Ledwij why the paintings looked clean, he was told they had been cleaned for the exhibition. Hawthorn was sceptical about anything Ledwij told him after waiting on payments for sales of his art, only for Ledwij to say the deal had fallen through.

Nobody purchased any drip paintings on exhibition. And Ledwij next offered Ken Reinhard, principal of Alexander Mackie College of Arts, a teacher training college in Sydney, to transport the exhibition to Sydney. Ken Reinhard later told reporters: "I have to admit I wouldn't have known an original Pollock from a bull's foot in 1978 but to get a chance to put on a free exhibition of Pollock's seemed too good to pass up."

Only when the exhibition was about to open in Sydney did some people doubt the authenticity of the decoratively paint-dripped works. Terry Ingram, the arts correspondent for *The Australian Financial Review*, was one, writing that "surely are not those of the great Jackson Pollock, we have come to know, the untidy, neurotic genius who lived in a pigsty and painted Blue Poles." Nancy Borlase, the art critic for *The Sydney Morning Herald*, was another doubter questioning the painting's provenance and the misspelt *Blue Polls*. Neither journalist was an expert in Jackson Pollock, but they knew how to contact one.

The experts weren't fooled for a minute. Clement Greenberg only had to see a copy of *The Australian Women's Weekly* to know that it was wrong. Pollock's widow, Lee Krasner, made a statement that the paintings were fakes and that the exhibition's proposition was wrong as Pollock did not paint studies.

Ledwij must have regretted the extent of media coverage when the *New York Times* reported "'Jackson Pollock' Exhibit to Be Checked". The Sydney exhibition was cancelled, and Ledwij removed his paintings. He claimed they were being sent to Los Angeles to be authenticated. "I am no expert and have never claimed to be, but I have documentary evidence these are genuine Pollocks." And announced libel action against *Willesee at 7*, *The Australian* and *The Mirror* for reporting his exhibition was fake.

It turns out that "Paintings by Jackson Pollock" was not the only fake exhibition at Fine Art Galleries that year. Ledwij also exhibited

David Mabbutt F.R.S.' (Fellow of the Royal Society), claiming that Mabbutt had art in the collection of the Queen, the Tate and the National Gallery, London. Only there never was an artist called David Mabbutt in the Royal Society, nor with art in the collection of the Queen, the Tate, nor the National Gallery.

It was all a con; Ledwij was a failed artist trying to prove his talent through fraud. How much of a con artist and how large the fraud was not exposed until he was arrested. Ledwij had sold 'half shares' in his enterprise to three men: Bunbury radiologist Dr Pratten, Dr Martin from the Perth suburb of Salter Point and Mr Colin from Mount Lawley. Ledwij had been pretending to be buying paintings for Dr Pratten; instead, he used the money to pay for his gallery, travel and private life.

Ledwij was held on remand because he was a flight risk due to the $70,909 in a Swiss bank account. He claimed to have no control over the account and that he was a negotiating agent for a tax scheme to donate a 'million dollar' painting to a public gallery. The police took possession of the allegedly 'million dollars' painting, *Arabesque 2*, the largest of the fake Pollock's at 10m x 1m.

In 1979, Bohdan Ledwij was found guilty of seven charges of stealing $436,156 ($2,092,000 today) from Dr Pratten. He stole $185,406, claiming it was for the purchase of paintings, $199,300 for the fake Pollocks and $51,450 for a deposit to buy the Tattersalls Club in Perth. Ledwij was sentenced to six years in jail, with a minimum of four years before parole. Completing a lying bastard quadrella, Ledwij was also charged with perjury for giving false evidence at his bail hearing.

> *"Bohdan Ledwij is a boy who likes art*
> *Some of his paintings seem odd at the start."*

One of Ledwij's schoolmates at Altona High School in Perth wrote this strangely prophetic doggerel verse for their school magazine. As the poem foretold, some of his paintings appeared odd at the start and then, after closer analysis, outright fakes. None of the money Ledwij obtained was recovered by the time of his trial, and a decade later, he was declared bankrupt. He listed his occupation as "art designer" in his bankruptcy declaration.

The problem of art forgers is often confused with ideas about artistic skill versus originality, failing to distinguish between fakes, forgeries, copies, appropriation and piracy. There is a popular, fatuous idea that there is a great skill and technical ability in being an art forger. The idea is often celebrated in popular culture. The forger and conman are portrayed as the little guy sticking it to the experts, the connoisseurs and other establishment figures. Collectors blamed for being greedy. Experts blamed for not knowing everything. It is entertaining until you realise it is victim blaming.

Blundell's innuendos

"They are not Brett Whiteley, full stop. They are impressions and innuendos. They were done on consignment for the deceased for decorative purposes. She was quite aware they were copies," Sydney's most notorious and blatant art faker, William Blundell, declared. His whiney nasal voice strained for emphasis as he gave evidence in front of Justice William Windeyer.

It was an extraordinary courtroom revelation in the Equity Division of the NSW Supreme Court. Not since Van Meegeren proved that he was an art forger and not a Nazi collaborator who had sold Dutch masterpieces to the enemy had an art faker needed to tell all in court.

Blundell had not been charged with any crime; he was in court to explain why Germaine Curvers included him in her will and her estate's actual value. The scrawny, fifty-two-year-old furniture dealer revealed that the assumed millions of dollars in paintings by Picasso, Pollock, Streeton and Whiteley in Germaine Curvers's art collection were all fakes. Of 161 paintings brought to court, only twenty-three were not by him.

Four days before her death from breast cancer, the seventy-one-year-old Germaine Curvers had made a new will. Blundell had typed out this will, and it was signed before witnesses. As her executor, she named William Blundell, left nothing to her estranged husband, the millionaire property developer John Curvers, nor her son Patrick or her daughter Sabrina. Instead, she left her estate to other relatives and friends, including Blundell, along with several charities – the Salvation Army, the AIDS foundation and, not surprisingly, the Cancer Council.

When she was alive, the Belgium-born Germaine Marie Françoise Toussaint Curvers was a larger-than-life Sydney socialite. Dressed in eye-popping colours, leaning forward to air kiss with a long cigarette holder in one hand and a champagne glass in the other. She enjoyed playing up her French accent. "Darling!"

Curvers met Blundell when she was decorating the bed and breakfast place she ran. Blundell was painting imitation Heidelberg School style impressionist scenes. She bought dozens of them, paying him a couple hundred dollars for each painting and about $50 for the antique frame. Blundell's paintings decorated the walls, and her guests were impressed. She then covered her Woollahra mansion walls in the same manner, and her many friends were impressed with her new art collection.

William Blundell calls his paintings 'innuendos' because they were suggestions of the work of famous artists rather than blatant forgeries. He says they are 'intended for decorative purposes', but he uses period pigments and attempts to age his work using coffee or, even less successfully, a microwave that left tiny holes in the paint's surface. It is not illegal to copy an artist's signature or create the effect of age on the artwork; there are innocent reasons why this might be done – for a movie prop or just for decorative effect. Blundell even signs the work with initials to suggest a "Streeton" or "Whiteley"; under common law, it is not illegal to forge a signature on art. It is only unlawful on documents.

Blundell claims that he has done over four thousand paintings and drawings in the styles of Charles Blackman, Arthur Boyd, William Dobell, Russell Drysdale, Sidney Nolan, Arthur Streeton, Claude Monet and Brett Whiteley. Over two hundred paintings and drawings suggestive of Brett Whiteley alone. Blundell might be exaggerating, but the number of his fakes in Curver's collection suggests he is not far off.

Unlike art forgers, Blundell doesn't create fakes out of a thwarted artistic ambition or greed; faking art seems to be a personal goal. Perhaps, as an identical twin, he always believed that all copies are equal. He studied with the Sydney-based impressionist painter James Ralph Jackson. He learnt to fake at the public expense, taking advantage of the Art Gallery of NSW's appraisal service to learn what was wrong with his early attempts. He staged an exhibition of his own impressionist-style paintings, 'Homage to the 9x5s', referencing the Australian impressionist exhibition painted on cigar box lids. And he has enjoyed the attention of being exposed as an art faker in three separate *Four Corners* programs in 1984, 1990, and 1999.

Blundell wasn't committing a crime; Curvers was exploiting his desire to paint copies. And after her death, he had the evidence, for in Curvers's handwritten ledger were recorded her sale of hundreds of his 'innuendos'.

Curvers saw fine art as high-end fashion labels; it was about names that said exclusivity and prestige. So she became a frequent buyer from Blundell, selling them as genuine works in her Windsor Street Art Gallery in Paddington in the 1980s and 1990s. She studied her clients, watching for people who consistently underbid at art auctions and believed that bargains existed in high-end art.

Curvers wasn't just selling fakes in Sydney; she travelled interstate to place Blundell's work in various art auctions. She sold about two hundred paintings through Brisbane's Isle Love Auction Centre until, in 1992, she was told that her consignments would not be accepted because of doubts over their authenticity.

Blundell's witness box revelation that Germaine's art collection was fake was a big surprise to her husband and children. Many more people were surprised how Germaine had gotten away with so much art fraud for so long.

There had been complaints about Curvers's art gallery ever since it opened. Although art fraud was being committed on a massive level, the police were only called in once; in 1994, over a dispute about the authenticity of Brett Whiteley paintings sold to a doctor. However, by refunding the sale price and claiming she had bought the paintings in good faith, Curvers made the police and the problem disappear in the eyes of the law.

The dispute over her will in the Supreme Court would not cause all of Blundell's fakes to disappear from the art market. On the contrary, in 2002, the Supreme Court ruled that the 917 paintings in Germaine Curvers's estate could be sold. William Blundell continues to paint, and his fakes keep turning up in the art market, even acknowledged and described as: "in the manner of Arthur Streeton & initialled 'A. S' lower right".

Faking Possum

"Not mine! Not mine! Not mine!" The renowned Anmatyerre artist Clifford Possum Tjapaltjarri, with his big grey beard and tangled hair under the wide brim of his brown leather stockman's hat, disclaimed eighteen paintings.

Tjapaltjarri was born around 1932, northwest of Alice Springs. His family had moved there after the Coniston Massacre in 1928. His mother also raised his cousin, Billy Stockman Tjapaltjarri (born c. 1927), who, as an infant, had survived the massacre. He was hidden shortly before his mother was killed along with between 30 and 200 other Warlpiri, Anmatyerre and Kaytetye people by the Northern Territory Police.

His family gave him the name 'Possum', and 'Tjapaltjarri' is his 'skin' kinship group. He had a traditional bush upbringing in the Mount Allan area. In the 1950s, following the example of his grandfather and two older brothers, he started wood carving for the tourist market. In 1972, he joined the men's painting circle at Papunya School and moved from tourism to the fine art market. Over the next three decades, his career as an artist flourished. His Western Desert 'dot' painting met with international acclaim. He had a retrospective exhibition at the Institute of Contemporary Art in London in 1988 and was in the collections of major Australian galleries.

The exhibition at the Christopher Day Gallery in Paddington hadn't even opened yet when, on Tuesday, February 23, 1999,

Tjapaltjarri denied the attribution of the eighteen paintings. That only left four paintings. The paintings came down and were moved to a Mascot warehouse.

Unlike most art dealers, the young British art toff, Patrick Corbally Stourton, didn't represent the artist whose work he was selling. He had bought all the paintings wholesale. Dr Ronald Fine, a Sydney-based art collector, had also purchased paintings from the same wholesaler, John O'Loughlin, and donated them to the Art Gallery of NSW and the Museum of Contemporary Art.

So instead of being the guest of honour at the exhibition, it became a tour to identify fakes. Tjapaltjarri pointed out two incorrectly attributed paintings in the Art Gallery of NSW's collection and five more at the Museum of Contemporary Art; all had been donated by Dr Fine.

Tjapaltjarri first met O'Loughlin in 1990. At the time, O'Loughlin ran an art gallery in the Sheraton Hotel. By the late 1990s, the Australian Indigenous art market was booming, and O'Loughlin now operated as an Indigenous art wholesaler. Indigenous art had become an important sector of the Australian art market, with international art collectors hot to buy. The presence of multiple Indigenous art wholesalers indicates how demand was increasing exponentially. Conditions were ripe for the faking of Indigenous art.

During the 1990s, O'Loughlin sold many authentic paintings by Tjapaltjarri before, but when supply didn't match demand, he took matters into his own hands. All he had to do was paint some Western Desert dot-painting-style canvases. Load them into his car, drive up to Alice Springs and persuade Tjapaltjarri to sign the backs of the canvases.

The old artist was under financial pressure. His extended family and his own drinking and gambling meant he lived a hand-to-mouth existence. And he was never punctilious about signing paintings, selling unfinished works to tourists and signing pieces by other family members. So it was easy for O'Loughlin to put the screws on him.

As Tjapaltjarri explained, "He give me fifty dollars for signing canvas with painting... not my work. I have never seen painting. He take me way out in the bush, way out, 30 or 40 miles out. I was scared he might be too bad for me."

"The second time he come back in 97, bring a roll of canvases and find me walking in street in Alice Springs and he take me bush and tell me, 'I pay you to sign em'. He tell me 'Your painting from long time', I was thinking in my heart you lie...that not my work. I sign...don't know... probably big one, must be ten, eleven paintings...because I was drunk. Once every canvas he take my picture as I sign, I was frightened...you know I was scared. I remember there were round ones and square ones...I remember not mine because they not my story. I was thinking that the fella might get rid of people that far out."

O'Loughlin photographed Tjapaltjarri signing the backs of the paintings. CLiFFoRD PoSSUM – all capital letters except for the small 'i' and 'o'.

Investigating detectives Paul Baker and Paul Simonsson of the Commercial Crimes Agency interviewed people in Adelaide and Alice Springs.

Geoffrey McMillan gave a statement along with a photograph showing O'Loughlin in 1993 painting in the style of Eunice Napangardi, an established Indigenous artist. When O'Loughlin found out that McMillan had given a statement to the police, he confronted him.

"I just want to know why you are trying to shaft me".

"What do you mean?"

"I've just read your statement to the cops and you have rolled over on me".

"What in the statement is not true?"

"Nothing, it's all true, but a mate wouldn't do that to another mate," O'Loughlin retorted. According to McMillan, O'Loughlin denies that this conversation took place.

And following a lead from a telephone intercept, Baker and Simonsson found O'Loughlin's secret studio in a tin shed on a property south of Adelaide, near the township of Willunga, with some completed and partially completed 'dot' paintings.

In October 1999, O'Loughlin was arrested, extradited to New South Wales, and charged with obtaining money by deception and using a false instrument. In July 2000, there was a four-day committal hearing before Magistrate Ian Barnett at the Downing Centre Local Court, Sydney, to determine if the matter should proceed to trial. And O'Loughlin was indicted on twenty-two counts of deception.

What exactly did Tjapaltjarri mean by "not mine!" Were all these paintings forgeries? Tjapaltjarri spoke six Western Desert languages, including Anmatyerre, but only a "little bit English". And he didn't deny that it was his signature on the backs of the canvases. Even with a translator, the sixty-eight-year old had a confusing time giving evidence. Without any familiarity with court cases, he couldn't understand what was being asked of him, especially why he should be questioned by O'Loughlin's council.

It was clear from the committal hearing that a trial for art forgery would be problematic for several reasons, not only because of how difficult it was for Tjapaltjarri to give evidence. This would not be a charge of forgery because you can only forge documents, not paintings.

Further complicating a forgery prosecution, O'Loughlin believed he had been initiated and, as a relative, had a right to make the images. It was a story that other non-Indigenous art dealers were telling at the time. It might have been an incorrect and self-serving belief. Still proving O'Loughlin had criminal intent when he painted the art Tjapaltjarri signed would be difficult.

Although Western Desert Indigenous culture has different concepts of authorship or responsibility for images, the owner of an image can instruct a family member to do the actual painting. This is not very different from the workshops of Rubens, Titian or other old masters of European art. However, you look at it, the paintings that O'Loughlin had asked him to sign Tjapaltjarri were "not my work...because they are not my story".

In a pragmatic and expedient move to secure a conviction, the DPP made O'Loughlin an offer. Plead guilty to five counts of obtaining money by false and misleading statements when he claimed that each of the works was entirely painted by Tjapaltjarri to detectives Baker and Simonson during police interviews, and to Corbally Stourton and Dr Fine when he sold them. In November 2000, O'Loughlin was given a three-month suspended sentence and placed on a good behaviour bond for three years. It wasn't a sentence likely to deter others. Still, it was Australia's first successful prosecution for faking Indigenous art.

The fakes that Tjapaltjarri identified did not exhaust the supply of fake Indigenous art. Fake works in the style of Emily Kame Kngwarreye, Turkey Tolson Tjupurrula, Ginger Riley Munduwalawala and other artists continued to be discovered at auctions. Some people thought it was open season for forging Indigenous art.

The Toorak forgers

Around 1926, in the Great Sandy Desert at Well 33 on the Canning Stock Route, a Kukatja–Wangkatjungka boy was born. It was just after 'the killing times' when European cattlemen massacred the Indigenous peoples. The last of such slaughters occurred only a year or two earlier at Bedford Downs Station, where station hands murdered a group of Gija and Worla men in retaliation for spearing a cow. The police assisted by burning the bodies. The boy would become a great artist, Rover Julama Thomas.

Like many Indigenous men in the Kimberley, Rover Thomas worked as a stockman on the region's vast cattle stations for most of his adult life. He saw the start of the Argyle diamond mine in the area – not that he profited from any of it. A slave in all but name.

In 1968, equal pay for Indigenous workers marked the end of their exploitation at cattle stations and a way of life for Rover. In 1974, he was living at Warmun (aka Turkey Creek) in the East Kimberley, 3009km northeast of Perth on the Great Northern Highway. It wasn't much of a place, just a couple of buildings with no running water.

The same year that Rover moved to Warmun, on December 25, Cyclone Tracy destroyed Darwin. The consensus among the senior Aboriginal men in the Kimberley was that the cyclone was a manifestation of the Rainbow Serpent. It was a sign of the neglect and decline in Australian Indigenous culture and religion. Their remedy was to create more culture.

Two senior men received dreams from dead relatives that taught them a 'palga', a narrative dance cycle. The first was Geoffrey Mangalamarra from Kalumburu in the far north Kimberley, who organised for his Cyclone Tracy palga to be performed in various Indigenous communities in the Kimberley. Rover Thomas received dreams from his recently deceased sister, instructing him on creating his Kurirr-Kurirr Cycle (aka Kuril Kuril ceremony).

At first, there wasn't much interest in Rover's ceremony. After he reworked it in 1975, the people at the Warmun community became enthusiastic about it, and it was performed across the Kimberley and into the Northern Territory. Rover's palga is now a cultural icon for the Miriwung and Kija people.

Rover's first paintings were part of his palga. They arc shown in sequence, designed to be carried on the shoulders of dancers, accompanied by a songman and a chorus. The painting *Roads cross* was presented when the songman sang about the shadow of people killed long ago by white people; the dark patch of paint on the lower right-hand side represents where the massacred Indigenous men's bodies at Bedford Downs Station were burned.

Rover didn't create the paintings for his first performances. His uncle, Paddy Jaminji, and other local artists painted them, but nobody doubted that these images were Rover's invention. Rover only started to paint in 1981. At first, his paintings were for his own community, only displayed during his palga and not intended for the art market or the tourist trade. They were rough, bold works painted in natural earth pigments with a bush gum binder on wooden tea chest panels, what the art market now refers to as 'composition board'.

Rover was introduced to painting on canvas by the other senior men who painted at Warmun. Collectively they are now known as the East Kimberley School of painting. Once he started painting,

Rover did more versions for his palga. He then painted other scenes about his country. There was no stopping him; he was prolific.

When he met Mary Mácha, art dealer and manager of the Aboriginal Art Gallery in Perth, he announced himself, saying, "I'm Rover Thomas, and I want to paint." Mácha promoted his work to the world, and in 1990 Rover Thomas's paintings were exhibited in the Australian Pavilion at the Venice Biennale alongside urban Indigenous painter Trevor Nickolls. In 1994 the National Gallery of Australia (NGA) held the exhibition: Roads Cross: The Paintings of Rover Thomas.

Rover Thomas died in April 1998. He is revered as a great cultural leader. In April 1999, Sotheby's sold his painting, *Juntarkal Rainbow Serpent,* for $147,375, well ahead of the pre-sale estimate of $80,000–$100,000. In 2001 when the NGA purchased his painting, *All that big rain coming from top side*, for $778,000 ($1,196,000 today), establishing a record price for Indigenous art. But while most eyes were on his paintings, some greedy eyes were watching the money.

The Libertos were an ordinary-looking couple of baby boomers in their 60s, both about the same height and wearing glasses. Pamela (aka Pamela Gothe) wore her hair in a long blonde bob or tied up in two pigtails. In their life, they moved from Barkley Street in working-class East Brunswick to the tree-lined Malvern Road in multi-million-dollar properties behind tall hedges in the affluent suburb of Toorak.

Ivan Liberto was getting close to retirement, and, like many Australians, he had a lot of debts; he was paying off mortgages on the Toorak flat and an investment property in South Yarra and making payments on his Mercedes-Benz. Luckily, he had another source of income: other than working as a mechanic in the outer eastern suburb of Diamond Creek, he was selling paintings at art auctions.

Between 2002 and 2006, Ivan made more than $300,000 from just six paintings. Philips Auction on Glenferrie Road in Malvern sold *Turkey Creek crossing* for $890; it would have been worth more if Ivan hadn't accidentally damaged it while transporting it in his car. A Sydney collector bought *Roads cross* (small) for $69,175 at a Sotheby's auction. *Roads cross* (large) sold for $130,000 at Christie's the following year. Ivan sold *Wolf Creek crater* through a Lawson Menzies auction for $106,000. Another painting, *Kankamkankami*, sold for $120,000. He could have made more if *Rainbow Serpent* and *Ungoll Turkey near crossing* had sold at Christie's. All of the paintings were purported to be by the notable Indigenous artist Rover Thomas.

When the Libertos brought their paintings into auction houses, polite enquiries were made about how they came to have early Rover Thomas paintings. Pamela Liberto claimed that her father had bought or been given five paintings from Thomas when they worked together doing fencing for the Argyle diamond mine, which opened in 1983. There was no bill of sale or other papers, but that was not uncommon for Indigenous art of that era. Pamela said she acquired the sixth painting for $100 from a Swiss woman at a market. Rover Thomas's signature was on the back of the paintings, and the auction houses accepted the Libertos' story at face value. The paintings were selling, and the Libertos were happy.

Tim Klingender, the blue-eyed, blond-haired head of Sotheby's Indigenous art department and a member of the auction house's board of directors, was not happy; he was suspicious. He was looking at a painting of a serpent that Ivan Liberto had presented for sale. Something just wasn't right. The image was distinctive; a black snake with a yellow ochre head and dots along its side divided the board. It looked like a giant, blown-up version of *Juntarkal Rainbow Serpent* that Sotheby's had sold in 1999. The paint was different; it was flat, not thick and gummy, with marks from paint cans placed on it like most of Rover Thomas's work.

Klingender first met the Libertos when they came into Sotheby's "off the street" with a small painting that looked like *Roads Crossing* by Rover Thomas. The pre-sale estimate of between $30,000 and $50,000 was exceeded by the auction price of $80,000. From Klingender's perspective, Pamela appeared to be the more confident of the pair, a nice woman who seemed totally genuine. Ivan appeared a bit nervous.

At the time, Christie's was moving into the Indigenous art market. When another almost identical *Roads Crossing* was put on sale at Christie's by the Libertos, Klingender thought it was odd they didn't mention they had a second painting when Pamela sold the first version at Sotheby's. The second version was almost two metres square. The provenance was the same; Mr Gothe, Pamela's father, had acquired them when he worked for the mine. Klingender went to see it first hand at the viewing and thought it looked 'flat'. It sold after the auction.

When the Libertos came into Sotheby's in September 2005 with another painting, Klingender was more than very suspicious. He had sold the original painting ten years earlier. While he was prepared to believe that the Libertos had a *Roads Crossing* because Rover painted many versions of that image, he did not believe their *Juntarkal Rainbow Serpent* was genuine.

Without agreeing to sell the painting, Klingender persuaded the Libertos to leave it with him for "further research". He then organised a meeting with the rest of Sotheby's board of directors. They would take a loss because Roads Crossing's buyer had to be refunded as Sotheby's gives a seven-year guarantee of authenticity. Then he went down to Prahran Police Station, waited at the front desk and asked to see a detective to report a million-dollar fraud.

Klingender contacted Robyn Sloggart at the Grimwade Centre for authentication. Although Klingender had worked for Sotheby's for decades and had seen thousands of works of Indigenous art, his connoisseur's eye did not provide enough evidence that the paintings offered by Ivan Liberto for auction were fakes. It was only his opinion. Rover Thomas could not be consulted, so authentication by forensic analysis was used.

It can cost around $15,000 to get a painting authenticated by the University of Melbourne's Grimwade Centre for Cultural Materials Conservation. However, as the paintings from the Libertos were selling for almost ten times that amount, it was worth it.

The Grimwade Centre was established at the University of Melbourne in 1989 to do art restoration and museum-standard conservation. That changed when art dealer Lauraine Diggins lost more than $200,000 ($344,000 today), refunding money for three fake paintings she had unwittingly sold. Two of the fakes were supposedly by Arthur Streeton, and one allegedly by Tom Roberts. Diggins had acquired them from the Queensland art dealer Leigh Murphy, who refused to refund her. Diggins felt her reputation as an art dealer had been damaged. In response, she did everything she could to attack art fraud: she went to the police and the media, printed and distributed stickers to redact her old catalogues. She knew that more had to be done and in 1998, she helped fund the Grimwade Centre to establish authentication services.

The evidence that the Grimwade Centre collects means it is not just one connoisseur's opinion. The Centre conducted attribution assessments to check the art in question against the verifiable characteristics of the artist's authentic work providing scientific evidence to prove whether or not art can be attributed to an artist.

Paintings are examined through non-invasive means, looking at the painting under ultraviolet (UV), infrared light and X-ray. Patching, repaints, glue and varnishes will fluoresce differently under

UV light, while infrared light is used to reveal underdrawings in pencil, charcoal or dark pigments. X-rays can reveal underpainting, especially white lead paint, and information about the support's construction, such as the type of nails used. The Grimwade Centre also uses polarising and fluorescent light microscopy, Raman spectroscopy, Fourier transform infra-red reflectography (FTIR), X-ray diffraction, X-ray fluorescence, gas chromatography-mass spectrometry, and even various synchrotron beamline techniques.

Destructive techniques can also be used for examining paintings where a small cross-section of paint, about the size of a full stop, is removed for microscopic analysis. Scanning electron microscopy (SEM) can then be used to determine pigments. Chemical spot tests can also be used to determine if a particular material, such as white lead, is present.

The Grimwade Centre examination of the Libertos' paintings concluded that they could not have been painted in Western Australia and therefore were not Rover Thomas's work. Their attribution assessment that compared the Libertos' painting to verified Rover Thomas paintings found many anomalies in materials and manufacture.

On close examination, it was clear that the painter intended to deceive the viewer as there were thin washes of paint over white dots to imitate the red desert dust. And on the back of the Libertos' paintings, red ochre chalk had been applied to simulate the iron oxide red dust of the Western Desert.

Meanwhile, Klingender kept making excuses to the Libertos about the delay in putting their painting up for auction, saying he was trying to determine the right price.

On Thursday, March 23, 2006, Senior Constable Brown arrived at the Libertos' house with a search warrant. Pamela's paints, brushes and other art materials were gathered as evidence. Art auction catalogues and magazines were found that showed the Libertos' interest in Rover Thomas's art. In a 1999 Sotheby's catalogue, there was a note beside one of Rover Thomas's paintings: 'previous $96,000'. There was a digital camera with multiple close-ups of Rover's signature. Most damning of all, there were two unfinished Indigenous-style paintings. It was all the evidence that the police needed; Ivan and Pamela Liberto were arrested.

Across the new Victorian County Court's facade is the steel silhouette of a woman holding scales and a sword, the *Lady of Justice*, by the sculptor William Eicholtz. It is a dynamic, progressive image of Justitia: scales in one hand to weigh up the case, stepping forward to interpret the law with her sword ready to defend it. Inside in October 2007, for Ivan and Pamela Liberto, the scales of justice were about to be weighed before Judge Roland Williams.

The Libertos were charged with four counts of obtaining money by deception and two counts each of attempting to obtain property by deception by forging four paintings: *Roads cross* (large), *Roads cross* (small), *Kankamkankami*, and *Wolf Creek crater*. Ivan and Pamela pleaded 'not guilty'.

The prosecution case was that the Libertos were conspiring to forge paintings. While Ivan managed the sales, Pamela did the actual painting – mixing in the sand and other materials to simulate outback painting conditions.

Along with the evidence gathered in the police raid of the Libertos' home, the prosecution case also had the expert testimony of Associate Professor Robyn Sloggett from the Grimwade Centre.

Robyn Sloggett is a petite woman with pale skin, a sharp nose, square blue glasses framing her blue eyes and hair in a bob. She trained as an art historian before studying materials conservation. And her lectures on art authentication and identifying paintings are accompanied by enthusiastic gestures.

Pigments found at the Libertos' house were compared to those on the suspect paintings using SEM, FTIR and particle-induced

X-ray emission. This established that the paintings and pigments found at their house contained Prussian Blue and Cassel Earth. An exact chemical 'fingerprint' could not be proved, but they were close enough to be identical on the balance of probability.

Under one of the Libertos' paintings, *Kankamkankami*, was paint from an earlier image. "This is an odd thing to be finding on this work," Professor Sloggett told the jury. "It is like it was started and did not quite make it, and the canvas has been re-used." It was not something that Rover Thomas would have done. Professor Sloggett showed the jury the painting underneath: a serpent head could be seen when light raked the canvas. It was similar to Rover Thomas' *Rainbow Serpent*, an image that the Libertos had copied for another painting.

The Libertos' defence was conducted by the experienced lawyer, Maitland Lincoln, who was about the same age as his elderly clients and had been a member of the Victorian Bar for more than forty-one years. The defence argued that Pamela, befuddled by drugs from chronic pain, could not paint anything substantial. Pamela Liberto stuck to her story that she had inherited five paintings and bought the sixth one at a market. The presence of art materials at their home was explained by Pamela: "My doctor told me to take up painting to help cope with the panic attacks."

On Friday, November 2, 2007, Pamela and Ivan Liberto stood in the dock holding hands. After only two hours of deliberation, the jury returned with a verdict. Four guilty findings, each of obtaining money by deception and two each of attempting to obtain property by deception. Pamela started to cry.

After the guilty verdict, there were pleas on health issues due to their advanced ages. Pamela was on medication to treat bowel surgery complications from twelve years earlier, and Ivan suffered from arthritis in his hands and knees. However, in sentencing, Judge Williams did not think that the Libertos were too ill to serve time and sentenced both to three years with a minimum of nine months. "You weren't too infirm to do the paintings, you weren't too infirm to approach auction houses, you weren't too infirm to make several property transactions and changes of address. You were still trying to get top price for *Rainbow Serpent* when you were arrested."

Judge Williams described them as "premeditated fraudsters" who had run a "highly planned operation over a considerable period of time". He elaborated: "You attempted to enrich yourselves dishonestly at the cost of innocent third parties and the integrity of the art industry, particularly the Aboriginal art industry, which must suffer when this sort of activity is brought to light." He noted that the couple had shown no remorse nor acknowledged any wrongdoing. "You did all this for your lifestyle. You quietly aspire, it seems, to the good things in life."

The Libertos' flat on Malvern Road was ordered to be sold to repay the auction houses' losses. Klingender of Sotheby's was pleased with the result because, in the end, it recouped the auction house's money. Pamela's forgeries were ordered to be destroyed so they would never again be mistaken for Rover Thomas's work.

Judge Williams considered it absurd for the auction houses to rely on the stories of the Libertos as provenance for the paintings. Academics blamed the auction houses or the art dealers, pointing out that all the fake art came through private dealers and no fraud connected to the Indigenous community art centres. The auction houses point to problems of distance, language and a lack of scholarship in Indigenous art, meaning that there are few complete catalogues of even notable Australian Indigenous artists' work for them to consult. Without people like Klingender, the prosecution of the Libertos would not have occurred. New technologies make it easier to detect forgeries; however, because of the expense, this kind of examination is not conducted unless serious suspicions are raised, and megabucks are at stake.

Prior to her trial, Pamela hinted to the media about conspiracies in the Aboriginal art market. She didn't have any new information and just repeated some of the same well-known stories about inauthentic Indigenous art. After the guilty verdict, Pamela Liberto continued to protest her innocence. In an ABC's *Four Corners* investigation, she told Quentin McDermott: "I believe the paintings are genuine, but then I'm not an art expert, but in my heart I believe they're genuine Rover Thomas paintings and I am quite sad, not [*sic*], sad is probably the wrong word, I don't think they should've been destroyed."

Art forgery is always a mixture of greed, envy of the artist being forged, and the forger's arrogance that they can scam others. Like other forms of fraud, it is a confidence trick. What gave the Toorak couple the confidence to embark on their forgeries of Rover Thomas? It is hard to believe that the forged Rover Thomas paintings were Pamela's first. Most forgers start small before they gain experience and confidence. Ivan and Pamala had planned and studied Rover Thomas's paintings, photographed his signature, gathered materials and information.

Pamela Liberto still nurtured a frustrated desire to be an artist. Less than a year after her conviction, on July 24, 2008, she uploaded a video to YouTube. In a strange kind of admission, the video shows one of her forged Rover Thomas paintings, followed by a mosaic of her portrait and then a slideshow of her insipid, uninspired daubs. However, the Libertos were still protesting, if not their innocence, then that they were prosecuted. According to Ivan, "We were the right people to nail, the easy people to nail at the right time."

Art forgery is sometimes considered the high point of art crime, combining artistic creativity and criminal cunning. The public enjoys stories of art forgeries because they seem to celebrate the defeat of the expert. Art forgery appears to be a complaint of affluence and indications of an overheated art market. The Libertos demonstrate that this isn't true; they were neither creative nor cunning. They just had the greed and the front to exploit the Indigenous art market. Pamela required no painting skill to copy a Rover Thomas painting with the broad expanses of paint and rough lines. The idea of a perfect copy of a masterpiece misunderstands that the art's historical value depends on its authenticity, not its looks.

The Liberto and O'Loughlin fakes are not the only indications of the extent of forgeries in the market. Fake works in the style of Emily Kame Kngwarreye, Turkey Tolson Tjupurrula, Ginger Riley Munduwalawala and other Indigenous artists continued to be discovered at auctions.

The art of investing

This story is not about art but the avarice it can spawn. Many people buy art in the hope it will be a superb investment. For there is a limited supply of work by famous artists, and demand can be so high that art, initially purchased for a few hundred, can be worth a fortune a few decades later. Beauty might be in the eye of the beholder, but Streeton, Whitely, Norman Lindsey and Pro Hart are names you could bank on. And in the first decade of this century, credit was cheap and easy, and the banks were desperate to lend people money.

As its name might suggest, the Ronald Coles Investment Gallery was a gallery specialising in art investments for self-managed superannuation funds. Investors could buy, store and sell art through the gallery located in a historic sandstone church on Porters Road in the semi-rural Sydney suburb of Kenthurst. Investors included radio commentator Ray Hadley, the former chief executive of the Parramatta Eels, Denis Fitzgerald, and former professional rugby player Brad Fittler. In the 2007-08 financial year, the gallery had an annual turnover of $20 million.

Under Australian tax law, art investments in self-managed superannuation funds could not "provide any present-day benefit". Art investments "made for genuine retirement purposes" could not be enjoyed by the owner hanging on the wall of their house but had to be kept in storage. It seems fair as other people can't live in their investment properties. It also meant that a business providing secure climate-controlled storage solutions was needed to store the art for people's self-managed superannuation funds.

The only problem with the security at the Ronald Coles Investment Gallery was that its silver-haired director, Ronald Coles had the key. Investors who left their artwork with him might never see it again, as Coles would sell it if he could find a buyer. Consequently, he had some unhappy customers.

The first public indication that everything was not right with the gallery came in December 2008. An exhibition the gallery organised was suddenly cancelled, and one disgruntled customer instigated court action. Coles responded by filing for bankruptcy.

NSW police "Strike Force Glasson" raided the gallery along with Cole and his stepdaughter's homes in Kenthurst on Wednesday, January 21, 2009. The police seized firearms and hundreds of works of art. Investigators found a truck with 107 paintings inside near Coles's stepdaughter's home.

The auctioneer Tim Goodman got the job of storing and creating an inventory of recovered art. Instead of art worth $5 million, Goodman valued the hundreds of works somewhere between $350,000 and $580,000. Instead of genuine art, he found some fake Whiteleys, Streetons, Pro Harts, David Boyds and d'Arcy Doyle (if you were wondering where some of Blundell's fakes ended up). Even worse, there were multiple owners for some pieces, as Coles gave various names to the same work. A Norman Lindsay painting could be titled, *Gossip,* or *Witches Carnival,* depending on which investor had purchased it.

Millions of dollars were missing. Coles's art investment fund was a Ponzi scheme where investors' returns were paid out of the new investors they attracted. Hundreds of investors and self-funded retirees had been caught up in a scam.

Ronald Coles admitted to multi-million-dollar fraud in the Parramatta District Court in August 2013. He pleaded guilty to fifteen counts of fraud and deception as a director and larceny as a bailee. And he admitted to a further eighteen instances of fraud and deception. After many delays due to Coles's heart condition, Judge Antony Townsden sentenced him to eight years in May 2014.

It takes greedy people and the right conditions to work a multi-million-dollar art fraud. The tax law on art investments for self-managed superannuation provided Coles with near-perfect conditions. Investors couldn't look at their art, and if nobody is looking at art, is it really there? And it is not just tax laws that can create such conditions; I am reminded of Ronald Coles Investment Gallery every time I hear about rip-offs and other frauds around NFT (aka Non-Fungible Token) art.

How to frame a Brett Whiteley

Jud Wimhurst's former boss, Aman Siddique, an art conservator, phoned him to say:

"There are some things happening, and maybe you will hear some bad things said about me. The police might want to speak to you."

"What should I do?" asked Jud.

"You tell the truth."

Although Siddique didn't elaborate on why the police might want to speak to Jud, the truth was he knew what Siddique was referring to. For Jud was the one who first found Siddique's secret studio and raised suspicions that his employer might be forging art.

With his square-rimmed glasses, goatee beard and long sideburns, Jud looks like a classic hipster artist. He makes sculptures that poke fun at the consumer world, toy soldiers in McDonald's and KFC colours battle it out, and is represented by a prominent commercial gallery. Even though he is thriving as an artist, he still has other jobs to make a living. Between 2005 and 2007, he worked part-time, three days a week, for Aman Siddique at Victorian Art Conservation.

Victorian Art Conservation was located in a two-storey, nineteenth-century red-brick warehouse at 26-28 Easey Street in Collingwood. On the same street are design studios, the community radio station 3PBS, Backwoods Gallery, and the End To End building's graffiti-influenced architecture with three train carriages sitting on its roof.

Mohamed Aman Siddique, known as Aman, was the owner and sole art conservator at Victorian Art Conservation. He was born in Uganda in 1949; his parents had been encouraged to move there from India when it was still part of the British Empire. Then, in 1972, the psychopathic dictator President Idi Amin expelled all Indians from Uganda. Aged twenty-three, Aman became a stateless refugee. His family lived in England, where Aman worked and saved to study at the Chelsea School of Art in London. Aman loved art, but it is difficult to earn a good living as an artist, and he wanted a good job where he could use his knowledge of art.

He found the answer when he received a scholarship to do a three-year postgraduate course in art conservation at the prestigious Courtauld Institute of Art in London. Art conservators are the surgeons of the art world, bringing damaged art back to life. The job requires fastidious attention to detail, exacting technical skills and a knowledge of art history. But however good Aman was as an art conservator, his instructors at the Courtauld told him that he was 'too dark' and that the English art establishment was too racist to accept an Indian-Muslim art conservator. So, once again, in 1983, Aman packed up his life and moved, this time to Australia, where he had been invited to do art conservation at Ballarat Art Gallery. After establishing his reputation in Australia, he went into business for himself.

A round-faced, middle-aged man with greying hair parted to one side, Aman Siddique acquired an excellent reputation as an art conservator. He restored Russell Drysdale paintings, Indigenous art, material from the Mary McKillop archive, and fire-damaged paintings for QBE Insurance. People trusted him with art of considerable value, and Siddique deserved it. On one occasion returning twenty-eight watercolours when a client thought there were only twenty-seven. Another time, Siddique identified a fake when cleaning a painting for James Bleasel, former head of the Australian Antarctic Division. Cleaning revealed that originally there was an 'after' before the 'signature', so the inscription read 'after Eugene Guérard,' rather than 'Eugene Guérard', exposing an old art faker's trick of painting over parts of a painting to make it more saleable.

Downstairs at Victorian Art Conservation, Jud Wimhurst dealt with the carpentry that supports paintings, repairing frames and re-stretching canvas. Upstairs, Siddique would work with the art, retouching and varnishing.

Sharing the upstairs workspace with Siddique, but operating as an independent business, was a third person, Guy Morel, a conservator of books and paper. Morel started as an apprentice bookbinder before studying chemistry and working for the Public Records Office as a conservator. He paid no rent because Siddique wanted to give him a start with his business, and there were other synergies involved, as each could recommend clients to the other.

Cleaning a painting that is only twenty or thirty years old, even revarnishing it, is not uncommon, depending on the conditions in which it has been kept. If it had been exposed to cigarette smoke, it would need a clean. Many art dealers and prestigious Melbourne galleries, such as Kimberly Gallery and Australian Galleries, would bring their work to Siddique to get it looking its best for sale. One of the art dealers who brought work to Victorian Art Conservation was Peter Gant, a short, blue-eyed man with a turned-up nose.

Peter Stanley Gant was born in 1956 in country Victoria and went to boarding school at Geelong College. He began a teaching degree at Rusden College in Clayton but left to open his first art gallery after two years. Since that first gallery, Gant ran several galleries in Melbourne and the James Street Gallery in Geelong. The last was Gallery Irascible, which operated at 1272 High Street

Armadale between 1993 and 2010. He also ran an art dealership, the eponymous Peter Gant Fine Art, in South Melbourne. It was not a big operation, just himself and a secretary, but they did sell the big names of Australian art. In 1987, Peter Gant Fine Art ran a newspaper advertisement to sell art by John Perceval, Sidney Nolan and five works by Brett Whiteley.

Peter Gant loves to gamble on horse racing, which is not a good idea if you are unlucky, and Gant has been very unlucky. He must be the unluckiest art dealer in Australia. He had the bad luck to sell a fake Russell Drysdale painting to a Sydney property developer, Robert Ojeda, in 1989. And the bad luck of going bankrupt in 1990 due to a dispute over the sale of a car. That dispute did not end well, and in 1993 he was convicted of motor vehicle theft. Due to this run of bad luck, Gant is very familiar with the inside of a law court. In 1993 he was charged with deception for selling a John Perceval painting he didn't own but was acquitted in a trial at the County Court. Four years later, in 1997, he was in trouble again when he sold a dud "Russell Drysdale" for $250,000; the hapless customer returned to Gant's gallery with some armed enforcers, locked the door and made the usual threats while demanding his money back. The following year Gant sold some suspect Sidney Nolan paintings, and once more, he refunded the money and resold some of the Nolans. While Gant denied they were fakes, he wouldn't talk about his source for the paintings; art dealers like to keep their sources a confidential business secret.

That same year, 1998, Gant was associated with a batch of irradiated Lalique glass. Irradiation can change clear glass to deep purple or amber; it does not result in the glass being radioactive and is almost impossible to detect. Irradiation has been used commercially for colouring glass since 1976, but the statistical increase in purple antique glass sales wasn't noticed until 1995.

In March 2007, Peter Gant was about to have more bad luck. He and Siddique had returned from Sydney, where they purchased a Brett Whiteley painting, *View from a window of a bay*, at auction for $1,650,000, for an unnamed client. Siddique conducted an expert inspection of the condition of the painting before purchase.

The curly, golden-haired boy of Australian art, Brett Whiteley, was born in Sydney in 1939. In 1956 he met his muse, Wendy Julius. He was seventeen; she was not yet sixteen. They fell in love, a relationship that would dominate the rest of their lives. In 1959 Brett won a travelling scholarship, and a determined Wendy soon joined him in Europe. They married in 1962 at the Chelsea Registry Office and had one daughter, Arkie, in 1964.

In the late '60s, Brett and Wendy were living a rock-star lifestyle in New York's Chelsea Hotel. Whiteley was an international super-star artist, a prolific, precociously talented, brilliant risk-taker with a kaleidoscope mind. He was like a lead guitarist with a paintbrush and, like many lead guitarists of that time, and probably for similar psycho-social reasons, he became addicted to heroin.

Brett and Wendy returned to Australia in 1969 and moved into a flat overlooking Lavender Bay on Sydney Harbour with views of the bridge. Lavender Bay was not named for any reason of colour but instead after George Lavender, the boatswain of the prison hulk *Phoenix*, moored there when Sydney was a prison colony. Wendy Whiteley still lives there, tending the garden she created adjacent to her home.

The couple separated in 1987 after Brett started an affair with Janice Spencer, whom he met at Narcotics Anonymous. Tragically Brett died of a heroin overdose in 1992, and there were multiple court cases to contest his several wills. Still, Brett and Wendy are forever linked by the fame of their relationship and Brett's many paintings of Wendy.

Whiteley is an attractive target for art forgers for several reasons. He is a prestigious late-modern Australian artist, a favourite of both the art establishment and the general public. His paintings of Lavender Bay are very saleable to people in Sydney, with expensive apartments overlooking the bay.

He was prolific even when he was a heroin addict, and his addiction didn't seem to subtract much from the quality of his work. What his heroin addiction means for art forgers is that there were chaotic periods in his sales records, gaps, and sales were sometimes made directly from his studio to pay for heroin. When he needed the money, he painted more, using the same images of birds, boats and palm trees.

Whiteley's studio assistant and co-addict, Chris Quintas, also sold Whiteley paintings, for which he received 10 per cent of the sale price. Whiteley liked this better than the 40 or 50 per cent a commercial art gallery would take. There could be genuine paintings by Whiteley that have only been seen by Brett and Chris Quintas, and, as both are dead, no one can confirm their authenticity.

View from a window of a bay shows a view from Whiteley's window in Lavender Bay. Signed and dated in the bottom centre: 'Brett Whiteley 91'. Whiteley did many of these large paintings. He did not sit at his window and paint but painted on the other side of town in his Surry Hills studio, where he would mix memory with desire to produce sexy landscapes.

It is painted on a couple of hollow-frame wooden interior doors. The doors consist of a timber frame around the perimeter with a honeycomb paper core and lauan plywood faces on each side. Whiteley preferred 'Corinthian' brand doors sold at his local hardware shop, Surry Timber, just around the corner from his studio at 2 Raper Street. His largest painting, the 16-metre-long *Alchemy* 1972–73, is made from eighteen doors. To make the support for most of his paintings, two doors would be joined together to form a large rectangle, with the crack in between them filled in.

His paintings were framed with what is commonly known as a slip or shadow frame. Whiteley called them 'baguette frames' because the frame sandwiched the painting. To make these frames, custom-milled timber that had been japanned black is nailed directly to the side of the door. Whiteley wanted this type of frame for his paintings because it allows the paint to be seen right up to the edge. It can also provide room for a piece of Perspex sheeting to protect any collage and impasto elements he often liked to incorporate into his paintings. Around this timber, a 23-carat water-gilded gold frame was fitted; water gilding creates a solid gold effect on the frames without displaying any cut lines on the corners. Whiteley wanted water-gilded gold frames because that's what Francis Bacon had on his paintings, and Whiteley was a great admirer of the British painter.

Between 1976 and 1992, Brett Liechtenstein framed many of Whiteley's paintings. Liechtenstein was not a typical high-street framer but a water gilder and a manufacturer of bespoke products. He was not the exclusive framer for Whiteley. Whiteley also used two other framers, Wolf Blitzmyer and Charles Hewitt.

Commissioned by a private collector in Sydney, *View from a window of a bay* was then sold to Gould Galleries in Melbourne, which sold it to a Melbourne company's collection. They sold it at Deutscher-Menzies auctions in Melbourne in 2001 to another Melbourne company, which sold it six years later, again at Deutscher-Menzies, to Aman Siddique and Peter Gant.

Jud Wimhurst remembers *View from a window of a bay* because, in April 2007, the sizeable Whiteley painting was delivered to Victorian Art Conservation by Transart Specialist Art Transporters. It then sat around at the base of the stairs until Siddique told him to remove its frame.

Wimhurst remembers that there was a shadow frame nailed to the painting. "The frame seemed rudimentary to me. I hadn't come across that style of framing before. We would have framed it very differently; I'll put it that way. It seemed as though it had parts of the frame nailed straight to the side of the substrate of the painting."

There were some other odd things to Victorian Art Conservation, which in retrospect, looked suspicious. Jud Wimhurst remembers a delivery of several unusually short hollow-frame wooden interior doors. Siddique said they were destined for Peter Gant's house. "Why is he building a house for dwarfs?" Jud remarked.

Richard Simon also remembers delivering several doors to Victorian Art Conservation because he argued with Siddique over a join in their surfaces. He claimed that Siddique said to him: "The artwork to be painted on these doors is worth over a million dollars; I can't have joins."

In November 2007 and January and April 2009, Siddique ordered three large water-gilded frames from Mario Rincon, who learnt how to make them when working for Lichtenstein. These were not cheap frames: the first cost Siddique $1850, the second $2439.80 and the third $1833.70.

When Jud finished removing the large gold frame from the Whiteley *View from a window of a bay*, it remained on the ground floor. The painting went upstairs via the picture lift, a type of narrow elevator for moving large paintings.

Jud distinctly remembers when he next saw the painting. He arrived early for work one morning and was opening up. He went upstairs to the office area to check the answering machine. That's when he noticed a storage area that was usually locked had been left open. His first thought was to wonder if there had been a break-in, so he investigated.

Looking inside the storage area, he saw a series of incomplete paintings in Brett Whiteley's style, painted on hollow-framed doors that were joined together. There were paints and paintbrushes, books on Whiteley lay open, and on the floor lay a cardboard template the same shape as a vase on the Whiteley painting, which was propped up to one side, as an example. A large blue painting was balanced on two paint cans. Jud didn't have a good look, but it didn't look innocent.

Jud had already made up his mind, for other reasons, to stop working at the Victorian Art Conservation. Before he finished up, on September 21, 2007, he raised his suspicions with the part-time paper conservator, Guy Morel. When Siddique was out, he encouraged Guy to stand on a stool to take photographs over the partition wall with his compact Nikon digital camera. While the middle-aged Guy balanced precariously to take his photos, the keys to the lockable storage area sat in the unlocked top drawer of Siddique's desk just a couple of metres away.

Guy was more than suspicious; he was shocked. Over the next few months, he took more photographs. What he appeared to be documenting was a forgery factory, with Aman Siddique, an experienced art conservator, producing the fakes.

He decided to contact the police, telling Detective Sergeant James MacDonald of the Fraud Squad, "I've got a concern about some forgeries that are ongoing." Detective MacDonald was the right man to investigate because, although he couldn't tell the difference between oil paint and acrylics, he was actually interested in art fraud. He also knew who to speak to about the forgeries, Associate Professor Robyn Sloggett from the Grimwade Centre for Cultural Materials Conservation, whose work in art authentication was essential in proving the Libertos forged paintings. MacDonald had already contacted Professor Sloggett because he was interested in getting some training on the subject of art fraud.

Guy Morel's photographs were enough to persuade Detective MacDonald to go to Victorian Art Conservation to see for himself. Siddique was conveniently out, and now Morel knew where to find the keys to the locked door of the storage area, so there was no need to peer over any partitions. MacDonald agreed it looked suspicious, but it was not enough to arrest Siddique.

As John Ribbands QC would later point out, with the benefit of hindsight, it is a shame that when Morel unlocked the door, the Detective didn't write his initials or the name of his dog or put a thumbprint in paint on the back of the large blue painting that was in progress. Instead, Detective MacDonald encouraged Guy Morel to continue photographing the work in Siddique's secret studio. So Guy continued to take photographs from 2007 to 2009, showing the progress of blue, orange and brown paintings. (What happened to all the half-finished art shown in Guy's photographs?)

Guy had some concerns about spying on Siddique for the police; after all, Siddique was a friend and a generous colleague who had helped Morel establish a business. He was also concerned Siddique's mental health was not the best and was worried that being exposed as a forger would make him suicidal. Indeed, Siddique was probably suffering from depression at the time.

With his white hair, blazer and white shoes, Robert Le Tet would look perfect in a movie playing the role of a venture capitalist or the director of a media company, both positions he plays in real life. His office looked the part, especially when its walls were hung with Australian art by big-name artists. He had known Peter Gant for decades, as his business had been lending Gant money to purchase art since the mid-1980s.

Gant was unusual in borrowing money to buy art, as most art dealers don't. Most dealers finance their art purchases by reinvesting their profits. This is because art is an illiquid asset that cannot be sold quickly, and art dealers don't want lenders to know the financial details of the gallery's inventory. None of this seemed to bother Gant or Le Tet.

Gant would leave art at Le Tet's office as surety for these loans. Gant would then send dealers and advisers to view the art, assuming that the painting was owned by Le Tet.

One of the people sent to view a painting was freelance art adviser Anita Archer, previously the head auctioneer with Deutscher and Hackett. She had been advising Andrew Pridham on his art investments. Pridham was the Australian managing director of investment bank Moelis & Company and the chairman of the Sydney Swans football team. He primarily collects Australian colonial artists, like John Glover, but he is also interested in other art with investment potential, such as Whiteley.

The painting Anita Archer was looking at on that day in Le Tet's office featured a vast expanse of cobalt blue with three orange palm trees and a white pier jutting out at the bottom. Various boats and white birds were scattered across the middle. In the upper left corner was a recognisable section of the famous Sydney Harbour Bridge and on the right was the curve of the bay with a couple of multi-storey buildings. It was large, 163.9cm high, and 255.7cm long, including the 6.5cm deep gold frame. Archer described the painting to Pridham as 'a trophy'.

Only a few months after Guy Morel had photographed the big blue painting in Siddique's secret studio, Andrew Pridham paid $2.5 million for a painting known by its description, *Blue Lavender Bay*. It was hung at the end of the entrance lobby in his glamorous Mosman residence. However, it wasn't long before Pridham began to doubt the authenticity of his new painting.

He invited Wendy Whiteley over for morning tea to have a look at it. Wendy wasn't comfortable with the painting. "I needed to feel sure, you know. It's a big deal to tell someone that they got a huge fake on the wall, you know. You don't make yourself the most popular creature in the building when you do that." What do you say when the proud owner of a work of art shows you something that you have doubts about? Do you crush their enthusiasm by raising doubts or remain silent? So Wendy said, "Well, if it is a Whiteley, it's a bad hair day Whiteley", meaning that the painting wasn't up to Brett's usual standards. Later she questioned its authenticity, as did Whiteley's framer Brett Lichtenstein.

The painting was framed in a new gold frame with a black shadow frame that protruded slightly onto the painting. Brett Lichtenstein had not made it, nor would it have passed Brett Whiteley's exacting requirements. Later, forensic analysis by Robyn Sloggett showed no evidence of nail holes belonging to an earlier frame. There was also some blue paint on the inside edge of the black shadow frame's rebate, which indicates that the new shadow frame must have been attached when the paint was wet. This would be an odd thing to find on a new frame for an old painting, but not impossible if it had been cleaned and an excessive amount of cleaning solvent had somehow accumulated on some paint, which had then scraped against the new frame.

It is usual to find all kinds of things on the backs of paintings, ranging from dealers' catalogue numbers to exhibition details. On the back of the big blue painting were some words. In the left corner was written '2520 Christian 212 4831'. And in the right corner was: 'C. Quintas 29 253 Goulburn Street Darlinghurst ph 2124831.' 2520 is Wollongong's post box/parcels code, and one of the framers that Whiteley used, Wolf Retzmeyer, lived in Wollongong. Also, at the bottom on a strip of tape: 'A39 – 349.5'.

The signature on *Blue Lavender Bay* is difficult to find because it is hidden. It was initially missed by Professor Sloggett and her team on their first examination of the painting. It is painted in white on the off-white paint of the pier, playing with the 'white' in his name in a typical piece of Whiteley's visual wordplay. The police couldn't determine if this signature was genuine as it was painted in block capital letters.

With questions now circulating about the authenticity of the multi-million-dollar painting, Gant was asked to provide documentation of its provenance. He created a document stating it was owned by Le Tet and that it had been purchased from Brett Whiteley's studio. The problem was that Le Tet was not happy to see the document. He was even less happy to see his signature forged, and instructed his solicitor to write a letter stating it was not correct, not prepared by him, nor did it contain his signature.

Gant tried to placate Le Tet over a few glasses of wine. He explained that the document was created out of commercial motivation since the painting had been viewed by the buyer in Le Tet's office. And that the signature had been forged by an unnamed colleague.

The terms of the sale included a full refund up to five years later if two recognised experts had doubts about the painting's provenance. So it was sent to the Grimwade Centre to be examined.

Orange Lavender Bay (aka 'Marmalade Sydney') was bought by luxury car dealer Steven Nasteski for $1.1 million in 2009. The alternative title is because 'Marmalade' is written on the back of the painting. Possibly it once hung in the West Sydney offices of Marmalade Films Pty Ltd, run by Robert Le Tet, which made TV commercials between 1982 and 2001.

At 121 x 215 centimetres, it is a little bit smaller than *Blue Lavender Bay*. Otherwise, it is similar to the blue painting, with many of the same elements: boats, a pier, Sydney Harbour Bridge and the sexy curve of the bay. Apart from the colour, the other significant difference is that along the lower section bit of land with, two blue palm trees and another tree with black foliage.

Various agents had arranged the sale, one of these was John Playfoot, who ran Gallery Moderne in Armadale. Playfoot has been an art dealer since 1973 and has known Peter Gant for around thirty years. He described Gant as a 'scallywag with a very good eye'. In 2007 or 2008, Gant told Playfoot that he was going to get a Whiteley that had previously been owned by Le Tet.

Playfoot then offered the painting for sale through various sub-agents to a variety of billionaire businessmen. Finally, he sold it to Steven Nasteski for $1.1 million, giving the money directly to Peter Gant. Nasteski was told that the work appeared in a catalogue and that copies of the catalogue existed; one was at the State Library of Victoria and the other at the National Gallery of Victoria's library. It turns out neither library has a copy. Trust was not improved when only a digital reproduction of the catalogue was produced.

With the news of Pridham's problems circulating in 2010, Nasteski was concerned about his orange painting and asked Brett Lichenstein to come to his house in Coogee to examine the frame. Brett told him that the gold frame was not one of his. Nasteski then sought a report from Robyn Sloggett at the Grimwade Centre. He also asked Playfoot for his money back, phoning him four times every day in June until Playfoot conceded. It wasn't that Playfoot agreed with Nasteski's doubts about the painting; it was simply good business practice.

After paying Nasteski a refund of the $1.1 million, plus interest and costs, Playfoot asked Gant to refund him. Gant refused, insisting that the painting was genuine. Fellow art dealer, Andrew Crawford, suggested that Playfoot get Wendy Whiteley to have a look at *Orange Lavender Bay* because "I think it's a scam". Not that Wendy Whiteley could always identify her former husband's work. As Peter Gant remarked about *View from a window of a bay,* the original Whiteley that he and Siddique had bought, "Well, according to, you know, Wendy, the expert, this was one; that was a fake until she was shown a photo of Brett Whiteley standing next to it."

On June 15, 2010, an orange painting was delivered to the Grimwade Centre. Just over a month later, on July 16, it was joined by a blue one. Then Detective James McDonald of the Fraud Squad called, stating that he had a series of photographs of what looked like a forger's studio producing Whiteley paintings. It was hard not to draw conclusions.

Professor Sloggett used infra-red photography to reveal the paintings' underdrawing, not that they had any infra-red photographs of Whiteley paintings with secure provenance to which they could compare them. They were examined under magnification. They were then compared to known Whiteley paintings. And the materials compared to those Whiteley was known to have used. However, in the end, their examination was inconclusive; there was no evidence to prove that these two paintings were not by Brett Whiteley, but there were too many doubts to say they were. Her report would conclude:

This work cannot therefore, on the evidence available, in particular on the basis of the lack of points of identification with materials and techniques known to be used by Whiteley and in the absence of any verifiable provenance that links the work to Whiteley, be attributed to the oeuvre, the body of work of Brett Whiteley. The evidence suggests rather that this work has not been produced by Whiteley.

Peter Gant's luck was running out, and he was spending more time in court again. In 2010 he was convicted of breaches of the Fair Trading Act for selling three works: two attributed to Charles Blackman, called *Street scene with schoolgirl* and *Three schoolgirls*, and one to Robert Dickerson, called *Pensive woman*. It wasn't a matter of whether Gant knew that he was selling fakes; what mattered was that he hadn't taken adequate steps to confirm their authenticity. In a landmark ruling, the Victorian Supreme Court ordered that the three drawings be destroyed so they could not enter the market again. In 2011 Gant was unsuccessful in suing *The Age*, Stephen Nall and Wendy Whiteley for defamation and declared himself bankrupt for the second time.

In August 2013, Gant sold *Orange Lavender Bay* to an engineer, Steven Drake. Drake was aware of the issues over the painting's provenance and offered $300,000, believing its value could more than triple once it was authenticated. In the end, Drake paid only $122,000. Playfoot received $110,000 for it, and Gant pocketed $12,000 commission on the sale.

On Wednesday, March 5, 2014, seven years after Jud Wimhurst saw Siddique's secret studio, police executed a search warrant on Victoria Art Conservation, which authorised the seizure of paints, frames, solvents and other items relating to fraudulent Whiteley paintings. No paintings in the style of Whiteley or copies were found on the premises. Two pieces of timber, parts of a gold frame, were seized for 'evidentiary purposes'. Paintings described as being by Howard Arkley, Charles Blackman and Arthur Streeton were also seized because Detective Senior Sergeant Michael Martin thought they might also be forgeries. The magistrate ordered the Streeton to be returned, but the Arkley and Blackman paintings would become the subject of more legal action as Siddique tried to get them back. Police searched Peter Gant's home the following day, but no Brett Whiteley-style paintings or copies were discovered.

In the police interview video, Peter Gant sits with his arms crossed, a well-thumbed paperback book in front of him. He appears exasperated about why he is there. The accusations are all 'crap'. He claims that he had bought all three paintings back in 1988 from

Quintas and had kept them in storage for twenty years without ever showing anyone. He doesn't want to talk about them. He is not prepared to say where *Through the window (Brown)* is, nor if it has been sold. Even if you doubt the paintings' authenticity, you can see why Gant is a bitter man. "Everyone who saw it loved it. A year later they all hated it." It was, in his opinion, typical of "stupid, unsophisticated, nouveau riche horrors".

When Gant is shown Guy Morel's photographs taken over the partition wall at Victoria Art Conservation. He is bewildered by the unusual angle and denies knowing the location where the photographs were taken. When questioned about fake Whiteley paintings, Gant tells the police, "I've seen a lot of fake Whiteleys, but they are bad."

When told that he was about to be charged with obtaining financial advantage by deception, Gant uttered one word: "Bullshit".

Gant wasn't the least bit concerned about his co-accused, Aman Siddique. He giggled at the idea of the hot-tempered Siddique getting upset at being questioned.

Siddique did not cope well with being arrested; he was shattered. The police were so concerned that they called in the police doctor to examine him.

At seven o'clock in the morning of June 27, 2014, police seized *Orange Lavender Bay* from Steven Drake's house. Drake helped them manoeuvre the large painting through his hallway. *Through the window (Brown)* is still missing; the police claim that it was offered for $950,000.

Courtroom 3 in Melbourne's Supreme Court is a two-storey high room with wooden panels on the lower level, a white plaster ceiling, and arched windows on the upper level. At one end, beneath a carved wooden awning, is the judge's bench beside the witness box, a small round wooden pedestal with steps and a railing leading up. There are wooden benches for journalists and writers. The jury box is on the opposite side of the room. At the other end of the room, behind two tables and three benches of lawyers and solicitors, is the dock where the accused sat, separated by a uniformed sheriff's officer. Above the dock, on the second storey, is the public gallery. Unlike the rest of the antique courtroom, the dock has a contemporary feature of a reinforced glass surround. For Gant and Siddique's court case, the front section of the surround was removed at the request of Gant's lawyer, Trevor Wraight QC, because it would give the jury the impression that the defendants were violent, dangerous men.

On most days of the trial, there were at least nine lawyers in court. The two men had their own Queens Counsel (QC), another barrister and a solicitor. The prosecution was led by Ms Susan Borg, the Crown Prosecutor for the Office of Public Prosecutions. In costumes to match the Renaissance-revival style architecture of the courtroom, QCs and barristers donned wigs and black robes; Justice Michael Croucher wore a wig and red robes edged with silver; his associate, Lachlan Carter wore a black robe but no wig; the tipstaff, John Vardy was dressed in the traditional uniform of a long grey coat with black brocade; while the solicitors wore their business suits.

Siddique and Gant's trial was one of the last cases to be tried in the Supreme Court, with the barristers and judge wearing traditional wigs. The tradition officially ended in Victoria on May 1, 2016. The crusty, grey-bearded barrister, Remy van de Wiel QC, who represented Aman Siddique, commented on this end of an era in his summing up to the jury. He noted the royal connections with the judges' red robes and, according to his history, the black lawyers' robes referenced mourning for Queen Ann, along with the 'mourning sleeves' on the QCs' robes. The history of the wigs dates back to the Sun King, Louis XIV of France. Remy's old wig looked like it is made out of horsehair, but the younger wigs in the courtroom were made of nylon. Van de Wiel used this historical point to emphasise to the jury: "You are here to apply the principles of law, and that's why we dress the way in which we do and it's the only justification for it – believe me; I do not go to bed wearing these clothes, I don't wear them around the house or certainly don't wear them walking my dog."

For the first week, before the trial proper started, there was a Basha inquiry. Named after a New South Wales case, a Basha inquiry is a pre-trial hearing that allows the defence to cross-examine new witnesses before giving evidence in front of the jury. Some of these new witnesses included Jud Wimhurst, Brett Lichtenstein and the art dealers John Playfoot and Anita Archer.

The two art dealers' problem was that if they were knowingly helping Gant sell a fake, they would be involved in the deception. Consequently, they had their own lawyers with them. When Playfoot testified, he stated that he was never suspicious but that his wife was. Suzanne Playfoot had good reason to be wary of Peter Gant because, in 1998, her husband had named Gant in a London court as the source of a batch of irradiated Lalique glass.

On Monday, April 11, 2015, the courtroom was packed with potential jurors. The accused were formally arraigned on charges of obtaining financial advantage by deception. Aman Siddique clearly responded to the charge with "Not guilty", and Peter Gant mumbled. Justice Croucher then addressed the potential jurors, summed up the prosecution and defence cases and read through a list of all the witnesses, court staff and other people involved in the case. One potential juror was a cousin of John Playfoot and was excused from jury duty.

A panel of fourteen jurors was then selected. The first juror chosen was a young man who looked like he was having a panic attack, pulling his hoodie collar up over his nose and hyperventilating as he sat in the back of the jury box. Most of the subsequent jurors were decades older, and a couple were retired. Fourteen were selected in case any of them became sick or couldn't sit for some reason; if this didn't happen, two jurors would be balloted off before the jury started deliberating.

The prosecution case was that sometime in the first half of 2007, Gant and Siddique had agreed to use their combined expertise as art dealer and conservator to create and deceive a buyer to pay top price for fake Brett Whiteley paintings. Siddique's defence denied there was an agreement with Gant and that Siddique had profited from this agreement. The defence did not dispute much of the evidence; what was in dispute was the paintings' authenticity.

"I think the paintings, like the accused, should remain innocent until proven otherwise," Trevor Wraight QC told the court. The two paintings were brought into the courtroom in the absence of the jury. With shrouds of bubble wrap hanging off them, the two massive paintings were carried in by the tipstaff and one of the defence solicitors. It would have been prejudicial for the jury to see how the paintings were handled, as this was not done by professional art handlers wearing white gloves. Although they were carefully manoeuvred around the court's antique wooden benches, it was certainly not done to professional standards, with bare hands touching the gold leaf frames and once or twice the paintings.

They sat in Courtroom 3 of the Supreme Court of Victoria for weeks, on the opposite side from the jury box, leaning against the wall on the back row of the benches where the media and members of the accused's family sat. Before their court appearance, the two paintings had been stored in a police warehouse. If the paintings proved to be genuine works by Brett Whiteley created in 1988, then they would have spent most of their existence in storage and their time displayed in court was their only public exhibition.

The blue painting, the larger of the two, was now called exhibit #20, and the orange one, exhibit #21. Both depicted scenes of

Lavender Bay and both were framed in water-gilded gold frames. Were they the paintings Gant had bought from Quintas or the fakes Siddique had painted upstairs at Victorian Art Conservation?

Over the next four weeks, the prosecution presented its case. Starting with their most persuasive witness, Guy Morel, and his photographs: exhibit #1, 'photo-book A', showing the development of the blue painting, and exhibit #2, 'photo-book B', showing the same for the orange one.

Wendy Whiteley described her occupation as a "gardener". Rather than having her objecting to any questions about drug use on the grounds that they might be incriminating, Justice Croucher explained that he would give her a blanket certificate for her evidence, even though the overwhelming probability was that her drug use back in the 1960s, '70s or '80s was not going to be of interest to any prosecuting authority.

As Wendy had separated from Brett when the two paintings were alleged to have been painted, she couldn't be sure that he hadn't painted them. It was just her opinion as someone who had known Brett and his paintings well. She had made an inventory of Brett's studio before the divorce in 1988–89, but he may have hidden them from her. During their multi-million-dollar divorce dispute, the discovery of a cache of paintings hidden in a studio wall added another $2.5 million to the asset pool.

If the prosecution was hoping that Professor Sloggett's evidence would be as conclusive as it had been in the trial of the Libertos, they were to be disappointed. Her testimony made her sound more like a connoisseur than a scientific expert witness: "The lack of spontaneity, the lack of wit, the lack of spirit – the lack of everything" and "it's dead, it's a dead hand".

Was it a battle between masterminds of one art conservator against another art conservator, or was there no evidence? The scientific evidence presented to the jury consisted of infra-red photography of sections of the paintings that showed underdrawings. Although similar to Morel's photographs of the paintings' progress in Siddique's secret studio, they proved nothing.

Problems for the prosecution case were mounting up.

There was Guy Morel's evidence, not as the photographer of Siddique's secret painting but as the expert on paper. Morel had examined the catalogue for Peter Gant's exhibition, A Private Affair, which featured the artworks in question. This was not unusual work for a conservator of paper. Morel had gone along with the request to write the report upstairs at Victorian Art Conservation to allay any of Siddique's suspicions. The catalogue was printed in high-resolution offset lithography. The copy shown to the court was remarkable because it was from a test run, what printers call a 'running proof', and contained handwritten notes by the printer. The catalogue had never been printed and distributed because the exhibition had been cancelled due to the tragic death of the gallery's 32-year-old co-director, Greg Korn, Gant's business partner. Although Morel didn't date the paper stock it was printed on, he concluded that the catalogue was genuine. And the photographer, Jeremy James, swore he had photographed the two paintings for the catalogue.

Now a yoga instructor, Gant's former gallery assistant, Rosemary Milburn, remembered, prompted by entries in the gallery's consignment book, a delivery of paintings. On Monday, October 3, 1988, at Peter Gant's Coventry Street gallery, there had been a large delivery of art that Rosemary had noted in several entries in the gallery's consignment book. One of the entries was about the delivery of three paintings. Written on consignment note #23 was 'Chris Quintas, 3 Whiteleys, packaged in bubble wrap and wooden crates, moved by Grace Fine Arts', along with Rosemary Milburn's signature. No expert evaluation of the handwriting was made of this consignment note, and Milburn does not remember the paintings in much detail.

She recalled that she could only see them through the packaging and that they matched the description of the three paintings that the prosecution alleged were forged.

There is also evidence for the existence of paintings fitting the description existing in 2006. Invoice #0175 in Siddique's books reads: '14/07/06 Brett Whiteley, Lavender Bay Blue, surface cleaning and varnishing approximate size 1600 × 2500 possible framing 4000/5000 plus GST'.

At the end of the prosecution case, the jurors were allowed to examine the paintings up close. White ribbons tied to the ends of the wooden benches 'roped off' the paintings. The jurors were not allowed to talk or point. First, they lined up to look at the fronts. Then, with the assistance of the judge's associate and the tipstaff who held the large paintings, at the backs.

There were definitely some reasonable doubts about the two men's guilt. At the end of the prosecution case, Justice Croucher took the highly unusual step of offering the jury a Prasad invitation. A Prasad invitation is sometimes used in cases where the identification of the accused is seriously in error because of good evidence that they were somewhere else. The judge asks the jury if they have heard enough and want to return a verdict of 'Not guilty' or if they want to hear more.

Out of the original fourteen jurors, only one had to be balloted off as another juror had already been excused from service because their parent, who lived abroad, had become gravely ill. The juror who was balloted off looked relieved and then very pleased when he learnt that he would be excused from jury service for the next ten years.

After sitting for eighteen days, the jury returned, not long after lunch, to tell a stunned court that they wanted to hear more.

There wasn't much more for the jury to hear. Gant's defence called no witnesses, and van der Wiel only called two witnesses to testify to Aman Siddique's good character.

The need to find both Siddique and Gant guilty if one was found guilty was an added difficulty for the prosecution. There was no evidence that Gant and Siddique had conspired to forge paintings. There was no evidence that Siddique had ever received any money for his part. Still, the prosecution's case was convincing enough that on Thursday, 11 May, the jury of six women and six men found Gant and Siddique guilty.

When you see a magician pull a rabbit from a hat, you don't know how it was done, but you know it is a trick. You applaud and enjoy the magic show. In a criminal trial, the defendants must be given the benefit of the doubt. If the prosecution can't show how the magician did the trick, it must be assumed that a rabbit might have been pulled from a hat or several Whiteley paintings had been pulled out of storage. The jury was sure that it was a trick, even if nobody had explained how it was done.

Even though the judgement would be appealed, the rest of the court case proceeded as if it was final. Arguments on appropriate sentences ranged from ten to twenty years, because of the two offences, to the possibility of a suspended sentence in the interests of justice. The court heard summaries of Gant and Siddique's careers from their respective defence lawyers. In determining a sentence, issues had to be weighed up, including general deterrence, the possibility of rehabilitation and adverse effects on the men. Both men had lost their businesses and were unlikely ever to work in the art world again. Should their sentences be the same or different? The prosecution argued that both men were equally culpable, as both were equally valuable to the process of fraud.

If Peter Gant was hoping to make a fortune by selling the paintings, he failed. What money he received quickly left his account, including payment of various matters relating to the sale, like transport. Gant was discharged as a bankrupt in August 2015. At his trial in the Supreme Court in 2016, he was represented by Legal Aid. He works in his daughter's catering business when not appearing in court.

But it was Aman Siddique who had lost the most and still had more to lose. A broken man suffering from depression and anxiety. As he is not an Australian citizen, he could be deported if he served a sentence of more than twelve months.

By September, Justice Croucher had not sentenced the pair, and both were still out on bail, a very unusual position for convicted men. Croucher considered whether he could just leave the sentence up to the Court of Appeal, but there was also the matter of compensation to consider for the victims.

On October 12, the trial recommenced, this time in the most ornate of Melbourne's Supreme Court courtrooms, Courtroom 1, the Bianco Court, where the Renaissance Revival style of the building's exterior is reflected in the interior, in its carved wood, detailed plasterwork, brass rails and huge chandelier. Although still dressed in their robes, the judge and barristers looked different without the now-redundant traditional wigs that made the top of their heads look flat. They still had their wigs with them, sitting on benches like strange soft toys; Justice Croucher entered with his on but then took it off.

There were more barristers than usual in the court because lawyers for Pridham and Playfoot were there to make their applications relating to compensation for loss. Pridham wanted $2.5 million from Gant and Siddique. Nasteski had received a refund from Playfoot, so did that mean that Playfoot was now a victim? What is the value of some wood moulding with gold leaf and painted doors? Does it even matter as Gant is bankrupt and Siddique has no assets of his own after exhausting his finances paying for the trial? Croucher dismissed applications for victim compensation by Pridham and Playfoot. Due to joint liability complications, he was concerned about the civil court matter between Pridham and his art adviser, Anita Archer. He ruled that Playfoot paid the refund due to 'good business practice' and not due to the deception.

The forgeries have not affected the prices paid for Whiteley paintings, nor has it put people off buying them since 2014 when the stories broke. Steven Nasteski has even purchased a new Whiteley for his house.

When Justice Croucher finally sentenced Gant and Siddique in November, he noted that the fraud was audacious and the pair was "sufficiently impudent to think the art world was greedy or gullible enough, or perhaps both, to fall for this ruse three times." He relished quoting the Australian art critic Robert Hughes: "Art prices are largely about voyeurism and toxic snobbery. They are what you see when you peer up the anus of culture." Then he sentenced Gant to five years imprisonment, with a non-parole period of two and a half years, and Siddique to three years imprisonment, with an order for ten months to be served and twenty-six months suspended. Both of their sentences were stayed until the men's bail could be determined by the Court of Appeal.

On April 27, 2017, the government's prosecutor, Daniel Gurvich QC, asked for Gant and Siddique's convictions to be set aside. Nobody disagreed, and the Victorian Court of Appeal quashed the convictions. The crucial point was that there was no rational basis for concluding that Milburn and James were both mistaken in their evidence. If Milburn and James were mistaken, that meant the entry in the consignment book and the catalogue's running proof were fakes, yet no expert evidence had been given about these documents to suggest this. Given all this, "there was simply no basis for the jury to have reached that conclusion." The Justices noted:

"It is sometimes said that juries 'always get it right'. Sadly, in this particular instance, that seems not to have been so. Trial by jury is of fundamental importance to both the rule of law, and to our system of criminal justice. It represents perhaps the greatest safeguard we have of the rights of the individual against the state. There have been literally thousands of criminal trials conducted over the years without anyone being able to demonstrate that the jury, assuming they were properly directed and the trial otherwise properly conducted, had wrongly convicted an accused person. This case is a rare and almost unique instance of the system having failed in that regard."

The court released both men and the two paintings; they are not guilty. *Orange Lavender Bay* returned to hang on the wall of Steven Drake's Toorak mansion. The ownership of *Blue Lavender Bay* was not so clear. Nobody will pay millions of dollars for either painting again just because they could be by Brett Whiteley. Especially when neither is included in art historian Kathie Sutherland's just published 2400-page *Brett Whiteley: Catalogue raisonné: 1955-1992*, a definitive list of Whiteley's work.

It looked like Steven Drake was the last victim, left with a dud; however, further revelations about his art collection came in a civil case several years later. In April 2021, County Court Judge Brimer ordered Drake to pay damages of $288,585.68, plus interest, to Alex Stanowitsch. In 2011 and 2012, Drake induced Stanowitsch into an investment scheme with Peter Gant. Gant provided nine paintings as security, claiming that they were by Howard Arkley, Charles Blackman, John Brack, Russell Drysdale, Sidney Nolan and Albert Tucker. However, all nine paintings were fakes. Brimer found that Steven Drake was a business associate of Peter Gant through buying and selling paintings and loaning him money.

Self-righteous Pricks

Norman Lindsay and the Witch of Kings Cross

Art in Australia, December 1930, sold very well at 3 shillings 6 pence – more than 5000 copies. A Sydney bookseller made the reason for the excellent sales of that issue explicit by advertising it as: "Pictures for Men only. Wonderful Art Book". This advertisement caught the prurient attention of the men in the NSW vice squad, the state's morality police. What they discovered surprised and excited them.

Six months after the edition had been published, the ever-vigilant vice squad raided two bookshops and the magazine's office. Protecting the public from even illustrations of exposed nipples, bare buttocks or pubic hair. Booksellers and publishers were charged with selling obscene material. Print blocks, stereotypes plates and unsold copies were seized.

Sydney Ure Smith established *Art in Australia* in 1916 to be the premier publication of Australian art in the early twentieth century. Published bi-monthly *Art in Australia* was markedly different from the art magazines of today. Most noticeable, it only has forty pictures, ten full-colour (including two advertisements) and thirty black and white. The ten pages of full-colour chromolithographic printing are really the only content. These fine art images were the whole point of the magazine. Typical of art magazines, there are pages of advertisements at the front and back. However, only two of the advertisements were for art galleries, for, at the time, there weren't many more in Australia.

The issue featured only one artist, Norman Lindsay, a man of many talents; illustrator, author and amateur boxer. The rest consists of an editorial, a boozy interview with Lindsay, and a photograph of him posing next to a model sailing ship he'd made. The magazine regularly had issues with single artists; in the past, it had ones on Margaret Preston and Norman Lindsay's older brother Lionel.

The cover is mostly text with a pen and ink drawing of a thin man wearing a long cloak and a tall wide-brimmed hat, an illustration for Lindsay's chivalric farce of *Micomicon*. The editorial and interview are defensive as if anticipating the attention of the vice squad. This was not surprising, considering that since 1904, Lindsay's art was censored and declared blasphemous, pornographic and obscene. Australian Customs banned his second novel *Redheap* (along with *All Quiet on the Western Front*, *Arabian Nights*, and other books). All copies were confiscated. The editorial points out Lindsay's novel *Redheap* (published in London that year and published in the U.S. as *Every Mother's Son*) was not banned in any other country. The censorial prudish attitude was unique to Australia. Lindsay says in his interview in the magazine, "There is something extremely disgusting in having one's work pawed by policemen."

Not all of Lindsay's thirty-eight illustrations in the magazine featured naked women. There are scenes of sailing ships, pirates drinking rum, cavemen fighting, and the pen and ink sketches for *Micomicon*. But Lindsay liked his art with plenty of nude women, and there were sufficient numbers in the magazine. Lindsay packs his pictorial space with nudes, crowds of voluptuous women, bacchanalian orgies and fantasy ballroom scenes. A bevy of curvy, topless beauties with lasciviously smiles. The sheer and diaphanous veil of literary reference was transparent for the excuse that it was. Lindsay didn't care; it was all in good fun and taste.

A few weeks after the raids, the charges against the book-sellers were dropped. However, the police proceeded with obscenity charges against the publisher and editor, Sydney Ure Smith and co-editor, Leon Gellert.

Then the new state Attorney General, Joseph Lamaro, declared: "*Art in Australia* cannot be branded obscene". At the mention hearing in the Local Court on July 8, 1931, the police presented no evidence. The case was dismissed, with all copies of the magazine and the printing plates to be returned. Under the separation of powers, the executive branch is not meant to interfere in the judicial, but in practice, Australian politicians often get involved when there are allegations of obscene art.

Lindsay was tired of the way that Australia treated him. So Lindsay left Australia at the end of 1931 with a public "to hell with this bloody country". He threatened never to return and heaped further scorn on Australian culture in American newspapers.

Lindsay returned to Australia the following year, and the police continued to interfere with his nudes. In 1966 Victoria Police's vice squad visited the Southern Cross Gallery to view an exhibition of his paintings. There had been yet another complaint. Lindsay's *Bacchanalian Festival* was removed from the window, and no charges were laid.

Lindsey was again a victim of the vice squad. And this is not a unique case; many artists and galleries have had their exhibitions co-curated by the police, acquiescing to the implied threat of state-sanctioned violence.

If Norman Lindsay's art was too much for the wowsers, they hadn't seen the work of one of his former models, Rosaleen Norton (aka Roie, aka 'the Witch of Kings Cross'). Whereas Lindsay depicted creatures of the light enjoying a naked frolic in the sun, Norton was a creature of the dark, a Satanist for free love who enjoyed sex magic and erotic communion with demonic forces in self-induced trances.

Rosaleen Norton studied art for two years at East Sydney Technical College, cultivating her style and arching eyebrows before settling down in Sydney's red-light district, Kings Cross. Her art is the kind that now adorns many heavy metal band album covers and T-shirts. Erotica with satanic themes. Demons with erect penises and nude women drawn with sensuous curving lines. Heavy-handed symbolism in vortexes of metaphysical space.

In 1949 Norton, her cat, Geoffrey, and her lover Gavin Greenless hitchhiked from Sydney to Melbourne, hoping for an exhibition. A mutual friend and student booked the gallery at the Rowden-White Library at the University of Melbourne's Student Union. And her exhibition opened on August 1.

It was only open for two days before two policemen, Detective John Olsen and Inspector A. S. Tannahill, came to see it. They were so interested that they took away four of Norton's works, the *Witch's Sabbath*, *Lucifer*, *Triumph*, and *Individuation*. Locking them in the strongroom at the Russell Street Police Headquarters to protect the morality of university students, they charged Norton with exhibiting 'obscene art that could deprave and corrupt the morals of those who saw them'.

The police decided to take legal action independently without consulting the Crown Law Department, the equivalent of the Office of Public Prosecutions. It was not the wisest of decisions.

The Magistrates' courtroom was so packed that the hearing was moved to the District Court to accommodate all the spectators. If anyone had come to see the allegedly obscene art, they were disappointed, for the four works of art were turned to face the wall. Norton's defence lawyer, A. L. Abrahams, successfully argued that a court was not the proper place to view the art. The magistrate and a crowd of spectators went to the student union gallery to view Norton's art in an appropriate setting.

Abrahams made the police's allegation that the painting would 'deprave and corrupt people's morals who saw them' look flimsy. The warden of the student union, R. R. P. Barbour, who had given permission for the exhibition, testified that he didn't find the drawings sexually stimulating or corrupting.

Stipendiary Magistrate Donald Addison judged that the minds of Melbourne University students did not need protection from corruption. He ordered that all charges be dismissed, the drawings returned and for the police to pay costs of £4/4 ($211 today).

The trial and associated publicity meant more university students visited the exhibition asking to see the "rudies". However, for the penniless Norton, hopes that this would result in more sales were not realised.

Australian law wasn't finished with Norton. In 1952 the publisher of limited edition, leather-bound, *The Art of Rosaleen Norton*, Wally Glover, and the printer, Tonecraft Pty Ltd, were charged with obscenity. The prosecution was briefer than a G-string. "That's my case, your Worship," D. J. Vine-Hall of Crown Solicitor's office said, submitting into evidence a copy of the book. And with that, the prosecution rested.

It was enough. The Magistrate described two of Norton's images as "an offence to chastity and delicacy". He fined Tonecraft Pty Ltd £1 for printing the book, Glover £5 for selling it and ordered that two of Norton's illustrations, *The Adversary* and *Fohat*, be blacked out in all copies of the book.

U. S. Customs went further, deciding that the whole book was obscene and burnt the copies sent to New York. Unable to export, advertise or distribute the book, Glover was stuck with the cost of producing the book and the advance given to Norton. He went bankrupt.

Was this simply wowsers using the law to enforce their faith and prejudices, or do the police have a deeper motive? Moral panic is the art of distracting the public from actual corruption within the police force and government by calling something else immoral. Attacking an artist over alleged sexual impropriety or going on a witch hunt is a traditional way to maintain the fig leaf illusion of decency.

The indecency of Mike Brown

In 1965 Australia was a deeply conservative country. Apart from the new decimal currency made at the new Australian mint in Canberra, little had changed since the 1930s. Robert Menzies had been prime minister for longer than many people could remember. And the Australian government censored everything from Disney movies to modern art.

In Melbourne, police raided the Austral Bookshop to seize copies of *The Trial of Lady Chatterley*. Although Penguin Books had been found not guilty of obscenity for publishing D. H. Lawrence's *Lady Chatterley's Lover* in England, it was still banned in Australia. And *The Trial of Lady Chatterley* had transcripts of the court case quoting the novel. It was ridiculous, but most Australians didn't want it to change.

In Sydney, Mike Brown wanted change in Australia. The lanky young drop-out from art studies at the East Sydney Technical College had already had considerable success when Brown and two other young artists formed a short-lived art movement laughingly called the Annandale Imitation Realists. The art critic Robert Hughes praised Brown's *Mary-Lou as Miss Universe*, an overtly sexual assemblage made from junk, as "uproariously funny, savagely satirical, and intolerably many-faceted comment on the mass-produced darlings of Hollywood." In 1963, Brown's *Mary-Lou as Miss* Universe was selected for a travelling exhibition before the invitation was withdrawn after complaints about its content.

This made Brown angry about censorship. He was also incensed about the prosecution of Sydney's *Oz* magazine; it was the third time the magazine had been charged with obscenity. This time it was for a photograph of the magazine's production team pretending to urinate in sculptor Tom Bass's *P&O Wall Fountain* captioned: "Pictured is a trio of Sydney natives P. & O.'ing in the Bass urinal". The inset curving channels and pools of Bass's biomorphic bronze on the P&O building's outside wall was almost at the right height to function as a urinal. *Oz* magazine was taking the piss, but Magistrate Gerald Locke sentenced them to three to six months in prison with hard labour for publishing obscenity. The magazine's production team was on bail, awaiting an appeal.

Brown felt that their prison sentences threatened his freedom and his art. Motivated by a desire to crusade for civil liberties and protest the laws against obscenity, Brown decided to create five new works for his upcoming solo exhibition. The new works were a protest against censorship. They included swear words, depictions of genitalia and quotations from books banned in Australia: *Lady Chatterley's Lover*, Vladimir Nabokov's *Lolita* and James Joyce's *Ulysses*. Each work had two sides and was hung on a wire so that they could be turned over.

Brown's exhibition, "Paintin' A-Go-Go!" at Max Hutchinson's Gallery A, was not exactly open to the public. It was for adults only, and viewers had to ring the doorbell to be admitted into the gallery. Rather than take the chance of the public making a complaint about his art Brown went to the *Daily Mail* to tell them about his exhibition.

The *Daily Mail* had a photographer waiting when Sergeant Frank Farrell (aka Bumper Farrell), chief of the vice squad in the

Darlinghurst division, visited Gallery A on Monday, November 22, 1965. A former rugby league player with cauliflower ears, Bumper Farrell was the kind of man that Australia had, all too often, looked to define decent behaviour.

Fortunately, Max Hutchinson hired a lawyer for Brown; unfortunately, he was a young inexperienced lawyer who advised Brown to cooperate with the police and answer questions. It was the worst advice he could have given. In the police interview, Brown admitted to riding in the truck that delivered the paintings to the gallery. This apparently innocent action formed the technical basis for the charge of "delivering...an indecent picture."

The charges against Brown were heard on November 28 and 29, 1966 in the Paddington Court of Petty Sessions. Bumper Farrell presented four of Brown's paintings to the court but not the fifth, titled *Hallelujah* because it sold during the exhibition.

Remarkably Mike Brown's obscenity case had many of the same people as *Oz* magazine, from Bumper Farrell to the magistrate, Gerald Locke. Only the defendants and defence teams were different. Art patron John Reed had arranged for new legal representation for Brown; the barrister Kenneth Gregory Horler who later established Sydney's Nimrod Theatre. It didn't help; Horler frequently clashed with Magistrate Locke over points of law, but it didn't make it worse. The result was predictable when Magistrate Locke eventually delivered his judgement in December.

"Not even artists are permitted to indulge obscenity for art's sake. I am concerned with nothing else," Locke declared. "Does society permit the flaunting of sex, the debasing of the female form, or are they being foisted on an unwilling community by a noisy and arrogant few?" He described Brown's paintings as "an orgy of obscenity" and sentenced him to three months hard labour for delivering obscene art.

Max Hutchinson had pleaded guilty to exhibiting the same allegedly obscene pictures and was fined $30 ($366 today). The difference between Hutchinson's fine and Brown's three-month sentence for delivering the same images is vast.

At the end of 1966, Brown was on bail awaiting appeal. The art dealer and civil libertarian Frank Watters set up a defence fund for the appeal and held a fund-raising exhibition in February 1967. Charles Blackman, Elwyn Lynn, Geoffrey Proud and John Pearl were amongst the artists to donate work. The vice squad responded by putting the gallery on its proscribed list.

While out on bail, Brown continued to exhibit, including some of the paintings found obscene, at Strines Gallery in Melbourne. Remarkably, as the gallery's director, Sweeney Reed, already had his own problems with obscenity charges. There had been three uninvited guests at Strines Art Gallery's inaugural exhibition in October 1966, all undercover members of the vice squad. Sweeney and the artist Ron Upton had been charged with obscenity for exhibiting Upton's work *Oops!* — a brush and ink drawings with collage elements.

John Reed paid for a lawyer to defend his adopted son, Sweeney, and the witnesses for the defence included the Anglican Bishop of Melbourne, Felix Arnott. In 1967 through some unusual legal logic, Upton's *Oops* was obscene because it emphasised sex and offended accepted community standards. However, Upton and Reed were found not guilty of exhibiting it.

The appeal against Brown's conviction was heard on June 5, 1967 in front of Justice David Levine in the Sydney Quarter Sessions. Levine had overturned the conviction of the *Oz* magazine defendants citing Magistrate Locke's bias against the defendants. And on July 26, Levine delivered his judgement on Brown's appeal. He upheld the conviction but accepted the work's artistic merit and reduced the sentence to a $20 fine ($250 today).

The Paddington vice squad had been disbanded in 1966, and Frank 'Bumper' Farrell was redeployed to suburban uniform duties. Max Hutchinson moved to New York in 1968, where he continued to work as a gallery director and curator. The NGV had two Mike Brown retrospective survey exhibitions, the first in 1976 and the second in 1995, two years before his death in 1997.

Even after his death, Mike Brown was still offending Australia's moral guardians. In 1999, the Catholic Archbishop of Perth complained in vain that Brown's painting, *You're Welcome*, at the state's art gallery was blasphemous. Even after vice squads were disbanded, police raided a Mike Brown-inspired art exhibition — an event that will be examined in a later chapter.

Warning signs

The theme of the 1982 Sydney Biennale at the Art Gallery of NSW was 'Vision in Disbelief'. When Juan Davila arrived for the exhibition opening, he had a vision of disbelief. The thirty-six-year-old, Chilean-born, Melbourne-based artist had been invited to exhibit his painting *Stupid as a painter*. Only it wasn't there.

Stupid as a painter is about how a quotation is removed from its original context. Its title quotes a French phrase that Marcel Duchamp hated and had fermented his desire to create cerebral, conceptual art. And Davila's art is more than an exercise in applying paint, more of a semiotics lecture than erotic evocation. Like much contemporary art, the huge multi-panel painting depicts a complex array of references. Kiss of the Spider Woman mixed with images of Marilyn Monroe, Pop art and the pornographic illustrations of Tom of Finland. It suggests multiple valid interpretations to the viewer rather than demanding a correct reading. It presents various interpretations and views which are the difference between art and pornography.

Stupid as a painter was selected to be part of the Biennale six months earlier. The organisers had seen it, and the painting hadn't changed. However, what had seemed like a good idea in the planning was suddenly censored by Edmund Capon, the Director of the Art Gallery of NSW, who refused to exhibit it. As a compromise, the Biennale organisers arranged for Davila's painting to be shown at Roslyn Oxley9, a new commercial gallery in Paddington that had just opened the year before. The unprofessionalism of the Biennale organisers and the Gallery of NSW is hard to imagine today.

Outside Roslyn Oxley9 at the entrance, there were notices saying the exhibition was unsuitable for 'underage' people. Inside, the painting was obscured from casual view behind an industrial screen.

Despite these precautions, on Wednesday, April 14, the vice squad came and took it away, claiming it was obscene. They had received a complaint from Reverend Fred Nile, leader of the ultra-conservative Christian political party, The Festival of Light. Nile was trying to get free publicity for his by-election campaign for a seat in the State parliament by acting as the state's moral guardian. He hadn't seen the painting himself, but he had sent some of his devotees along to Roslyn Oxley9.

Although Sydney's Gay & Lesbian Mardi Gras is now world famous, this was only four years after the first Mardi Gras. It had started as a protest march in 1978, calling for the repeal of all anti-homosexual laws. The homophobia behind Nile's complaint and the police confiscating *Stupid as a painter* is blatant. *The Daily Telegraph* ran the headline: "Porn Art". And, Davila wondered if this really was his art anymore, or had it become: "a *simulacrum* of the many other cases in the history of Australian art where works have been censored." (And in this chapter, it has become that *simulacrum*.)

Only the intervention that evening by Premier Neville Wran put a stop to the police action. Wran was constitutionally opposed to the censorship of the arts. Before he went into politics, when he worked as a solicitor, Wran represented the *Oz magazine* editors in their English trial for obscenity. "I am surprised that in this age, when nudity, obscenity and pornography – rightly or wrongly – are available, that an art gallery should be raided." The gravel-voiced Premier went on TV to describe the vice squad's seizure as an "invasion" and declared that "art has nothing to do with the vice squad."

Furthermore, demonstrating his knowledge of art censorship, Wran said, "Aubrey Beardsley would turn in his grave." This was an oblique reference to a decade-old case in Melbourne in 1971. A magistrate declared posters featuring two drawings by the nineteenth century English illustrator and writer Aubrey Beardsley's *Lysistrata* and *Cinesias pursuing Myrrhina*, were obscene and ordered them to be destroyed. An appalling judgement that was overturned on appeal.

Wran's police minister, Bill Anderson, followed his leader and ordered an end to the police action. To prevent this, Nile appealed to the Supreme Court – and failed. Davila's painting was back on exhibition by Friday, this time at the Powers Gallery of Contemporary Art (now the Museum of Contemporary Art, aka MCA) in Sydney.

Juan Davila's assessment was: "The discussion about *Stupid as a painter* in the press and in the art scene was predictably 'Is it art or is it pornography?' only a repetition of the long history of censorship in Australia." This would not be the last time police would seize art from Roslyn Oxley9 Gallery, and it would not be the last time the police would return the same artwork without laying any charges. Nor would it be the last time the police went after Davila's art. Nothing was resolved, legally or politically; it was just another round in Australia's culture war. The most remarkable part is the way that it repeats.

Two years later, in 1984, NSW police confiscated three more works by Juan Davila. This time they were being exhibited in a council-run art gallery at Lake Macquarie: *Australian Landscape*, *Photo-romance* and *Photographic Cubism*. Although a magistrate ruled that they were obscene and ordered them destroyed, they were saved by the NSW Governor Sir James Rowland, who granted them mercy. While Australian law was happy to destroy art, the political establishment didn't yet want to be seen as philistine vandals.

Regional values

The Mildura Prize for Sculpture began in 1961 to promote tourism to Victoria's wine country. In 1970, it became the Mildura Sculpture Triennial bringing minimalism, non-objective art, performance art and earthworks to the Murray River region. The growth in regional art galleries in Australia in the 1960s, '70s and '80s meant more people had access to contemporary art. It also meant that art censorship was no longer the sole concern of police and magistrates in capital cities.

The Tenth Mildura Sculpture Triennial went from April 2, 1988 to May 31, 1988, with sculptures installed around the city. Jill Peck's site-specific construction made from reclaimed iron bark, *Hut*, can still be seen in its original location. But only a few people ever saw another one of the sculptures.

The triennial's curators had invited Cath Phillips to show a vulva-shaped construction in a bush setting. It was the accompanying text: "She ran her tongue like fire across my nipples, she slipped her hand in my cunt and grinned" that got some locals' knickers in a knot.

The police in Mildura maintained they had a legal requirement to protect the public from lesbian themes and the word 'cunt'. And the thirty-three-year-old New Zealand-born sculptor thought she had a right to exhibit it.

She received no practical support from the Mildura Sculpture Triennial, who threw up their hands and acquiesced to the police censorship. It was common practice in regional Victoria. That same year the police decided that Don Stewart's sculpture, *Cameraman and Old Man with Young Woman*, was too explicit and ordered it removed, effectively co-curating an exhibition at the City of Hamilton Art Gallery.

Cath Phillips was not going to allow some men, police or otherwise, to decide what she could exhibit. Nor was she about to let her art quietly be censored. She wanted the right of reply to the censorship and to being described as an "obscene artist". When the police covered up her work, Phillips uncovered it. The police then charged her with obscenity.

The magistrate fined Phillips $400 ($880 today) after deciding that community standards are different in regional Victoria; that the standard of obscenity was not the same as applied to metropolitan sculpture shows. The idea that there is a difference in law enforcement in regional and metropolitan Australia means there is not one law of the land but many.

Cath Phillips refused to pay the fine and spent two days in the Mildura lock-up, the only artist ever jailed for exhibiting 'obscene' art in Australia. That year, 1988, was the final year of the Mildura Sculpture Triennial. Phillips became the first lesbian president of the Sydney Gay and Lesbian Mardi Gras organisation.

Trial by media

The Melbourne-based artist Bill Henson has been exhibiting his large-format photographs of naked adolescents and crepuscular landscapes since the 1980s. He has been shown worldwide, from the Guggenheim in New York to the Venice Biennale. He is in many significant Australian art collections, including the NGV, the Art Gallery of NSW and the Australian National Gallery.

Henson's art is about moments of transition and points of heightened emotion between day and night, child and adult, seen and unseen. The images are mysterious and dramatic rather than revealing. His photographs are slightly out of focus and under-exposed, dark images lit in a way that makes pale skin look translucent and almost blue with the cold.

His exhibition at the Roslyn Oxley9 Gallery consisted of forty-one large photographic prints, 127 by 180 centimetres. About half the images were landscapes, and the other half were nude children. The exhibition's invitation featured *Untitled (#30)*, a naked pubescent girl walking out of the darkness.

Before the opening of an exhibition at Roslyn Oxley9 Gallery, some nerves and anxiety are perfectly normal. However, on that day in May 2008 the hostile phone calls, the threats from some callers and the crowd of reporters outside the gallery concerned Roslyn Oxley enough that she considered calling the police. After seeing the exhibition invite, some radio and newspapers had been fuelling anger all day.

Before anyone at the gallery called the police, two NSW police officers arrived at the gallery. Their commanding officer Superintendent Allan Sicard arrived shortly after. Superintendent Sicard looked at the growing crowd outside the gallery and the art inside. His first comment was: "I'm really concerned about the potential damage to the work." Roslyn Oxley, Bill Henson and Superintendent Sicard were concerned about the art and gallery staff's safety. At 5:15 pm, forty-five minutes before the exhibition was to open that Thursday evening, the decision was made to cancel.

Then Sicard raised the issue of the legality of the images; he wanted to make more enquiries. A fourth policeman arrived, and Henson provided his address, telephone numbers, the model's names, ages and parents' details.

The police then wanted to photograph the exhibition, but Roslyn Oxley objected. Detective Senior Constable Martin Kierman was sent to get a crime scene warrant. However, the presiding magistrate, Jason Day, rejected the application. The police asked Oxley again if they could photograph the exhibition, hoping she had changed her mind. And again, they were told no.

Everyone left the gallery, and the roller door at the entrance was locked.

Just after seven o'clock the following day, Prime Minister Kevin Rudd made his regular appearance on Channel 9's breakfast television show, *Today*. He was shown the invitation to the Henson exhibition.

Channel 9 had modified the photograph, adding salacious black bars over the girl's body to imply that censorship was necessary. The text at the base of the screen, along with the time and weather, displayed a clear message: 'Outrage over child porn-art'.

"I find them absolutely revolting," was the reaction of the ever-self-righteous Prime Minister. Rudd took the opportunity to preach: "Kids deserve to have the innocence of their childhood protected. I have a very deep view of this. For God's sake, let's just allow kids to be kids. Whatever the artistic view of the merits of that sort of stuff – frankly I don't think there are any – just allow kids to be kids." Finally, claiming expertise where he had none, Rudd declared that the photograph had "no artistic merit".

NSW Premier Morris Iemma declared he found the exhibition "offensive and disgusting" and issued a statement condemning the artist and the girl's parents. NSW Opposition Leader Barry O'Farrell followed the trend appearing to have no memory that he attended the major retrospective "Bill Henson: Three Decades of Photography" at the Art Gallery of New South Wales.

Midnight Oil's tall, bald frontman Peter Garrett, the Minister for the Arts, worked very hard to keep a low profile. Garrett had made the election promise to talk more about the arts, but he remained silent on his term's first serious arts issue. In an open letter leading writers, filmmakers, musicians and artists called on the Minister for Arts, Peter Garrett, to "stand up for artists" against the "encroaching censorship, which has resulted in the closure of this and other exhibitions". Garrett ignored their letter and maintained his right to remain silent.

The only politician who didn't join the choir was Malcolm Turnbull, who owned two landscapes by Henson. He alone talked of 'freedom' and 'the law' while his colleagues on both sides of Parliament were about to form vigilante gangs and lynch mobs.

Although the media, politicians and the public were all now screaming that Bill Henson was a child pornographer, it didn't make it so. The Australian Classification Board (ACB) had already determined that Henson's photographs were 'mild and justified' and gave them a PG rating. This meant that they were suitable for viewing by children over sixteen. And they weren't child pornography, as there is no such thing as PG-rated child pornography.

Twenty-four years after the police removed Juan Davila's *Stupid as a painter*, there was a repeat performance. Instead of consulting with the ACB, NSW police rushed to enforce the Prime Minister and Premier's opinion and seized thirty-two of Henson's large-format photographs from the Oxley Gallery along with a stack of invitations to the exhibition, threatening to lay child pornography charges. More Henson works were impounded at the Australian National Gallery in Canberra.

A few weeks later, the 'ongoing' police investigation was going nowhere. No victims of Henson's alleged crimes had been found. Rather several of his previous models, now adults, spoke to the media about how comfortable they were working with him and their pride in appearing in his photographs.

After dragging their feet, on Thursday, June 5, 2008, the NSW Department of Public Prosecutions (DPP) announced they would not be recommending charges. NSW police followed the DPP's advice and returned Henson's photographs to the Roslyn Oxley9 Gallery.

In October, the next round started with a non-controversy when it was revealed Henson had visited a Melbourne primary school to find models. The Victorian government reprimanded the school principal, presuming wrongdoing and prejudicing the process, before discovering that there had been no breach of any protocols. The polemics of state and federal politicians had convinced some people that art was simply a cover for paedophiles.

Politicians made new laws, and art exhibition organisers worried about nudity. Labyrinthine legal processes were created around exhibiting any images of children, and the definition of child pornography in NSW was broadened. The effects of the political furore would go on for years and have impacts across Australia.

Just over eighteen months after the Bill Henson censorship fiasco, the Sydney Children's Hospital Foundation refused to accept a work for a charity auction by the Archibald prize-winning artist Del Kathryn Barton. This was because her six-year-old son, Kell, was shown bare-chested. (Instead, another charity, Midnight Basketball, which runs workshops and tournaments for at-risk youth, benefitted from Del Kathryn Barton's generosity.) The Sydney Children's Hospital Foundation administrators were not prudes; they were just protective of their foundation's reputation. They have no way of knowing if the image would be controversial because what was apparent in the Henson fiasco was that it was an arbitrary action.

This is the chill effect – a form of soft censorship where people avoid hot topics. It is hard to observe because people not doing something out of fear leaves little or no evidence. Artists and curators working with nudes in Australia now fear being demonised. The lingering trepidation of controversy and police action will continue to affect artists, curators and exhibition sponsors' decisions.

In some ways, the attack on Henson's art was just a repeat of the pandemonium over Davila's *Stupid as a Painter*. It was also an escalation in the allegations, the number of politicians promoting them, and the time the police held on to the art before not bringing any charges. Again, nothing was resolved, with both sides claiming to hold the moral high ground. An ominous sign of yet more repeat performances.

A troll in St Kilda

At a meet-the-artist event at Neon Parc, a person innocently asked the clichéd question to Paul Yore: 'What was the most unexpected reaction to your work?' About forty people collectively took a deep breath because they knew the answer.

The most unexpected reaction was Victoria Police raiding Yore's installation at the Linden Centre for Contemporary Arts (aka Linden Gallery, Linden or now Linden New Art). Even after Magistrate Amanda Chambers dismissed all the charges against him, his name was still linked to child pornography. In her judgement, Magistrate Chambers was particularly critical of how the police had handled the search warrant when they had cut out parts of Yore's installation with a knife.

It continued a tradition of the police acting on complaints from 'the public', in other words, 'trolls'. Not the kind of trolls in fairy tales, but one of the many types of trolls alive today, the ones you encounter online. In Paul Yore's case, the troll was named Adrian Jackson, a former member of the Australian Army whose political opinions are so inflammatory the Liberal Party refused to renew his membership in 2003. His hobbies include making incendiary comments online, attending local city council meetings and running unsuccessfully as an independent conservative candidate in local council elections.

One of Jackson's petty ambitions was to end local council funding for the Linden Gallery, for reasons he explained in a letter to the *Port Phillip Leader*:

> *Ratepayers should not be treated as cash cows for a handful of contemporary artists living out their dream. I do not think we ratepayers are getting value for money at the council-funded Linden Gallery. I question the amount spent on maintenance, air-conditioning and wages. There is little income from this gallery and no admission fee is charged.*

Linden is a converted neoclassical mansion in the bayside suburb of St Kilda, best known for its annual exhibition of postcard-sized art. It is one of Melbourne's oldest local council-funded art galleries with a reputation for quality exhibitions. Its income comes from artwork sales, sponsorship, philanthropy and government funding, including local government; in 2013, it received $246,700 from the City of Port Phillip, up from $226,361 the previous year.

On Saturday, May 18, 2013, an exhibition paying homage to Mike Brown, "Like Mike", opened at Linden. The day after it opened, Adrian Jackson went looking for something to help him end the council's funding. He must have thought that he had found it in Gallery 2 because Paul Yore's installation, *Everything is fucked*, is utterly over-the-top glitter-gun-rainbow gay. Jackson walked around Yore's installation but couldn't imagine that he could enter 'the grotto'. After finding out that he hadn't seen all of it he returned a week later to look inside Yore's installation and then rang St Kilda police. Jackson knew that words like 'pornographic' and 'obscene' would no longer motivate the police into action, but after Rudd's attack on Henson, he knew that the phrase 'child pornography' would push the right buttons.

Paul Yore is a successful young Melbourne-based artist who makes tapestries, patchworks of printed fabrics, and mixed-media installations out of found material. He exhibited at Heide Museum of Modern Art in 2009. His *Playdough's Cave* was installed in the Atrium at Federation Square in 2012, and in 2013 he won the $8000 Wangaratta Contemporary Textile Award.

His art is a mixture of juvenile humour and childish joy with the explicit and adult. Funny, irreverent and ribald, *Everything is fucked* could be positive, joyful sex or a negative worldview. The visitor is immersed in his queer psychedelic aesthetic.

At the front of the installation is a fountain depicting a pissing teenage heart-throb singer, Justin Bieber. The sound of running water from the fountain joins the chaotic mix of mechanical and recorded sounds that are part of the installation; a tinny electronic version of a jingle keeps repeating. Mechanical prayer-wheels made from old record players ring bells, adding to other sounds made by toy instruments.

The installation has exterior and interior spaces. "The internal and external aspects of the work balance the work," Yore explained. "The structure itself, the main part of the installation, you can actually enter inside it. I mean, when you first walk in, it looks like a mountain of junk or something. You can enter into the work on this other level."

Made of multi-coloured plastic children's toys, television sets and other excesses of consumer society's 'final days', the work is a sensory overload of colours, images, words and sounds, reflecting a culture that has achieved peak stuff.

Yore's phallocentric, psychedelic worlds appear crazy and cha-otic, like the world. Contrasting, contradicting, transforming even as you comprehend them; a spinning message of 'no' upside down becomes 'on'. There is so much to look at, so many images, messages and flashing strobe lights.

Yore transforms found material from the hetero-world into a celebration of queer culture with lots of phallocentric imagery.

He cannibalises his previous installations, fragmenting, reusing and recycling parts, reconstructing them using 'bad carpentry' skills. In altering these elements, he demonstrates the power and potential for transforming the spectacle of mass consumerism.

On Saturday, June 1, two police detectives went to the gallery before it opened, took some photos, returned to the office and obtained a warrant. They executed the warrant twenty minutes before midday, just before opening. Detective Samantha Johnson cut out seven pieces of Yore's installation with a Stanley knife, effectively creating her own collage. She bagged them and returned to her office to start on the documentation.

That day the Linden Gallery remained closed, and Yore responded to journalists' questions to say the raid "borders on homophobia".

Jackson's agenda was made clear the following day in a comment he made in *The Leader*, a free newspaper for real estate advertising:

> *Mission accomplished – the kiddy art exhibition is now closed. Next step is getting the Linden Gallery to be self funding instead of behaving like a parasite on ratepayers. Currently $100,000 PA is spent by Port Phillip Council on maintenance and equipment in the Linden which has been a ratepayer owned building for the last 25 years or so. This money does not appear in the Linden's annual Statement of Affairs (see their website) as far as I can see but what is included is about $250,000 PA in ratepayer funds in 'operating cost'. All this for 6 or 7 exhibitions per year involving about 6 artists per exhibition. The large post card exhibition could be moved to the town hall and the Linden closed if it can't be self funded. Other galleries in Port Phillip can fund themselves so why can't the Linden committee.*

On Monday, June 3, at ten past three, Paul Yore, accompanied by his solicitor, was interviewed by detectives from the St Kilda

Crime Investigation Unit. If the police were expecting to gain any information or a confession, they would be disappointed – Yore gave a "no-comment" interview.

That evening there was an emergency board meeting at Linden. On legal advice, an application for classification of the exhibition was sent to David Emery, the Manager of Applications at the Classification Branch of the Australian Classification Board (ACB).

The Linden Gallery remained closed to the public for the rest of the week. On Saturday, June 8, about 100 people rallied at Linden, demanding it reopen and stop pandering to censorship. Linden reopened on Tuesday with extended opening hours as a form of compensation for the closure; however, the room with Paul Yore's work remained closed.

On June 16, Linden Gallery announced in a media release that the ACB had classified Paul Yore's installation as 'Classification 1 – Restricted.' This means that the work is considered to contain adult content and should be restricted to 18 years and over. At this point, the police case should have abandoned any prosecution because even submitting the installation for classification by ACB is an absolute defence against producing or possessing child pornography let alone being given a classification. For if the ACB classifies something, then it cannot also be child pornography. However, as the St Kilda police had no experience investigating cases where art was labelled as alleged child pornography, they had no idea what to do. They never asked Melinda Martin, the Gallery Director for Linden, about the ACB classification of the exhibition.

Tensions between the art world and the police were high in 2013. Early in the year, a South Australian police detective publicly urged Premier Jay Weatherill to stop Henson's participation in the 2014 Adelaide Biennial. Bill Henson announced he had withdrawn from the Biennial; it would be South Australia's loss, not his. After the police raid on Linden, art fair director Barry Keldoulis went through the Sydney Contemporary 2013 art fair with lawyers to determine if the art could be shown in NSW. A few hours before its VIP preview, Keldoulis announced the fair would not show Yore's work nor the paintings of a Queensland artist Tyza Stewart.

Yore continued to exhibit without any further incidents or allegations in 2013. Clearly, most senior curators in Australia believed the accusations against him, like those against Henson, had no substance.

The prosecution was also feeling uncomfortable. In an attempt to avoid media scrutiny, Paul Yore was charged with the production and possession of child pornography on Saturday, September 7, 2013, the day the federal election was announced. Next, there was a mess of court dates. On November 25, 2013, the mention hearing was adjourned by the prosecution. On January 10, 2014, another mention hearing was again adjourned by the prosecution. On February 14, 2014, there was another hearing for Yore's defence team to say that he would be pleading 'not guilty'. For more than a year the prosecution delayed proceedings as the police and Office of Public Prosecutions couldn't agree on how to proceed.

The charges were finally heard on September 18–19 before Magistrate Amanda Chambers.

A large number of lawyers were in court on the first day, not just Yore's defence team but lawyers for each member of the staff and board of directors of Linden, who had all been called as prosecution witnesses. They were concerned about exposure to allegations of possession of child pornography arising from their testimony. The court gave them certificates that their evidence would not be used against them. It was clear from this that the prosecution only had Paul Yore in its sights. If he was found guilty, there was the potential for a ten-year sentence.

The prosecution was conducted by a young policewoman, Acting Sergeant Kirei Wall. She decided that viewing a video of Yore's installation was the best place to start. This was the defence video because she admitted it was of far better quality than the police video. Then for about six minutes, the magistrate watched the psychedelic rainbows of colour and ultra-violet lighting, along with an interview with Paul Yore explaining his installation and describing the sickly-sweet surface of the spectacle of mass consumerism.

Most of the police case consisted of Exhibit #10; seven pieces of cardboard, paper and tinfoil cut from Paul Yore's installation. These pieces were collages with children's heads, with or without Pokemon stickers stuck over them, near or on the naked bodies of adults, again with or without Pokemon stickers stuck over them. The prosecution contended that the proximity of the children's heads to the naked adult bodies created an indecent context, and therefore it was child pornography.

The crucial evidence that would decide the case came from the very first prosecution witness. Melinda Martin, the director of Linden, explained that it had been classified as 'Certificate 1, restricted to people over 18'. At that point, the magistrate asked the witness to step outside the courtroom.

The case never had a chance of succeeding. And Acting Seargent Wall was hopelessly outclassed by Yore's defence team of prominent barristers Neil Clelland QC and Rowena Orr QC. Yore's defence was not based on contesting the police timeline of events or any police evidence. Neil Clelland QC was focused on the statutory definition of child pornography. The defence wanted to know how the concept of the production of child pornography was being proven, because all Paul Yore had done was stick photographs from magazines together with tinfoil and Pokemon stickers.

The Victorian *Crimes Act* defines child pornography in the following manner: 'child pornography means a film, photograph, publication or computer game that describes or depicts a person who is, or appears to be, a minor engaging in sexual activity or depicted in an indecent sexual manner or context.' And 'publication' means 'any written or pictorial matter', according to the *Commonwealth Classification (Publications, Films and Computer Games) Act 1995*.

"Is it your case that if a person sticky tapes a child's face onto a men's magazine that is producing child pornography?" The defence's question to Detective Johnson was ruled hypothetical.

Arguing that the law regarding child pornography must be interpreted in a way compatible with freedom of expression and not only a technical classification, the defence wanted to know how Yore's fundamental human right to freedom of expression was balanced against the harm that was sought to be avoided. As Yore's art does not raise any issues of risks to children, there is no reason to limit his freedom of expression.

The defence case consisted of three expert witnesses, or 'witnesses with specialist knowledge' in the current legal speak. Each had prepared a report for the court on Yore's art.

Jason Smith, Director of Heide Museum of Modern Art, had seen an earlier version of *Everything is fucked* at Heide and considered that it had great merit for being innovative, radical, humorous and critical. His opinion of the police exhibits cut from the exhibition was that they had corrupted the artist's message, and he would only comment on the whole work. When asked about the artistic merit of Exhibit #10, Smith replied, "This is not an artwork. This is part of an artwork."

Antonia Syme, Director of the Australian Tapestry Workshop, knew Paul Yore from his residency at the Australian Tapestry Workshop. She praised his strong track record in exhibitions. In cross-examining the defence witnesses, Acting Seargent Wall attempted various contorted and leading questions about the defence of artistic merit. Eventually, the magistrate put this line of questions out of its misery by asking Antonia Syme, "What if Leonardo da Vinci made child porn? Does it follow that because he is an artist, the work has artistic merit?"

"Putti? Leonardo did lots of naked children."

The last witness, Max Delany (aka Mark Newman Delany), Senior Curator at the NGV, explained Paul Yore's use of collage and assemblage in his artworks. Delany's testimony on collage is well worth considering, not just concerning the trial but in understanding contemporary art. We all think we know what a collage is because we have been doing them since primary school. Collage, assemblage and installation are modern art techniques fundamental to contemporary art. Where art is created not only by altering materials but by changing the context in which the materials are displayed. The obvious cuts distinguish collage from decoupage, photomontage or a 'Photoshopped' image, where the cuts are hidden. Delany explained to the court that 'collage is unnatural' because it removed the image from its context, so it no longer functions according to the original context. "Taking an advertising image in a collage, the adverting image no longer functions as advertising."

In the cross-examination, the police prosecutor showed Delany Exhibit #10, the seven pieces of cardboard. He was asked if he recognised them as Yore's work. Delany replied that he recognised them as parts removed from Yore's installation but that they were the work of the police. Asked about the artistic merit of Exhibit #10, Delany answered that he couldn't comment as the paper and cardboard were now not part of Yore's art and were being presented in the context of a court of law.

Desperately defending her case, the police prosecutor, Acting Seargent Wall, argued that the ACB had only classified the submission on Paul Yore's installation and not the whole installation. She also suggested that the ACB could not classify collages or art installations because they are non-photographic images. She attempted to explain about the unknown and unidentified children who were hurt because their pictures were placed with photos of adults (also unknown and unidentified) in sexual poses, or a sexual context, without respect for their rights. If she thought her case had any chance of succeeding, she would have to wait for over a month for Magistrate Chambers to make her judgement.

On the morning of October 1, Courtroom 4 of the Magistrates' Court was packed; every bit of public seating was taken. Paul Yore's family was there, along with Max Delany, myself and many journalists, to hear Magistrate Chambers dismiss all the charges and order that the Chief Commissioner of Police pay all costs in what she described to be "clearly unusual proceedings".

The police claim that they were caught in the middle, legitimately responding to complaints from members of the public, members of the public who so often turn out to be trolls with right-wing agendas as obvious as a Mardi Gras float. However, using the courts to determine what is obscene or child pornography does not stack up. The police's ignorance of the law cannot be an excuse as they also ignored the advice from the experts, the Office of Public Prosecutions, that they couldn't win the case.

In the end, the troll in St Kilda accomplished little, and Linden remains funded by the City of Port Phillip. Still, it costs him nothing to try. Taxpayers paid for the court time, the police and the defence case, costs that would have made Linden's annual budget look like beer money.

Paul Yore's successful career as an artist has continued. After the court case, he travelled across Europe looking at folk art, outsider art and junkyard art. On his return to Melbourne, he had an exhibition where he assembled another version of *Everything is fucked*, adding several fucked pigs.

Bloody Vandals

Stabbings in Melbourne

The former premier of Victoria, Sir James Patterson, was stabbed in the chest. Fortunately, he was already dead, and it was his portrait by Gordon Coutts that was struck. It was not seriously injured, and it remained on the gallery wall of the National Gallery of Victoria (aka NGV, the National Gallery). It was Melbourne's first recorded art crime.

It was called the National Gallery because the states of Australia had not yet federated. Like the Art Gallery of South Australia, it was housed at the State Library. Unlike South Australia, there were more rooms: Swinburne Hall, the painting school studios and four galleries: the McArthur, Cowen, La Trobe and the Buvelot wing (some of these rooms at the library are still used for exhibiting art).

Patterson's portrait was hanging in a bay in the Buvelot wing out of sight of the gallery attendants. Named after the colonial artist Louis Buvelot, it was also known as the 'portrait gallery' because of all the portraits hanging in it. It was on Little Lonsdale Street, on the opposite side of the building from the rest of the gallery.

On Wednesday morning, February 24, 1897, a gallery attendant dusted the portrait at 10am. He then left to help with some unpacking in the main part of the gallery. When he returned at noon, the painting had a 3-4 inch cut in it.

Patterson's portrait has been restored and now hangs in the Parliament of Victoria. Its artist, the Scottish-born Gordon Coutts, kept travelling and painting figures and landscapes. He achieved international fame in his own lifetime. However, his style is no longer fashionable as his desire for distant and exotic locations that had brought him to Australia ultimately diminished his art.

There were speculations about the stabbing motivation, but people were sure it was about Patterson and not Coutts or his technique for creating an oil painting from a photograph. The next time art was stabbed at the NGV, people weren't so sure.

During opening hours, on Thursday, August 2, 1917, Max Meldrum's *A peasant of Pacé* was stabbed with a small knife. It was also hanging in the Buvelot gallery. Again, there were no witnesses to the crime; the custodians only discovered the damage when locking up for the evening.

Some kind of blade, possibly a penknife, had made a long scratch, followed by a jagged 76-millimetre cut in the lower right-hand area of the canvas. Why would anyone want to do that?

Painted in 1908, *A peasant of Pacé* depicts an old man, a peasant from the municipality of Pacé in northwestern France near Rennes, seated beside a table. It is a traditional, representational oil painting that could have been painted a century or two earlier.

It was painted by the Scottish-born, Melbourne-based artist Max Meldrum, a talented painter who studied under Frederick McCubbin and Bernard Hall at the National Gallery School. In 1899 he was awarded a travelling scholarship and moved to Paris, where he married a woman from Pacé. He eventually returned to Melbourne in 1912. In 1916, he established the Meldrum School of Painting in competition with the National Gallery School.

Although Meldrum was a conservative artist, politically, he was a liberal and a pacifist. After the stabbing, some people speculated that Meldrum's pacifist statements, made when Australia was at war, inspired the attack. Was the attack a cowardly stabbing of the art of a brave pacifist? Or was it part of a quarrel over Meldrum's presidency of the Victorian Artist Society?

Fortunately, the damage did not affect a significant part of the painting. The broken threads were realigned to fix the tear, and the canvas was patched on the reverse. After the repairs, *A peasant of Pacé* was returned to exhibition. In 1931 it was removed and consigned to the gallery's immense storage, where it resides to this day.

This would not be the last time, or the most notable time, that art at the NGV was vandalised. Art vandalism is, unfortunately, too common to examine all the incidents in Australia.

Dickheads

Surely Poseidon, the god of the seas and earthquakes, will have drowned or buried the dickhead who used a hacksaw to castrate his statue. The castration of the god's classically small genitals happened one night in 1959 at the University of Melbourne. The vandal was arrested and convicted but successfully appealed his conviction.

In 460 BCE, a Greek sculptor, believed to be Onatas of Aegina, made a bronze statue. Around 100 BCE, it was already an antique and was being exported when it was lost in a shipwreck. In 1928 fishermen off the Cape of Artemisium found it in their nets, and it is now in the National Archaeological Museum in Athens.

Two bronze copies were made of the statue, and on the occasion of the 1956 Melbourne Olympic Games, the Greek Orthodox Community presented one to the University of Melbourne. At the time, it was believed that the bearded man represented Zeus with his raised, now empty, hand about to hurl a thunderbolt. After further research, it is now thought to be Poseidon wielding his trident.

The sculpture was displayed outside the Beaurepaire Centre until the vandalism. Although university students are frequently suggested as responsible for the vandalism of sculptures, this is probably the only time a student actually did. Did he think that the minds and morals of his fellow university students needed protection from nudity? If he did, he would have given himself, if not the statue, a fig leaf of an excuse. Probably he was just a dickhead.

After the sculptor Eric Thake recreated Poseidon's penis, the statue was moved to a more secure location, the inner courtyard of the Elisabeth Murdock Building (aka the Old Pathology Building). Some sites make public art more vulnerable because some places are visited by more idiots than others.

Every year in Australia, public art is stolen, intentionally damaged, or both. It is a crime, and for the sake of completeness, I have looked at a ton of examples. Stupidity is not a legal defence, but at least some idiots are contrite and attempt restitution, sometimes even before they are tracked down. Just as there are many opportunistic thefts and vandalism, there are plenty of regrets and returned stolen sculptures.

The Boy With the Turtle was created by an unknown artist around 1850. It sat in one of the many ponds in Fitzroy Gardens in Melbourne for over a century. In 1977 it was nicked from Fitzroy Gardens. It was recovered two and a half years later, abandoned in a Richmond car park.

Changes in public art practice mean that there is more public art than ever before and, often, without plinths putting the sculpture closer to the public. And some members of the public are drunk, kleptomaniacs and vandals. The unstoppable stupidity of drunken kleptomania and the sheer destructiveness of these idiots stand in contrast to the irrepressible creativity and extreme generosity of many artists.

In 2016 the plinth of Bruce Armstrong's sculpture, *Owl* at Belconnen Way and Benjamin Way in Canberra, was vandalised with crude words and pictures in spray paint. Unfortunately, with or without spray paint pointing this out, Armstrong's *Owl* does look like a dick.

Statue Wars

In 1992 an unknown vandal used gelignite to blow up a memorial 43km west of Cloncurry on the Mount Isa Highway in Queensland. That year the High Court's Mabo decision recognised native title, heating the already tropical atmosphere of racist Australia. The memorial was to the Kalkadoon (aka Kalkatungu) and Mitakoodi warriors who fought a battle in September 1884 against colonial forces. It was one of the few memorials of Australia's frontier wars. It has since been rebuilt. Since its rebuilding, the brass etching of the bust of a Mitakoodi warrior in the monument's centre has been shot numerous times.

For millennia sculptures have been used to make triumphant political statements, glorifying the person whose statue is raised on a pedestal. They are marks of ownership and a declaration of how something is to be remembered and regarded. They come from the pre-historic world of magical practices. And Ancient Egyptians, Romans, Jews, Christians and Muslims have defaced, pulled down and destroyed statues. The politics and intention of defacing sculptures are brutally clear, for the figures are symbolic representations, magical effigies that transmit praise or condemnation to the person represented.

'Statue wars' is the name given to the conflicts over removing statues of colonial heroes, racists and enslavers. It is a war that has broken out in many countries. Although it has only recently become a common term, it is evident from the bombing, the bullets and decapitations that the statue wars started in Australia in the 1990s. Only as it was conservatives destroying statues and memorials, the media was not as interested in the battles as they are now.

Two naked figures were seated on a park bench by Lake Burley Griffin in Canberra. They were Greg Taylor's *Liz and Phil Down by the Lake*, part of the National Sculpture Festival, a temporary exhibition organised by the Australian National University in 1995. Naked, the wrinkly, old Liz and Phil looked the very opposite of regal – frail and human. Only the crown on Liz's head reminded the viewer who was being depicted. Made of cement fondue coated with iron oxide, the figures had a rusted appearance.

The word 'republic' was rumbling in the gas-filled bowels of Australian politics. The fact that neither capital punishment nor *lesemajeste* is in Australian law didn't stop Returned Service League chief Bruce Ruxton from calling for Taylor's execution. Other monarchists' reaction to Taylor's sculpture was more extreme, taking revenge on the sculptor through his sculpture.

Overnight Liz's head was swiped. The police log read: "the Queen has lost her head and doesn't know where to find it." Sub-editors worldwide wrote playful headlines and Australian newspaper cartoonists used it as a meme.

After the beheading, a former Sydney policeman decided to cover the sculpture in bedsheets printed with the Australian flag. Censoring the offending image while remaining technically within the law.

The following night, the Duke's head was removed, and further vandalism severed both figures' legs and caved in Phil's chest. The offending image had been destroyed, and the exhibition organisers removed the wreck a day later.

In a secondary controversy, the Australian Federal Police issued a denial that Liz's head had been found in a right-wing militia member's home. It was true that they had raided a right-wing militia member who had infiltrated the computer and communications sections of the Defence Department and possessed an arsenal of weapons. But he didn't have the missing head.

Yagan was a Nyoongah warrior who had played a notable role in resisting British colonial settlement in the area now known as Perth. The government offered a bounty for him, dead or alive, and in 1833, he was shot at point-blank range by eighteen-year-old William Keates. Yagan was then decapitated, and his head was sent as a trophy to England. The ghoulish souveniring of body parts would be a war crime if it was done today but at the time was a popular practice amongst English colonialists. Keates was later speared to death in revenge.

After passing through multiple British hands, Yagan's head was buried in an unmarked grave along with another Indigenous Australian body, some dried viscera and a Peruvian mummy in a corner of Everton Cemetery in Liverpool in the 1960s. In 1997 Yagan's head was returned to the Nyoongah people for a proper burial.

Robert Hitchcock's statue of Yagan has stood on Heirisson Island in the Swan River in Perth since 1984. It had been vandalised before: painted white, its spear stolen and an attempt made at castration. Then, in the same week that Yagan's head was returned from England, the statue of Yagan was decapitated by a vandal in a symbolic re-enactment. The vandal responsible identified themselves as a 'British patriot' to the media.

The statue was restored with a new head, only for it to be decapitated again in 2002, leading to a second restoration and another slightly different head. The cartoonists and sub-editors in the West Australian media treated the decapitations as opportunities for humour.

The statue wars continue with symbolic attacks on bronze idols and stone monuments. This time, the symbols of the racist colonial establishment have been attacked. Around the post-colonial world, statues of racists, enslavers and other colonialists who oppressed minorities and Indigenous people are being pulled down from pedestals. Statues of Christopher Columbus, Confederate generals and slave traders have been removed in the US and England.

A phalanx of police protected the statue of Cook in Sydney during the Black Lives Matter protests in 2020. Compare this to their response to actual sculpture thieves who steal for profit. There have been some calls to remove a few statues in Australia: William Wentworth, James Cook and Lachlan Macquarie. Paint has been thrown and sprayed on some: Cook, Macquarie and Queen Victoria. However, unlike in other post-colonial countries, only the statue of the former Tasmanian Premier and body snatcher, William Crowther, has been removed by Hobart City Council.

This fact didn't stop then-Prime Minister Malcolm Turnbull in 2017 from making hyperbolic comparisons to Stalinists trying to alter history. If Turnbull was correct, then the US Army removing statues of Saddam Hussain in the invasion of Iraq was engaging in Stalinist history revisionism. But he is not correct; statues are not about history. They are about honouring idols in a secular state religion. It is about politics more than crime – part of the continuing culture war – so it is likely the statue wars will continue in Australia for many more years. This chapter may look like a brief introduction.

In a separate culture war, in the outer Melbourne suburb of Rowville, sometime between 5:30pm on Friday, November 12 and 5:30pm on Saturday, November 13, 2021, there was an attempt to decapitate a statue of Mahatma Gandhi at the Australian Indian Community Centre.

Holy monkey thieves!

The flight across the Pacific, from Los Angeles to Melbourne, takes most of a day. So, the tall 47-year-old American artist Andres Serrano had plenty of time to consider the storm of controversy he was flying into. It would probably be a repeat performance of the show he had witnessed in the United States, only with different actors with different accents. He would not have expected the level of violence from his opponents nor the treachery of his allies.

Serrano's art is limited edition, large-format photographs, around 51 centimetres × 76 centimetres. These are taken using conventional photographic techniques. They often have shocking subjects but are not judgemental: the homeless in the subway, a dead body in a morgue, a Klu Klux Klansman, Donald Trump, or, most famously, mixes of various bodily fluids.

Born in New York City in 1950 to Honduran and Afro-Cuban parents, Serrano was raised a Roman Catholic. This is only relevant because, in 1987, Serrano created his most famous image, a photograph of a plastic crucifixion submerged in urine, *Piss Christ*. Printed in an edition of four, the artist retained one, and three others are privately owned. It was part of a series titled 'Immersions', photographs of statues in various bodily fluids, including milk, piss and blood. It was not the first time he had photographed bodily fluids, and it would not be the last, but it became the image Serrano is known for.

"As a former Catholic, and as someone who even today is not opposed to being called a Christian, I felt I had every right to use the symbols of the Church and resented being told not to." Serrano explained that "*Piss Christ* is a representation of the pain and suffering Christ underwent for all of us. My use of a fluid like blood or urine is a way of humanising him, identifying with his indignity and sorrow. The intent was neither to desecrate nor to offend, but if it does, it should invigorate your belief, not diminish it."

'Immersions' won a national competition with a $15,000 prize and a travelling exhibition paid for by Equitable Life Assurance, the Rockefeller Foundation and the National Endowment for the Arts (aka NEA). The NEA is a US taxpayer-funded federal endowment, and this is where politicians come into the story.

The battle over 'Immersions' was at the start of what became known as the 'culture wars' – battles to save the United States' soul from the evils of a liberal future. *Piss Christ* became a symbolic battle about whether taxpayers funded the views of people other than the old white men in charge. Should a photographer receive taxpayer's dollars if the majority didn't like their photographs? Many Republicans thought that the taxpayer shouldn't fund the arts at all. In the chamber of the US Senate on May 18, 1989, US Senator Alphonse D'Amato, in an iconoclastic demonstration of what he would have liked to do to the actual photograph, tore up a copy of *Piss Christ*.

In October 1997, there were two exhibitions by Serrano scheduled for Melbourne: at the NGV, there was a retrospective, "A History of Andres Serrano", and at the Kirkcaldy Davies Gallery, an exhibition of his recent photographs, "History of Sex". But before either had even opened, the then Archbishop (now Cardinal) George Pell (aka Pell Pot) sought an injunction restraining the NGV from exhibiting one of Serrano's photographs on the grounds of blasphemy.

When Serrano arrived at Melbourne Airport on Thursday, October 9, he put his best foot forward: he was going to love his enemy.

He told the media that he understood why Pell, as a conservative Christian, felt that he needed to protest, but "Fortunately, when it comes to belief, the Archbishop cannot and doesn't speak for all Christians." He challenged Pell to at least come and look at the exhibition to understand what he was protesting about. Pell did not take up Serrano's offer.

The son of a heavyweight boxer, George Pell, was born in Ballarat in 1941. In his youth, on the football field, he played ruckman, a position reserved for the tallest player on the team. Ever since, the former football player turned priest loomed over people, rising through the ranks of the Catholic Church, ignoring allegations of sexual abuse as he hoped others would ignore the accusations by altar boys against him, to be appointed Melbourne's Archbishop in 1996.

Archbishop Keith Rayner AO, the Anglican Archbishop of Melbourne and Primate of Australia, joined Pell in the legal action to block the NGV exhibition. The Islamic Council of Victoria wrote to Premier Jeff Kennett and NGV Director Timothy Potts to protest the Serrano exhibition. Jewish leaders joined the choir of disapproving religious voices.

Not that Serrano had managed the miracle of uniting Melbourne's diverse religious communities. The Uniting Church Moderator, Reverend Pam Kerr, had a different view: "If there were to be any good to come out of all of this, it might be that it reminds us Christians that the cross was a highly offensive event and that Christ himself was treated brutally."

Melbourne's media got excited about Pell's blasphemy claim – perhaps too excited. In South Yarra, journalists staked out Kirkcaldy Davies Gallery, watching the trams going along Malvern Road and waiting for a police raid that never happened.

Words of complaint were not about to alter NGV Director Potts' exhibition plans. Potts claimed that it was about free artistic expression. He told the media: "Since quite a lot of contemporary art is tough-minded and issues-based, it is bound to be inherently controversial."

Outside the Supreme Court on Wednesday, October 9, 1997, religious groups, including the multi-faith Religious Alliance Against Pornography, demonstrated. Inside the Supreme Court, a three-hour injunction hearing was held before Justice David Harper. Archbishop Pell was represented by the eccentric barrister Clifford Pannam QC, best known for his expertise in racing law. The NGV was represented by the well-known human-rights barrister Julian Burnside QC.

Pannam wanted an injunction restraining the Gallery from exhibiting the work, not only because it was blasphemous but because it was in breach of the indecency provisions of the *Summary Offences Act 1988*. A difficult task because he couldn't point to any actual legislation prohibiting blasphemy. Instead, Pannam argued that a common-law misdemeanour of blasphemous libel was evident in a couple of old English court cases.

In an affidavit, Pell stated: "Both the name and the image *Piss Christ* not only demean Christianity but also represent a grossly offensive scurrilous and insulting treatment of Christianity's most sacred and holy symbol. It is calculated to outrage the feelings of Catholics and other Christians."

When Julian Burnside spoke to the court, he pointed out the practicalities. The image of *Piss Christ* had already been shown publicly in Australia, in *The Australian* newspaper, in Robert Hughes' *American Visions* on the national broadcaster and in publication, in public schools, public libraries, and many church libraries around Australia. And there was no evidence that its public appearance had caused civil strife or destabilised society. Burnside told the court: "It is simply not enough to say it might be criminal, and we'll stop it."

Justice Harper did not immediately grant an injunction but announced that he would deliver his decision on Friday morning once he'd had time to consider both sides' arguments.

On Friday, October 10, Justice Harper rejected Pell's plea for an injunction. He was not convinced the photograph was indecent or obscene. While Justice Harper agreed that *Piss Christ* was offensive to Christians, he noted that "a pluralist society such as contemporary Australia operates best when the law need not bother with blasphemous libel."

He did not accept Pannam's arguments that blasphemous libel existed in common law. Instead, Justice Harper determined that "not only has Victoria never recognised an established church, but now Section 116 of the Australian Constitution forbids the Commonwealth making any law for establishing religion." Without an established religion, what was blasphemous? Although blasphemy is an offence under the common law in England, only blasphemy against the established religion, the Church of England, is prohibited.

NGV Director Potts was not surprised at the court's decision. "It would have been a startling and inexplicable result if the injunction was granted because it would indicate that art that has been seen and debated in Europe, Japan and the US is unsuitable for Melbourne."

On Saturday, October 11, Pell's arrogant response to the court decision was published. Although he stated that he respected Justice Harper's decision, he went on to say that the NGV "mistakenly believe they could insult the state's Christian majority with impunity by hiding behind the curtain of 'artistic expression'." Pell was vague on how the NGV to be punished now that he had clarified that it didn't have 'impunity'. He concluded his response by stating that he was defending a principle that Christians or any other religious or racial group should not be publicly insulted at the exhibition paid for from the public purse. In effect, he was demanding veto power over every public institution.

From feminist Germaine Greer to criminologist Alison Young, everyone was keen to offer their opinions on *Piss Christ*. Young noted that apart from the title, there was no proof that the yellow liquid was urine. She also asked the public to remember their outrage at the assassination attempts of fundamentalist Muslims on publishers, translators and Salman Rushdie when his 1988 novel *The Satanic Verses* was declared blasphemous by Ayatollah Ruhollah Khomeini.

Premier Jeff Kennett advised people who thought they would be offended to "stay at home, see Rembrandt or have a game of tennis. It is not compulsory." Not everyone heeded Kennett's advice.

In his home in outer suburban Chelsea Heights, Anthony watched his mother crying during the evening TV news. She was upset that Justice Harper had failed to support Archbishop Pell's call to shut down a blasphemous art exhibition. Anthony decided that something had to be done and that he and his friend Timur were the men to do it. Like many people, Timur and Anthony wanted to look like heroes, and, like many people, they weren't sure how to go about it. Now the Archbishop had shown them the way.

Are God's laws higher than Australian law? When the courts fail to sanction a charge of blasphemy, faithful fanatics and extremists are willing to act outside the law – people like Anthony who want to make their mother and the Archbishop happy. If Australian law could not protect the honour of their faith, then the faithful would do it – by destroying what Archbishop Pell had declared to be a blasphemous image.

On Saturday, October 11, two groups gathered at the NGV. Outside the waterwall entrance of the NGV on St Kilda Road, about 200 demonstrators, many holding crosses, gathered outside to pray and protest the Serrano exhibition. Inside, at the official opening of A History of Andres Serrano, the NGV's curator of photography Isobel Crombie said without a hint of irony, "I am very pleased that we were able to entice the artist to this country and to arrange such a warm welcome for him."

The warm welcome boiled over just after the official opening concluded. A scrawny 51-year-old angry man with blue, bloodshot eyes and tight lips, John Allen Haywood, walked up to *Piss Christ*, took it down from the wall and kicked it. He did little damage to it or the security guard he fought with as he was dragged away.

The following Sunday, at half past three, Timur and Anthony went to the NGV. They bought two $6 tickets and entered the Serrano exhibition. The exhibition's entrance was signposted: 'Suitable for people eighteen years and over'. And security was checking ID at the door. Anthony's fake ID was questioned, but security allowed the two boys to walk in.

Anthony had a hammer in his belt. He and Timur spent almost an hour at the exhibition working out a strategy. The problem was how to lure the two security guards away from *Piss Christ* long enough to destroy it.

On the opposite side of the gallery, Timur kicked the partition causing Serrano's *Klansman (Great Titan of the Invisible Empire)* to fall off the wall. He picked it up and let it drop again. This distracted security guards away from *Piss Christ*. Timur caused $500 damage to the frame of *Klansman*, but nothing more.

With the guards occupied. Anthony pulled out his hammer and started to bash *Piss Christ* eight or nine times.

When Timur was restrained, the other guard rushed back to deal with Anthony and quickly overpowered him. As Anthony dropped his hammer, it hit a guard on the knee.

The guard's knee was bruised and sore from the hammer's impact but did not require medical treatment. Serrano's two photographs had been far more seriously damaged; Anthony's hammer blows created webs of cracked glass.

The other people in the gallery froze, stunned, at the short, violent outburst. Then they were ushered out by gallery staff.

That Sunday, Premier Kennett accused religious leaders of lacking leadership for not condemning the three vandals. Of course, Pell did not damn the attackers and explained his position to the media with the smug satisfaction of someone whose word could not be questioned. "I understand that sense of outrage that has promoted these attacks on the image and I repeat my support of peaceful and legal protest only."

Then NGV Director Potts decided to stop talking about artistic freedom and close the Serrano exhibition. The cost to the NGV of shutting down the Serrano was just under $100,000, including all the legal fees. Never before had the NGV closed an exhibition early, and there are no other examples outside of a pandemic. A gallery director is meant to defend the art they have chosen to exhibit, not censor it. To make it look better, Potts framed it as concern for the safety of visitors and staff, emphasising that a security guard had been injured when Anthony dropped the hammer.

Many people condemned Potts's decision, from former arts minister Race Matthews to the Museum of Modern Art at Heide's curator, Ms Juliana Engberg. Some suggested that Potts was more concerned about the cost of insurance for the upcoming Rembrandt exhibition. Serrano felt betrayed by Potts. Potts's claim to have adequate security was obviously false. Serrano was particularly unimpressed with Potts caving in to censorship, telling the media that "The damage that was done to *Piss Christ* is nothing compared to the blow the National Gallery has dealt to the arts and freedom of expression in Australia." He urged the public to boycott the Rembrandt exhibition at the NGV.

Premier Kennett was now urging Serrano to leave the country. Kennett wanted to get away from the controversies and back to his public relations spin of advertising Victoria's strength in the arts.

Visitors to touring blockbuster exhibitions are a substantial benefit to the city's income.

Serrano was in no hurry to fly back across the Pacific. His other exhibition, "History of Sex", was still showing at the Kirkcaldy Davies Gallery.

On Monday, October 14, the first of the vandals, John Haywood, appeared in the Magistrates' Court on criminal damage and burglary charges. He told the court he was remorseful, pleaded guilty to two criminal damage counts and burglary, and received a suspended one-month sentence. The court was told he had sought psychiatric treatment since his marriage ended a couple of years earlier.

Outside the court, Haywood was a different man. He gave an impromptu press conference, demonstrating his remorsefulness and understanding of Christian love and forgiveness. When asked what he would say to Serrano, he replied, "I wouldn't like to say nothing to him. I'd just like to punch him on the nose. You can only go so far with taking the piss, you understand. It riles me, it really gets me very upset." He was happy to have been an encouragement to Anthony and Timur.

In December, Anthony appeared in the Children's Court. He pleaded guilty to one count of criminal damage. His lawyer told the court that he had attacked the photograph because: "He saw the work as a deep and bitter attack on all that Christians held sacred and its destruction as the only means of venting his outrage." His lawyer brought to the court's attention that Anthony worked part-time at a veterinary surgery. Anthony was released on a $2000 one-year good behaviour bond; ordered to pay $640 to the court fund and get counselling.

Unlike Anthony, Timur appeared in the County Court as he was eighteen at the time of the offence. In April 1998, he pleaded guilty to two counts of damaging property. Unlike most people in this story, Timur was not a Christian. He told the court he was not offended by *Piss Christ* but had been angered by the *Klansman* photograph because he was 'really against racism'.

The magistrate adjourned the proceedings for a year on the condition the offender agreed to specific terms – the 'undertakings'. If an offender does not keep to the 'undertakings', they are re-sentenced for the original offence and fined for the 'breach'. It didn't take long before Anthony encouraged Timur to participate in another crime. What they did was so stupid and pointless that it gave perspective to their moral character, demonstrating that these were not misled choirboys vandalising art for God but lawless yobs.

On Monday night, June 29, Anthony, Timur and another final-year high-school student broke into Melbourne Zoo. This was not a spur-of-the-moment drunken escapade; the boys had a plan. They had studied the zoo on an earlier reconnaissance mission. They were prepared and brought a bolt cutter, some fruit and a carry bag.

Timur assisted the other two boys in scaling the outer perimeter wall of the zoo. The third boy used bolt cutters to cut through the padlock on the zoo keeper's entrance to the rainforest enclosure. They wanted to steal a 'cute' monkey for a pet because Anthony 'loved animals'.

Hekel, a Bolivian squirrel monkey (aka *Saimiri boliviensis*), was 15 years old. He was inquisitive, used to humans and easily enticed by the fruit that Anthony offered. Hekel ended up in a carry bag; at only 35 centimetres in length and weighing about 1100 grams, he could offer little resistance. The boys took a tram and a train back to Timur's home on the other side of Melbourne in the depths of South Oakleigh. Hekel then spent the next 24 hours locked in a bungalow in the middle of Melbourne's cold, wet winter. He was alone and far from his family and the warm rainforest-style home at the zoo.

The unusual break-in at the zoo made the TV news the next day. After watching appeals for Hekel's return, the boys had a change of heart and decided to return him. They put him in a cardboard box with air holes and wrote 'sorry' on top. They attached a note: 'Common squirrel monkey. Melbourne Zoo. Please return to Melbourne Zoo. Heckles'. At around 7 o'clock that night, the box containing Hekel was left at the Oakleigh Police Station. Hekel survived the ordeal and was reunited with his family.

The boys were caught and pleaded guilty to burglary and theft at the Magistrates' Court. They were placed on a twelve-month community-based order to do 150 hours of unpaid work. Consequently, the following year in May 1999, Timur returned to the County Court for a breach of an adjourned undertaking for the damage to the Serrano exhibition. The names of juvenile offenders would normally not be public knowledge. However, because of Anthony and Timur's subsequent conviction, their full names and previous offences became public knowledge because they still had outstanding good behaviour bonds and other undertakings. I have decided not to give their surnames, even though their full names are on the public record, as they were young and reckless then, and I hope they have reformed.

After surviving multiple attacks in Australia and, again, in Sweden, *Piss Christ* was destroyed while on exhibition in Avignon, France, on Palm Sunday in 2011. The Archbishop of Vaucluse, Jean-Pierre Cattenoz, demanded its removal. Although protected by two security guards and a plexiglass screen, four young Christian extremists, disguised with sunglasses and armed with hammers and screwdrivers, slashed two works by Serrano, damaging both beyond repair. The other work was a photograph of a nun seated with her hands in her lap, titled *The church (Soeur Jeanne Myriam)*. As the vandals fled, they threatened three guards.

After the attack, the gallery director, Eric Mézil, did not close the exhibition but kept the damaged work on display "so people can see what barbarians can do."

Zealots demand that an image or statement only be understood in one way, their way. Andres Serrano proposes another way to interpret responses to his notorious photograph. "So, if *Piss Christ* upsets you, maybe it's a good thing to think about what happened on the cross."

Taggers, Renks and 70K

Inner-city Melbourne has a reputation for graffiti and street art, aerosol paint, stencils and paste-ups along train lines, over factories and in the many service lanes that run behind buildings. The most famous of these lanes runs between Flinders Street and Flinders Lane, Hosier Lane. The bluestone paved lane got its name when it was part of Melbourne's garment-making district; now, it is one of Melbourne's top tourist attractions. For years people have been painting in Hosier Lane. Every surface is covered in layers of multi-coloured aerosol paint, beautiful, dynamic hip-hop style pieces and witty stencils. In some places, the accumulated paint is several millimetres thick. People paint walls in Hosier Lane day and night. Many visiting graffiti writers paint there, including Banksy and Blek le Rat. Overlooking the lane is a three-storey-high face of an Aboriginal child painted on the side of a building in 2014 by the Melbourne artist Adnate. It is a vibrant place and a favourite photography location for tourists, school groups, and wedding and fashion shoots.

Some people wonder why you can't have attractive street art without tagging. The reason is that they are treated the same by the law and the artists. It is illegal to paint or paste things to walls without the owner's permission: it leads to the offence of 'criminal damage' in *Crimes Act 1958* s197(1) and in the *Summary Offences*

Act 1966 s10 'posting bills and defacing property'. And most street artists and writers have had some interaction with the police.

Although Hosier Lane might look like a chaotic, colourful, lawless area of outlaw art, it is not a free paint zone. It is curated to some extent. The owners of the buildings have given permission for ongoing painting. Rutledge Lane, a small crescent just off Hosier, is more of a free paint zone, but even that requires the building owners' permission to continuously repaint their walls.

Graffiti writers are known by their tag rather than their legal name for the obvious reason that what they do isn't legal. To be known means getting your tag up. A 'tag' is a *nom de rue*, the name on the street; it is also a verb to write your tag.

Many people write their names without permission on things around the city aside from graffiti writers. Most of us have tagged something at some time, even some of the people who say they hate tagging. It is a common desire to express your identity in public. Crime journalists carved their names into the wooden bench of the Melbourne Supreme Court. Steve Butcher, the senior court reporter for *The Age,* Channel Seven reporter Kate Osborne, and Wayne Flower, a *Herald-Sun* journalist who, along with his colleague Anthony Dowsley, won the 2012 Quill Award for 'Best Coverage of an Issue or Event' for their articles about the murder of Jill Meagher. Most graffiti writers would consider it ethically wrong to tag a historic building like the Supreme Court. However, graffiti is a massive movement, and there are rebels and extremists within it.

All graffiti writers tag, but then there are hardcore taggers who just tag and tag a lot. Playing hide-and-seek and dare comes with an addictive adrenaline rush. Unsurprisingly, some graffiti writers are not just vandals but audacious urban outlaws risking their liberty and life. Risking the industrial scale dangers of the railways and railyards, derelict factories full of asbestos or climbing up to the tops of buildings, 'the heavens', as graffiti writers call it, just to leave your mark.

'RIP Sinch' read the many tribute pieces in Brunswick when this prolific tagger and train surfer died at 26. You can still see Sinch's tag all over Melbourne years after his death, written in aerosol spray paint, fat marker pen or sprayed with an old fire extinguisher filled with paint.

And among the many dangers hardcore taggers face is violence. There are fights between them over walls, and they are also likely to be beaten up and abused by the railway's Asset Protection Officers or even vigilante citizens who take the law into their own hands. The rules of the graffiti game are simple; you only live once, and the player with the most exposure of tags wins. It is a game where you can be out in the lead and yet never win in the end.

While many inner-city councils and businesses embraced the endeavours of Melbourne's outlaw artists, those in the outer suburbs did not. Politicians from these areas were calling for harsher measures against graffiti.

In 2007 specific legislation against graffiti, the *Graffiti Prevention Act* was passed in Victoria. Four new offences were listed: possession of a graffiti implement, possession with intent to mark graffiti, advertising a prescribed graffiti implement for sale and selling aerosol paint to anyone under 18. It also provided for prison sentences. The new laws gave the police greater powers for search and seizure by reversing the onus of proof for possessing a 'graffiti implement'. This means a person must convince the police officer that they have a legitimate reason for having those items or receive a penalty notice of around $550. The reversal of the onus of proof is used in the offence of 'going equipped for stealing', but is graffiti as serious a problem as burglary?

The Director of Public Prosecutions (DPP) was keen to see these new laws enforced. Soon after the legislation was enacted, they appealed against the sentence imposed in the Melbourne Magistrates' Court against a 25-year-old from the seaside suburb of Mt Eliza.

Renks (aka Noam Shoan) graduated from the College of the Arts and worked as a graphic designer. He was also part of the notorious 70k crew along with Stan, Bonez and Bo. '70k' stands for '70s kids', as most of the crew were born in the 1970s, except for the youngest member, Renks. The 70k crew describe themselves as 'anti-graffiti taggers' because they were not about beautiful graffiti pieces but creating ugly but recognisable tags and throw-ups (a throw-up is something more substantial than a tag, using a couple of colours but less than a complete piece).

Renks was accused of painting seventy-two train carriages, a tram, a rail bridge and an overpass. He was convicted of multiple counts of criminal damage committed over five years. Although Magistrate Sarah Dawes agreed that Renks was 'a talented artist', she sentenced him to 250 hours of community service and ordered him to pay $30,299.17 in restitution. But it wasn't enough for the public prosecutor who appealed the verdict to the County Court. Regardless of his guilty plea, artistic talents and youth, in August 2007, Judge Tim Deneys Woods in the County Court overturned the previous verdict and sentenced Renks to three months, telling him, "It is not your right, in the name of art, to damage the property of others."

Renks appealed his sentence to the Court of Appeal, which was slightly more sympathetic. Judging that Renks had "unilaterally imposed his notions of art and decoration on the rest of the world". Justice Peter Buchanan upheld the conviction but suspended the remainder of his sentence. Renks served only forty-one days of his original three-month sentence.

Jailing Renks did not deter others or diminish the quantity of graffiti in Melbourne any more than swatting a fly at a BBQ prevents others. Melbourne's walls continue to be covered in layers of aerosol paint, stickers and tags.

The Ballad of Utah
and Ether

This is a love story about a woman, a man, trains and lots of aerosol paint.

Utah and Ether are graffiti writers on the run. Dubbed 'the Bonnie and Clyde of graffiti' by the US media, they have much in common with the American Depression-era bank-robbing couple Bonnie Parker and Clyde Barrow. A young, attractive, skinny, white American couple who live a nomadic life on the run from the law, posing for photographs while on a crime spree and using modern technology to stay ahead of their pursuers. But unlike Bonnie and Clyde, all they want to do is paint trains.

Utah (aka Danielle Bremner) was born in 1982 and studied at the Fashion Institute of Technology in New York before meeting Ether (aka Jim Clay Harper). He is three years younger and was studying at Bowling Green State University in Ohio. They fell in love painting trains. Although there are tens of thousands of young men like Ether spray-painting, there are not many women. In the mid-2000s, Utah was probably the most active female tagger in the United States.

Unlike the impossible-to-read wildstyle, popular with many graffiti writers, Utah and Ether paint in a bold, legible traditional blockbuster or bubble-style. Their objective is more about reputation and painting on trains than calligraphy.

Utah and Ether joined Chicago's MUL (aka Made U Look) Crew in 2006, painting trains in the United States and Canada. On Christmas Eve 2006, the MUL crew painted ten New York City subway cars. It required the kind of audacity, organisation and planning of a bank heist; only the objective wasn't money but fame.

While Utah and Ether got the fame they were looking for, it came with another kind of recognition, identification. After a string of convictions for felony criminal mischief and burglary for breaking into train yards, they were jailed in 2009 for six months in New York Rikers Island Correctional Centre and a further six months in Boston. They were also ordered to pay $US10,000 in remuneration, given five years' probation, and a five-year ban on travelling to Boston.

When Utah and Ether were released on probation, they had six months left to serve on their sentence. Still, five years on probation meant that even possessing paint and marker pens during that time would violate their parole. They decided they were graffiti writers, and that's what they were going to do. They wanted to create hardcore illegal graffiti as art, as they explained in artspeak on their website: 'a dialog between the safety of the gallery setting and the vitality of painting in the streets illegally.' 'Freedom is not defined by safety' became Utah and Ether's slogan. Outlaw painters are only restricted by their ambitions. Rather than stop, they decided to go large. Local reputation was not enough; they wanted international brand-name recognition.

Their passports had not been revoked, but leaving the United States would violate their parole. In 2011 they decided to live life on the run and headed off around the world on an intercontinental spree focused on spray-painting trains in about thirty countries.

They loved the art of the heist, employing their skills and knowledge of the railway system to their own ends. Their online videos show them breaking into and spraying in the railway yards.

Then the finished product comes into a metro station. Utah giggles behind the camera as the painted carriage pulls up. The coordination is impressive, with an electro soundtrack emphasising the precision and speed of the writers. 'Utah', 'Ether', 'MUL', and 'Yawn Face' are sprayed across metro carriages; 'Probation Vacation' fills two more.

They were both caught in China and deported to the United States. However, the Chinese put them on a cheap flight to New York, which landed at Newark Airport, just across the river from Manhattan Island, in the state of New Jersey rather than New York State. Consequently, there were no New York police waiting for them on arrival.

Utah and Ether laid low for a few days recovering and then flew to Europe to continue painting trains.

"Why the fuck would I want to go to an island with no metro systems?" was Ether's initial opinion about visiting Australia. Ether is correct; there are no metro systems in Australia. There are only five public transit train systems in the whole country. But after six years of travel, Utah wanted to visit Australia, hoping to relax in an English-speaking country for five weeks. She was also keen to become part of the 'Gentlemen's Club' by painting trains in all of Australia's five major cities and awarded a Top Hat emoji online by her Australian peers.

Utah won over Ether's objections. The tag team arrived at Melbourne Airport on Thursday, April 21, 2016, on a flight from the United Arab Emirates. They were preparing themselves for the disappointment of being deported after a long flight, but the Australian Border Force proved ineffective at keeping out two Americans with several criminal convictions between them.

Utah and Ether were not the only graffiti tourists coming to Melbourne for a spray and a vacation. Many people come to Melbourne to do graffiti and street art – dubbed a 'spraycation' by Melbourne's media. Many interstate and international graffiti writers come to Melbourne. The famous British street artist Banksy visited Melbourne in 2003 and left behind many of his stencil images. It's hard to imagine how many graffiti and street artists there are in Melbourne alone. All the Surrealists could fit into one café in Paris; all of the Abstract Expressionists could drink at the Cedar Bar in New York, and they did, but you would need a stadium to fit all the graffiti writers and street artists who have painted in Melbourne.

Utah and Ether are internet savvy and photogenic. Lots of photos; 'high quality, mass quantity' is Ether's objective. They have pages on Facebook, photos on Instagram, videos on Vimeo and YouTube, and their own webpage. Their *Probation Vacation* is in print and video format, available online at their website, along with other merchandise: limited edition zines, T-shirts, posters, sticker sets and box sets.

In Melbourne, they met up with their Australian friend and fellow graffiti writer, Nokier, who has been active in Melbourne graffiti for about a decade and was happy to show visitors around. He is a 30-something white man of average height and build with short dark hair and blue eyes. Utah and Ether had painted trains with him in Tunisia and India. And they spent the next fortnight couch surfing, painting trains, exploring the city, painting more trains and slapping up their vinyl stickers. Black stickers with their names in big, bold, sans serif white letters in two rows: 'Utah Ether'. Nokier added his sticker alongside theirs.

They went to AC/DC Lane, where two parachuting rats stencilled by Banksy were still visible. AC/DC Lane, named after the Australian heavy rock band, is part of a network of inner-city service lanes that provide access to the rear of buildings for deliveries and garbage collection, and make great locations for graffiti. Nearby are Banksy's rats and other street art and graffiti work, including a disintegrating paper paste-up by renowned US street artist Swoon.

Nokier, Utah and Ether stuck up their stickers in the lane, and Nokier wrote his tag in silver marker pen on one wall.

Ether and Utah enjoyed walking around the city because, as Utah explained, "It's a really nice city to walk around and also because the train is pretty expensive and full of Protective Service Officers." They sprayed some walls, and, of course, they broke into a couple of rail yards and sprayed some trains. They can throw up a piece incredibly fast, a spray can in each hand, one outlining in white, the other filling in the colour. They were painting trains at Bayswater depot on Sunday night, April 24. On Monday night, they were painting more trains in Williamstown. Then, on Friday, April 29, between midnight and thirteen past, they painted more trains at South Kensington train station and still more the night after in Pakenham depot and stabling yard on Saturday, April 30.

Early on the afternoon of May 4, as Utah was off getting a tattoo, Ether and Nokier filled in time, slapping up more stickers as they wandered around Fitzroy. After all their experience, you'd think they would be a bit more careful than to go tagging in broad daylight. Maybe relaxed by Melbourne's inner-city atmosphere, they had let their guard down. It was a small mistake that was about to have enormous consequences for Ether.

The exterior wall of the Babka Bakery cafe on Brunswick Street features a babushka doll in aerosol paint. Just inside the cafe, observing the activities of Ether and Nokier was a vigilante, described as a 'man on the street' or 'a single father from Fitzroy'. He followed them for about a block along Brunswick Street, whinging about their behaviour and photographing them on his mobile phone. Most graffiti writers don't like their faces to be photographed for obvious reasons. Ether and Utah are a bit of an exception to that rule; clear and undistorted photographs of their faces appear on their own website, but being photographed by an aggressive stranger was another thing.

"You're in fucking Fitzroy, mate! If you don't like it, go back to the 'burbs!" Nokier retaliated.

There are places in Melbourne with more stickers, tags and aerosol art than Brunswick Street, Fitzroy, like Hosier Lane, but not many. Fitzroy's graffiti and street art is dense and intense, blocks of it, legal walls and illegal pieces. The back of every street sign is covered in stickers. Every pole is plastered with them. The redundant red post-box is now just another surface to be covered in stickers. There are large painted walls up Rose Street, both east and west. There are plenty of tags around. It must rank among one of the most unlikely places on earth for anyone to complain about graffiti.

As Nokier argued, Ether tried to stop the man from photographing them on his mobile phone. The man's phone case also contained cash and credit cards, so he wouldn't let anyone lay their hands on it. There was a scuffle, hands and arms flailing around. Ether punched the man in the head. His glasses were knocked off, and somewhere in the struggle, they were broken. During this altercation, the man accidentally dialled his sister. Hearing the sound of fighting over the phone, she called the police. By then, the man had Ether pinned down in a headlock on the footpath. He could hear the police siren in the distance.

"Let me go!"

"You punched me in the face, dickhead! I'll let you go when the cops get here."

Nokier fled the scene; Victoria Police have no idea of his identity. He phoned Utah to tell her that Ether had been arrested. Ether was charged with attempted robbery, unlawful assault, attempted theft, bill posting and criminal damage. After Ether refused to provide an address to the court, he was denied bail because he was a flight risk.

Utah and Nokier waited outside the police station until midnight, hoping Ether would be released. The following day they headed west to Adelaide. Utah was still keen to continue on their mission to paint all the capital city trains in Australia and collect the Top Hat emoji. In Adelaide, they painted trains, shoplifted sushi and arranged for Adrian Lewin, a Melbourne lawyer who has worked exclusively in criminal law since 2009, to represent Ether. After Adelaide, Utah and Nokier continued west to Perth, back across the continent to Sydney and then north to Brisbane, all the time painting more trains. Utah and Nokier joined the 'Gentlemen's Club'.

As she was departing at Brisbane Airport, Utah's name was flagged in the immigration computer system, and Australian Border Force interrogated her. She had nothing to say and had nothing on her that could be used as evidence: no phone, no computer, no hard drive, and no contact information. "I knew that there was a pretty high possibility that I'd have a problem while leaving, and the last thing I wanted was for my problem to turn into anyone else's." She was not arrested and was allowed to catch her flight to Hong Kong.

Meanwhile, back in Victoria, the police had done their research and were well prepared when they interviewed Ether. They had plenty of photographs of Ether, Utah and Nokier's work. They suspected that Ether was connected to 'MUL', 'Nokier' and 'Sailor'. Ether looked bored during the interview as his side consisted of "No comment". He only varied from this when he was asked about TGT or TGF graffiti. "I don't know anything about that." (Ether released the video of his interview on YouTube as proof that he didn't rat on anyone.)

There are months of backlog cases for the courts and little space in Melbourne's remand system. At first, Ether was held in 'the sub', the subterranean Melbourne Custody Centre, for a few days. Next, he was moved to Moonee Ponds Police Station and then Heidelberg Police Station for about two weeks.

On May 12, another hearing at the Melbourne Magistrates' Court with new charges: recklessly causing injury, assault in company, possessing a controlled weapon without excuse and thirteen counts of criminal damage. The 'controlled weapon' was a boxcutter that Ether had in his backpack.

On May 31, 2016, Ether appeared before Magistrate Carolene Gwynn and pleaded guilty to eight damage charges, attempted robbery for trying to take the vigilante's phone and recklessly causing injury. According to the prosecutor, Tracey Ramsey, he had come to Melbourne specifically to do graffiti. He had done more than $4000 in damage with paint to trains in Bayswater, Williamstown, Kensington and Pakenham, as well as an RMIT University building and Etihad Stadium.

Ether's defence lawyer, Lewin, countered Ramsey's claim. Arguing that Ether's graffiti was just a side activity and his real reason for being in Melbourne was to meet up with friends. Lewin compared Ether's graffiti practice to yoga, a hobby you continued while on vacation, rather than the specific reason.

Magistrate Gwynn disagreed, judging that Ether "has come to Australia with the sole purpose of committing these offences." She gave Ether a six-month sentence minus the twenty-seven days he had been held in remand. He was also ordered to pay Metro trains $1595.08 and $280 for the vigilante's broken pair of glasses.

Ether was held at the Melbourne Assessment Prison for two weeks and then sent to Port Phillip Prison. He worked in the prison laundry where he claimed to have made and sold a few shivs made from cutlery that came in with loads of tablecloths and serviettes. Then, he was moved to Middleton, a new privately operated, restricted, minimum-rated prison in Castlemaine, central Victoria.

Prisoners at Middleton live in self-catered, cottage-style accommodation within the Loddon Prison Precinct. Ether was requested to paint a mural on a large wall inside the prison during his time there. He agreed to this request and did the same work inside that landed him there.

While in Middleton, Ether claims to have witnessed events that led to Hizir Ferman's (aka Hez) death. Ferman, a Coburg motor mechanic who had previously done time for armed robbery, assaults, drug trafficking and weapons charges, was near the end of his sentence for extortion and threatening to kill. Ether provides a detailed account of how Ferman was beaten to death by the 'toggies' (aka Security and Emergency Services Group), the heavily armoured prison riot squad, after Ferman assaulted two guards on Thursday, July 28, 2016. It is an account that contradicts the evidence given to the State Coroner that Ferman's death was an allergic reaction to pepper spray. Still, Ether's not coming back to Australia to provide this evidence under oath.

While Ether was in remand, Australian Border Force caught up with him, and his visa was cancelled on May 19, 2016. On his release, Ether would be deported to the United States. He knew he faced a further six months in Rikers Island Prison in New York for outstanding offences plus any additional time for breaking parole. He decided he was not going to do that, even if it meant sprinting across a runway; maybe a friend could slip him a ticket to Iceland when he was in transit at LAX.

He delayed signing the papers agreeing that he was fit to fly because that would announce to the US police when he would be returning to the United States. Luckily for Ether, it was the weekend before the Melbourne Cup, and many people in Melbourne take the Monday off before the public holiday on Tuesday for the horse race that stops the nation. That Monday, he was deported from Australia, sitting in the back row of the plane with a Serco guard on either side of him and one in the next row.

> *"I knew that even with having delayed my release info*
> *being sent to the U.S., there was a chance that when I*
> *landed I'd be met by the authorities at the gate. So I was*
> *pretty relieved when I was able to pass through customs*

*and exit the airport. Some friends picked me up and as
we drove towards the city center, I began to silently go over
the logistics of leaving America as soon as possible."*

Utah and Ether are still on the run. In early 2019 they were spraying trains in Georgia, Armenia and Azerbaijan.

Other Bastards

The Communist in
the cage

Sydney Road in Brunswick was busy on Friday evening, May 19, 1933. At twenty minutes to nine, a horse-drawn cart stopped in front of a hotel on the corner of Phoenix Street. One wheel was chained and padlocked to the hotel's iron balcony post. The horse was led away.

Bolted onto the back of the cart and covered in hessian was a disused elevator cage. The tall, wiry 19-year-old young man locked inside the iron cage was not an escape artist but a self-taught artist and communist named Noel Counihan. The cart and cage was a planned operation by the Unemployed Workers Movement and the Communist Party. The hessian covers were thrown off the cage and off the signs on the side of the cart: 'We Want Free Speech' and 'In gaol, 18 class war prisoners, for free speech.'

At the time, under the leadership of the extreme right-wing Chief Commissioner Thomas Blamey, Victoria Police were arresting anyone who dared to publicly criticise the government. It was not that making a public speech was illegal, but it might as well have been, as the police would charge any speaker they didn't like with the offence of obstructing traffic. According to the law, the police only had to claim the potential for impeding traffic to arrest someone for obstructing traffic, even if there was no traffic – like when they spoke on a dead-end street in Brunswick.

The police were expecting trouble that evening on Sydney Road. Shortly after eight o'clock, there had been a bold attempt at free speech. Reginald Patullo (aka 'Shorty' Patullo) had climbed up on top of one of the cable trams that ran along Sydney Road. This was before the introduction of electric trams with their overhead wires, so Shorty could stand on top of the tram and address the crowd as the police gave chase. Shorty was 'accidentally shot', arrested and eventually taken to Melbourne Hospital (now called the Royal Melbourne Hospital) by the police.

Although it was after dark, the long shopping strip of Sydney Road was still busy; it still is today. Opposite the Duke of Edinburgh Hotel was the Coles grocery store, open late on a Friday night. Looking down the road, Counihan could see a patrol car and a mounted trooper heading towards his cart.

Armed with an old HMV gramophone horn to amplify his voice, he spoke about issues close to him. Unemployment; although he wasn't unemployed at the time, he was about to be, as his impending arrest would result in him losing his job in a garment warehouse. He spoke about homelessness; he had recently left home when his conservative and alcoholic father burnt his left-wing books. About the injustice of police attacks on meetings and the need for freedom of speech in a democracy. And about the rise of fascism in Europe and about those who supported it in England and Australia, like Chief Commissioner Blamey.

Being in the cage prevented him from being arrested while making a speech defending the right to free political speech. But it must have been difficult to hear what Counihan said with the police shouting, climbing and banging on the old metal cage. Traffic was definitely being obstructed by a growing crowd of onlookers as mounted constables tried to disperse the crowd.

After their first attempts to get through the doors of the elevator cage failed, the police commandeered a 2.5-metre length of solid red gum to use as an improvised battering ram. When they had bashed a large hole in the cage, Counihan feared that he might be crushed by the next blow and surrendered. It had taken the police half an hour to end his demonstration.

Counihan was charged with offensive behaviour and obstructing the traffic. He was put in the lock-up for the weekend. On Monday, he appeared in the Brunswick Court of Petty Sessions. There he represented himself, arguing that the cart and the cage were not an obstruction. To the surprise of nobody, the magistrate sided with the police. Counihan was fined £5 ($476 today) or one month in prison for obstructing traffic. For offensive behaviour, he was fined £10 ($952 today) or two months. Counihan asked for time to pay, but the court refused. A comrade was able to pay the fine for obstructing traffic for Counihan. The Communist Party advised him to appeal the charge of offensive behaviour, and Counihan agreed.

As he was only nineteen, Counihan was held in the remand yard for minors in Pentridge Prison until his family arranged bail. If he had been a few months older, he would have ended up in the adult remand section.

Counihan's action and arrest made *The Sun News-Pictorial* under the headline: 'Two Exciting Arrests Stir Shopping Crowd in Brunswick.' Two days later, *The Herald* reported 'Speech from Steel Cage – Young Artist Fined £15' and included parts of Counihan's defence speech to the court, along with a photograph of the cart.

On appeal, with proper legal representation, Counihan won his case. His speech in the cage was the turning point for the media and public opinion. By the end of the year, the *Street Meetings Act 1933* gave some protection to demonstrators. It redefined obstructing traffic to 'undue obstruction ... having regard to all the circumstances of the case'.

Art, unlike the law, is poorly defined and often defies categorisation. Artists from the Dadaists to Pussy Riot have worked at the intersection of art and political protest. Although Noel Counihan became a notable social-realist artist, honoured with a retrospective exhibition at the NGV in 1973, he is most remembered for his protest. And considering the following two artists in this book, Ivan Durrant and Angus McLennon, whose protests are art, Counihan's cage, in retrospect, should be considered alongside.

Beverley's body

Ivan John Durrant placed Beverley's body in front of the NGV on St Kilda Road. He had slaughtered Beverley in a cattle yard in Wheelers Hill, just north of Monash University, on Monday morning, May 26, 1975. Loaded her body onto the back of a truck and drove into Melbourne. He informed the NGV's front desk staff that he was donating a sculpture and asked if they could leave it in place for a few days.

When it came to slaughtering cows, the twenty-eight-year-old artist Ivan Durrant knew what he was doing. He had worked as a slaughterman while studying to complete his high school matriculation. He hadn't finished high school as a child because he was in state care, if 'care' is the right word for the ill-treatment he received for much of his childhood. He went on to study economics at Monash University before deciding to become an artist.

Durrant is primarily a realist, even hyperreal, painter and sculptor, but this was the 70s, and art happenings were a happening thing. Durrant had intended to slaughter a cow on stage at Monash University three days earlier. But the invited news media leaked what was going to happen, and the university cancelled the event. So he asked the media to record him as he moved Beverley's body onto the NGV's forecourt.

Durrant explained that his *Slaughtered cow happening* was about "Taking responsibility for your own actions. If we are going to eat meat, a cow dies for that. And we have to face it." British celebrity chefs would make the same point decades later when they took television cameras into the abattoirs.

Modern Masters: Manet to Matisse, the first of the NGV's blockbuster exhibitions, was due to open that night. The NGV urgently needed to send a clean-up team to the forecourt to remove a dead cow.

Durrant was charged with littering for dumping Beverley's body. He pleaded not guilty, arguing that Beverley might be a sculpture or food, but was not litter. Stipendiary Magistrate J.W. Dunn told Ivan he had done this to "further your own ego as a successful artist", and fined Durrant $100 and ordered him to pay $157 in costs ($1705 today).

The NGV had a different opinion about Durrant to the magistrate. Three years later, they purchased a new work by him, *Butcher shop*, 1977–1978. A life-sized model of a butcher's shop window, complete with replica pigs' snouts, imitation black pudding, and trays bearing reproductions of lambs' brains, cutlets and chops. The NGV had it installed next to the entrance of their restaurant for many years.

Although he is a pacifist, Durrant is not a vegetarian; he uses meat in his art to represent death and brutality. Cows continue to be a central subject of Durrant's art. In 1978, he painted on five live cows and three calves at the Warragul cattle market. He does non-cow-related art and, in 2009, won the $20,000 Sulman Prize with an out-of-focus photorealist painting of the annual MCG Anzac Day football match. And in 2020, the NGV gave him a retrospective exhibition. However, Durrant is still best known for his now legend-ary, *Slaughtered cow happening*.

Proudly unAustralian

When the police first saw Azlan McLennan's *Proudly unAustralian*, they probably didn't know it was art, but they knew they didn't like it.

It was eleven days before Australia Day. *Proudly unAustralian* had been displayed on an external wall in central Footscray for two days. The 'billboard' space was managed by Trocadero Art Space, an artist-run space known for its politically oriented exhibitions. It was not a regular commercial billboard; it was more like a small sign of about 2×3 metres which was hard to notice among the many shops on Leeds Street.

Senior Constable Jay McDonald disliked it so much that he took immediate action on Friday, January 20, 2006. He went into the two-storey building but discovered the gallery was closed that morning. Demanding access from another tenant, he climbed onto the second-level awning of the two-storey building on the busy corner of Leeds and Hopkins streets in Footscray to take it down. He made no effort to contact the gallery, entered private property and removed property without explanation, permission, or warrant.

For *Proudly unAustralian* was the remains of a torn and burnt Australian flag.

In the first decade of the new millennium, the horror of living in a country with a history of the genocidal treatment of its Indigenous population that kept refugees in indefinite detention and illegally invaded Iraq drew outrage from some Australians. One of them was a thirty-year-old Melbourne-based artist, Azlan McLennan.

In 2004 Melbourne City Council painted over his work, *Fifty six*, on a Flinders Street shopfront art space after complaints, even though the art was approved by the council. It was the fourth time in two years that authorities had acted to censor McLennan. Sometimes he was censored by the very same body that commissioned his art in the first place.

McLennan's *Proudly unAustralian* was a follow-up to a work he'd shown in Un-Australian and Proud, a group exhibition in Trocadero, Footscray, in September 2005. His artist's statement about his work is clear, concise and free of any confusing, postmodern art-speak:

> *Proudly unAustralian is an artwork designed to counter the continent's upcoming anniversary, celebrating 219 years of European intervention. The burning of the Commonwealth flag exercises Prime Minister John Howard's public, yet begrudging reluctance to outlaw Australian flag burning in 2002, with his admission: "... I guess it's part of the sort of free speech code that we have in this country."*
>
> *The flag burning symbolises the locally and internationally deplored treatment by the Australian government of its indigenous peoples, asylum seekers, its industrial relations and education reforms, US collaboration in the attacks in Iraq and Afghanistan and the incitement against Muslim and Arab populations at home and abroad.*
>
> *This act is compounded by Howard's denial that there is no underlying racist sentiment in Australia following the racial tensions in Sydney in December and more*

*importantly, the government's clear role in this division
of class.*

Politicians poured petrol on the public hysteria. Flag burning was tantamount to treason, declared Queensland National Party MP Bruce Scott and the national president of the Returned and Services League (aka RSL). Major-General Bill Crews agreed flag burning should be a criminal offence. Inspired by this, Liberal MP Bronwyn Bishop introduced a private member's bill to make it an offence to engage in 'burning, mutilating or otherwise destroying' the flag, punishable with an $11,000 fine. However, Prime Minister John Howard stuck to his position that it should not be a crime and Bishop's bill failed.

The police claimed McLennan's *Proudly unAustralian* was an 'exhibit', but it would only ever be exhibited at an art gallery and never in a court. Inspector Craig Walsh admitted, "[We are yet] to establish if any offence has been committed."

They never did.

Just after Australia Day, the police returned the burnt flag to the gallery. It came with no apology, no explanation, no sign of embarrassment from the police, just something like, "All right, you've made your point."

McLennan sold *Proudly unAustralian*; he needed to pay his rent. Repeated censorship has not stopped him; he continues to create and exhibit art with clear political messages.

Courtroom Artists

Fay Plamka had an eight-year career as a court artist for the ABC and Channel Seven. The little, round woman with curly white hair was often seen wheeling her small suitcase of materials into court as she sketched the various and numerous court appearances of Melbourne's gangland war generals, lieutenants and soldiers: Carl Williams, Roberta Williams, Andrew "Benji" Veniamin, Mario Condello and Evangelos "Ange" Goussis.

In Australia, cameras are generally banned from the courts, so the news media employ courtroom artists to get an image of a defendant. Courtroom art results from two competing demands — the news media to have pictures to go with courtroom reporting and the court for reasons of justice to control what images are made and published. For there are some people, like the jury, the court does not want depicted.

The law about sketching in court varies according to the jurisdiction. It is also an issue of order in the court as a person drawing is not always unobtrusive and can be a distraction. Often it depends on the judge or magistrate in that particular case.

Fay Plamka was born to Jewish parents in the Föhrenwald Displaced Persons camp in Bavaria, Germany. She was only eighteen months old when she arrived with her parents in Australia. She studied art with the painter John Brack at the National Gallery School and then with Ernst Fuchs, of the Vienna School of Fantastic

Realism, before moving to Israel in 1968, where she worked as a portrait artist. She moved back to Australia, married and had children while working in graphic design and advertising. In 1989 she founded Illustrators Australia, a not-for-profit association to support professional illustrators.

There is often not much warmth between the courtroom artist and their subject. Generally, the subject has more to worry about than how the courtroom artist portrays them. Most frequently, the vibe of hostility the courtroom sketcher feels comes from the relatives of the accused. But Plamka and gangland murderer and drug trafficker Carl Williams was an exception. Plamka was once rebuked by the prosecutor for joking with Williams. She explained to the court that she needed Williams's cooperation to do her best work. After all, a defendant could make it impossible for a sketch artist by covering their face with a hand.

After making her sketches in the courtroom, Plamka returns to her studio and works on them some more. She has reference photographs of people she uses as stand-in models to work on her outline sketch of the accused. Not that she has much time to finish them before they have to be scanned or photographed for use on the evening news.

In 2008 a witness objected as Plamka started to sketch him. Plamka was not barred from drawing; instead, Chief Magistrate Ian Gray ruled that the informer's identity should be suppressed and advised her that no sketch could be published under his order. The reason for this suppression order was to protect the safety of a witness.

Plamka decided to continue sketching the witness; the television station might have wanted the image for the news, even if they had to pixelate the face. Then wrote his name under the sketch. Writing the witness's name led to her breach of the suppression order; without the name, the drawing could have been anyone.

Fay Plamka met Bobby Galinsky (aka Robert Lewis Galinsky) at a dinner party. Bobby would turn out to be a bad influence on Fay.

Fay was trying to sell some of her courtroom sketches; she hoped to make enough money to afford a trip to Paris. After the media have photographed the sketches, they belong to the artist. Some people and institutions collect these sketches; the National Museum of Australia has almost two hundred courtroom drawings by Veronica O'Leary of the 1982 trial of Lindy and Michael Chamberlain.

Bobby Galinsky is a US script doctor from Hollywood who moved to Sydney in 1994 and then to Melbourne in 2000. In 2009 he produced his first Australian feature film, Prey, a supernatural horror starring Natalie Bassingthwaighte. He was enthusiastic and decided his next production would not be another movie but an exhibition of Plamka's sketches. The exhibition was titled 'Melbourne's Underbelly Archives', a reference to the *Underbelly* books by John Silvester and Andrew Rule.

Galinsky rented the Steps Gallery in Carlton. He paid for the drinks at the opening and printed the invitations. The invitation had a touch of the script doctor's flair, announcing that: 'Refreshments *will* be served. Weapons *will not* be provided.'

Established in 1992, Steps Gallery is a large, square, white-walled room on the ground floor of 62 Lygon Street in Carlton South. Unusually for a Melbourne gallery, it is owned by the Meat Industry Employees' Superannuation Fund. It is not a bad investment as the gallery is a rental exhibition space; individual artists like Plamka or groups like the Wildlife Art Society of Australasia rent by the week for their exhibitions.

Amongst Plamka's sketches in the exhibition was the one she had made of the man whose identity was under the suppression order. Both Fay Plamka and Bobby Galinsky should have known better. Not only had Plamka been warned by Chief Magistrate Ian Gray when she did the drawing, but the Australian Federal Police had told Galinsky about it before the exhibition. Then at the exhibition opening on Wednesday evening, April 15, 2009, Channel Seven reporter Kate Osborne, who was also aware of the suppression order, questioned showing the sketch and the name.

Plamka and Galinsky argued about the drawing of the informant at the exhibition opening. Galinsky thought a bit of controversy was a good thing, but Plamka was worried. Quick corrections were made at the exhibition. In the catalogue, the name was crossed out with black Texta, and the name on the drawing was covered with a piece of paper. The paper had the word 'suppressed' on it, proving they were aware of the court order.

Even then, they didn't hide the man's name very well. You could still see printing in the catalogue through the marker's ink. It wouldn't have taken a police detective to uncover the name, and it was corrupt police who wanted to discover the name of the informer who had exposed police corruption.

Later in the evening, Plamka prevailed, and the drawing was taken down.

Both Galinsky and Plamka were charged with contempt of court. In the Melbourne Magistrates' Court on Tuesday, November 17, 2009, Plamka pleaded guilty to breaching the suppression order. She was represented by Trevor Wraight QC, who pointed out Plamka's good reputation, her contribution to the legal community and that she had "taken steps to ensure this will not happen again".

In a victim impact statement to the Melbourne Magistrates' Court, the man depicted in Plamka's sketch wrote that it had contributed to his 'fear and anxiety'.

Magistrate Susan Wakeling described herself as 'utterly bewildered' by Plamka, who should have been aware of the court order. Plamka was fined $2000 without conviction.

During his trial at the Brisbane Magistrates Court for wilful damage in 2015, the thirty-six-year-old internationally renowned street artist, Anthony Lister, sketched the magistrate. Lister had been caught painting on a wall in Brisbane and was found guilty of wilful damage and ordered to pay $440 in fines and perform five hours of community service. After the sentencing, Lister gave the magistrate the sketch as a present. The magistrate accepted the drawing provisionally. Saying that, he would have to make enquiries of the chief magistrate if he could receive the gift; after all, Lister could be back before him again in the future.

This is not a conclusion

At the start of the twenty-fourth day of the Gant and Siddique trial, 'in the absence of the jury', Justice Croucher announced that:

"My tipstaff said that last night as they were going out that one or more of the jurors, I think, indicated that they were concerned that they were being sketched...I think I might have been the subject of a sketch or two, not that I care about that, and so might one or more of you, which you might not care about. But what does concern me is that a juror might be concerned or more about being sketched.

"Section 77 of the Juries Act says that: 'a person must not publish or cause to be published any information or image that identifies or is capable of identifying a person attending for jury service.' And then it sets out a penalty... It says, amongst other things, that 'an offence against this section is an indictable offence'."

Sitting on the press bench on the opposite side of the court to the jury box, the person who had been sketching was Bill Luke, a tall, lanky, middle-aged man and former courtroom artist. I was sitting next to him and whispered, "Don't sketch the jury". He ignored my advice.

Luke was watching the forgery trial because he was researching a book like me. He had even attended their committal hearing at the Magistrates' Court the year before. His was a marathon effort in attendance that only the two defendants matched.

Luke apologised to the court and offered this excuse; he remembers "Magistrate Reardon saying he's seen so many of these sketch artists in court, none of them look anything like the people that were accused." Luke explained that his sketches "don't look like the people, they are just faces, hairstyle might be similar – so they're generic. I have done one sketch of the jury, of a jury member...The rest [were] just generic people, and some have been comical and almost cartoon."

After examining Luke's notebooks, Justice Croucher destroyed three sketches of the jury. Even though Luke had no intention of publishing these sketches, there was still the potential that they might be published. Luke was not disappointed at the loss of his drawings. The following year he was in the 2017 Archibald Prize exhibition with a portrait of another person he sketched during the trial, the crusty old defence barrister Remy van de Wiel QC.

This is not the end; things seem to keep repeating. This is not a conclusion; it's more of a reference to René Magritte's painting "this is not a pipe". I want to finish this book before a new art crime is reported in Australia... Too late...looted artefacts from Thailand and Cambodia acquired from notorious antiques dealer Douglas Latchford have been found in Australian collections. There have been more stolen sculptures and two attempted decapitations of sculptures in Melbourne.

This isn't much of an ending. Better security has not prevented art thefts or vandalism, new technology has not convicted more forgers, and the culture wars have used the police and law as weapons against artists. In telling a history, you would hope for a crisis and a resolution and not a century of repetition.

If you are expecting justice, you will be disappointed. Most art theft stories bring little sense of justice as the clear-up rate of these crimes is weak, and there are few arrests. The lack of proportion in the punishments is appalling; why should anyone do time for graffiti when the people who stole an ancient Indigenous petroglyph from Tasmania would only be fined if caught? And the vandalism of ancient Indigenous rock art continues across Australia with, more or less, impunity.

Examining art thefts is disheartening, frustrating and disappointing because the sad fact is that most stolen art is not recovered. Contrary to what the police tell the media after a theft, stolen art is not easy to trace. Australia is not part of the international art loss register and is unique in the developed world in not having its own stolen works register. While there are specialist art crime investigation units in Europe and North America, there are none in Australia.

If researching art thefts was disheartening, art forgery was worse. Although there have been a few successful prosecutions for art forgery, they do not inspire confidence. In art forgery, the risks are low, and the rewards can be very high. And art forgery is the art crime that continues to damage Indigenous cultures. When a fake is uncovered, the art market cools because buyers are less willing to take the risk, and the overseas market for Indigenous art can be devastated by fakes. But it is not just the market that suffers. Indigenous cultures are based on a complicated relationship of customary rights, laws and obligations, and art frauds damage these rights and traditions.

The prosecution of John O'Loughlin or the Libertos did not end art fraud in Indigenous art, only serving as a warning for continued vigilance. Fraud and related illegal activity are still commonplace in the Indigenous arts sector. In 2008, the Australian Competition and Consumer Commission (ACCC) prosecuted two Queensland art galleries for misrepresenting artwork by three non-Indigenous artists. The ACCC continues prosecuting companies for selling 'Aboriginal' paintings, boomerangs and didgeridoos imported from Indonesia.

By considering art crimes the same as any other theft, fraud or vandalism, the law often fails to recognise the cultural and historical damage these crimes cause. Under the law, art crimes often remain property crimes, and the cost to culture is ignored.

The art business is neither clean nor is it entirely innocent. The unregulated and secretive nature of the art market facilitates money laundering and other crimes. The secrecy of art dealers around the consignor's identity is a pathway for art forgery and illegally acquired art. No licences or qualifications are required to be an art advisor, art dealer or art valuer in Australia. When people are trusted with valuable artworks, where the security is lax or non-existent, and where penalties are vague or the crime hard to prove, sometimes, for some, the temptation is too much.

Most disheartening and frustrating is how the police have been used to fight the culture wars. Art has become a battleground for the culture war as right-wing forces censor and vandalise art. Art and culture suffer because the media and right-wing politicians want to create scandals to continue the culture wars. And from these deep divisions grew resentment, hatred and violence.

For all the attempts of censorship from Norman Lindsay to Paul Yore, nothing has been resolved. The conflict started before Lindsay had picked up a paintbrush and has still not been settled. Some people believe any nudity or reference to sexuality is morally damaging and that the law should enforce their faith in this claim, putting them in conflict with those who understand art history and hold more nuanced beliefs about using the law to enforce morality. And Australian law is an incoherent and unprincipled mess of unsuccessful attempts to resolve this contradiction.

The classic example of the limits of free speech is shouting 'Fire!' in a crowded cinema. Politicians and police claiming that an artist is exhibiting 'child pornography' does more long-term damage. Not only does it harm the individual artist, but it creates a chilling effect that continues to refrigerate the arts in Australia. And Australia continues to have an uneasy relationship with art due to the large numbers of vandals, wowsers, zealots, bigots and trolls.

I don't have any recommendations aside from those so obvious they would insult the reader's intelligence. The only way I can see to bring this book to a close with a dash of optimism is to point out that not all art crimes are about greed; there are some carried out for reasons of passions and politics. And that some artists question the role that artists should take in politics and society.

A year after that long forgery trial, in December 2017, I was in Collingwood, and I happened upon a rented van on Easey Street that was being loaded with paintings. And there was a real estate agent's sign on the red brick building that used to house Victorian Art Conservation. Aman Siddique was moving out.

I wondered where all the people in this book are now. Bill Henson, Paul Yore, Ivan Durrant, Juan Davila and Azlan McLennan are still exhibiting their art. Trevor Wraight, the defence lawyer who appeared for Peter Gant and courtroom artist Fay Pamalka, is now a County Court judge. Australia has returned thirteen antiquities connected to Subhash Kapoor to India. On Melbourne's streets, a few stickers, tags and bombs are all that remain of Ether, Utah, Nokier and Renks. Bohdan Ledwij, the painter of fake Pollocks, is dead, the Libertos are still alive, Peter Gant works part-time for his daughter's catering company, and others have vanished from the public eye: only Bob Ferguson is still laughing about *La Belle Hollandaise...*

THANKS

Many thanks for the assistance, advice, interviews and information to (in alphabetical order): Fletch 'Facter' Anderson, Bruce Armstrong, Wendy Black, Julia Burke, Eddie Butler-Bowdon, CDH, Gabriella Coslovich, Spencer 'Spud Rokk' Davids, Sean Doyle, Chris Dyson, Linda Ely, Bob Ferguson, Yvonne George, Ray Gill, Michael Hamel-Green, Peter Greenberg, Ian Harrison, Pamela Irving, David Jack, Tim Klingender, Bill Luke, Azlan McLennan, Duncan Mc Nab, Ray Mooney, Geoff Newton, Kenneth Polk, Sandra Powell, Loretta Quinn, Van Rudd, Catherine Voutier, Brendan Wilkinson, Dan Wollmering, Barry York and Alison Young.

Thanks for the assistance in research: Caroline Oxley (Research Officer, Victoria Police Museum and Historical Unit, Victoria Police) and Lisa Zito (Liaison Librarian National Gallery of Victoria). Apologies, if I've left anyone off this list.

Trove from the National Library of Australia, Australasian Legal Information Institute www.austlii.edu.au, and the *Australian Dictionary of Biography* were all used extensively, along with gallery collections and artists' websites.

Historian Thomas Blake's online calculator was used to calculate the current relative value of money. thomblake.com.au/secondary/hisdata/query.php

Page numbers for articles in online editions are not given.

The abstraction at the Art Gallery

"The theft from the art gallery" *Express and Telegraph*, 17 November 1885, p.2

"The theft from the art gallery" *South Australian Advertiser*, 18 November 1885, p.3

"The theft from the art gallery" *South Australian Advertiser*, 17 November 1885, p.5

"Art Gallery entered and robbed" *Adelaide Observer*, 21 November 1885, p.35

"Adelaide art gallery robbed to show how easily it could be done" *Chronicle*, 7 February 1935, p.14

"Police Courts" *South Australian Register*, 18 November 1885, p.3

"Police Courts" *South Australian Register*, 8 May 1886, p.3

A swag of art thefts

"Theft from Art Gallery, Wilkie Painting Missing" *The Argus* 23 August 1926, p.10

"Valuable Painting Stolen" *The Age*, 23 August 1926, p.8

"A stolen picture" *Evening News*, 5 August 1913, p.4

"First art burglary – no trace of Melbourne Rembrandt" *Advocate*, 28 May 1932, p. 6

Liam Cavell' Lyric Essay: How to steal a \$1.4 million painting' *Alternative Law Journal* v.35 n.33(2) 2008

Andrew T Kenyon, Simon Mackenzie 'Recovering Stolen Art – Australian, English and US Law on Limitations of Action' *University of Western Australia Law Review*, March 2002

"Art Gallery Theft" *The Age*, 29 September 1938, p.10

New Scotland Yard, Police Gazette, v.XIV n.20, 7 October 1927

"Stolen Painting in Court" *The Argus*, 29 November 1946, p.3

Geoff Maslen "Art galleries and collectors framed by criminals" *The Age*, 27 June 1998, p.10

Gabriella Coslovich "Picking up Paintings for a Steal" *The Age*, 8 May 2010

"Two gallery thefts may be work of art crank" *Daily Telegraph*, 26 June 1945, p.5

Peter Mohoney "Art world worried by thefts, forgeries" *Sydney Morning Herald*, 30 May 1976

"Missing art works found" *Canberra Times*, Friday 24 October 1980, p.3

"$20,000 art theft" *The Sydney Morning Herald*, 30 December 1985

"$300 Art theft" *The Sydney Morning Herald*, 3 March 1974

Barbara Muhvich "Crooks with a quick eye for art" *Sydney Morning Herald*, 21 January 1979

"Antiques Stolen From Art Show" *The Argus*, 13 March 1947, p.5

Susan Wyndham "Stolen Rees and Dobell works found" *Sydney Morning Herald*, 28 March 1985

"$30,000 art robbery at Manuka gallery" *Canberra Times*, 3 July 1985, p.7

"Fears for stolen artwork" *Canberra Times*, 26 March 1988, p. 9

"Stolen paintings" *Warwick Daily News*, 4 October 1940, p. 5

"Stolen paintings recovered" *Daily Mercury*, 4 October 1940, p.7

"Thief of two Dobell paintings may be art fanatic" *Sunday Herald*, 23 January 1949, p.4

"Art haul – found in garden" *Canberra Times*, 12 November 1964, p.1

"Stolen paintings – two valuable works" *The West Australian*, 22 January 1947, p.11

"Art theft blamed on student" *The Sydney Morning Herald*, 26 November 1955

"Valuable Pictures Stolen" *Sun*, 1 February 1947, p.3

"Art dealer charged with picture theft" *Barrier Miner*, 26 April 1951, p.3

"Picture theft charge denied" *Brisbane Telegraph*, 30 April 1951, p.6

"He didn't know it was loaded" *Sun*, 19 August 1951, p.44

"Dealer not guilty" *Sydney Morning Herald*, 19 July 1951, p.5

"Missing oil painting – theft charge" *Sydney Morning Herald*, 1 May 1951, p.5

"Dealer's alleged theft of 18th century oil painting" *The West Australian*, 25 April 1951, p.1

"Stolen Painting" *Newcastle Morning Herald and Miners' Advocate*, 25 April 1951

"Theft report to stay secret" *Canberra Times*, 3 September 1968, p.3

"Askin gets theft report", *Canberra Times*, 31 August 1968, p.7

"Askin to see theft report" *Canberra Times*, 28 August 1968, p.8

"Famous works of art vanish" *Canberra Times*, 6 November 1967, p.1

"Art-case charges 'on the way'" *Canberra Times*, 7 September 1968, p.3

"$500,000 art robbery" *Canberra Times*, 9 July 1990, p.2

La belle Hollandaise

"For trial over art theft" *The Age*, 15 July 1967, p.6

"$200,000 Picasso' hidden in bush'" *The Age*, 13 July 1967, p.6

"Picasso Theft Charge Remand" *The Age*, 27 June 1967, p.7

"No burglar alarm at Picasso theft scene" *Canberra Times*, 15 July 1967, p.8

"New flurry in art world over gallery" *Canberra Times*, 9 June 1967, p.2

"In Queensland this week" *Canberra Times*, 17 October 1963, p.2

"Missing Picasso found by police" *Canberra Times*, 13 June 1967, p.3

"Donor's Widow had Picasso" *Canberra Times*, 15 June 1967, p.3

"Major Rubin at Sotheby's" *Canberra Times*, 18 May 1959, p.6

Artnapping

"Ringleader in $3.5m art theft gets 11 years" *The Sydney Morning Herald*, 8 October 1987

"Charges over Capon art theft" *The Sydney Morning Herald*, 30 April 1992

"Three for trial on assault, art theft charges" *The Sydney Morning Herald*, 25 July 1973

"3 cleared of art theft charges" *The Sydney Morning Herald*, 15 February 1975

Dominic Cansdale "How Ballarat's forgotten art heist changed regional galleries" *ABC* 22 August 2019

The stolen exhibition

"Theft of 42 Pro Hart works 'devastating'" *Canberra Times*, 24 August 1991, p.12

Bruce James "Who Stole the Show?" *The Sydney Morning Herald Good Weekend* 20 July 1996

Andrew T Kenyon and Simon Mackenzie "Recovering Stolen Art – Australia, English and US Law on Limitation of Action" Faculty of Law, The University of Melbourne, Public Law and Legal Theory, Working Paper #23 2002

"Heysen art worth $½ stolen" *Canberra Times*, Monday 27 March 1995, p.1

"No insurance for theft of paintings" *Canberra Times*, 28 March 1995, p.5

Sky Blue and Joseph Brown
Ray Mooney, *The Ethics of Evil* (Bow Wow Productions, 2016)
Report of the Board of Inquiry into Allegations Against Members of the Victoria Police Force Vol. 3 Victoria Legislative Assembly 1978
Robyn Sloggett's interview of Ray Marginson: "High drama and…comedy: Developing the cultural collections of the University of Melbourne" *University of Melbourne Collections*, issue 5, November 2009, p.12–21.
Paul Robinson "Car crash kills Stephen Sellers, notorious Melbourne criminal" *The Age*, 7 May 1988
"Thieves take major art collection" *The Sydney Morning Herald*, 3 January 1979
John McDonald "Wanted: more dealers to bring art out of the supermarket" *The Sydney Morning Herald*, 20 May 1989
"Sledgehammer raids by police fail to find stolen art" *The Sydney Morning Herald*, 3 February 1979
"Fortune in stolen paintings recovered" *The Sydney Morning Herald*, 10 September 1979
"Art worth $400,000 recovered" *The Sydney Morning Herald*, 11 September 1979
"Police raid ACT houses for art" *Canberra Times*, 3 February 1979, p.1
"Woman found guilty of receiving paintings" *The Age*, 30 October 1981, p.18

Whose law? Whose culture?
"Paintings stolen to stop them 'leaving country'" *Canberra Times*, 8 March 1979, p.8
"Aborigines not guilty of theft of sacred art" *Canberra Times*, 5 November 1980, p.15
Felicity Ogilvie "The art of stealing" *ABC News*, 10 November 2019
1.08 Loti's Renoir
Keith Gosman, Candace Sutton, Cindy Jones and Karen Davey "Mystery remains over $1.5 million art heist" *The Sydney Morning Herald*, 24 March 1991, p.18
"Guilty of receiving a stolen Renoir" *Canberra Times*, 26 May 1985, p.1

The Picasso ransom
The Age, 5 August 1986, p.6
Patrick McCaughey *The Bright Shapes and the True Names; a memoir*, (Text Publishing, 2003)

Michael Shmith "It is goodbye to Patrick McCaughey" *The Age*, 10 July 1987, p.1

No evidence of art theft group: police" *The Age*, 7 August 1986, p.3

Letters to the editor, *The Age*, 26 December 1985

The Age 5 August 1986, p.1

Patrick McCaughey "The woman in locker 227" *The Sydney Morning Herald*, 16 August 2003

Christobel Botten "Gallery offers two art prizes as a lure to Picasso thieves" *The Age*, 9 August 1986, p.3

The Age, 11 August 1986, p.3

Fiona Athersmith "Mathews says all galleries could be targets" *The Age*, 12 August 1986, p.1

Fiona Athersmith "Photofits released as new search fails to locate stolen Picasso" *The Age*, 12 August 1986, p.4

Margaret Symonds "Picasso found safe in railway station locker" *The Age*, 20 August 1986, p.3

Thomas Dixon "Picasso's Weeping Woman: The agony and the ecstasy of the art theft" *The Sydney Morning Herald*, 23 July 2016

Debbie Cutherbertson "Picasso's Weeping Woman: Could mystery of 1986 NGV art heist be solved?" *The Age*, 23 July 2016

"News Diary" *The Age*, 21 August 1986, p.2

"Police say painting was in the hands of experts" *The Age*, 21 August 1986, p.3

"Picasso: police seek two women after sighting" *The Age*, 22 August 1986, p.3

"Studio raided for Picasso clues" *The Age*, 25 August 1986, p.6

"Police raid eliminates suspects in Picasso case" *The Age*, 26 August 1986, p.10

Justin Murphy, "Stolen Picasso" *ABC News* (broadcast 19 September 2004)

Christobel Botten "Sixty security cameras to be installed in gallery" *The Age*, 15 May 1987, p.6

"No evidence of art theft group: police" *The Age*, 7 August 1986, p.3

The Age, 16 August 1986, p.88

"Picasso-theft artistic parody pilfered" *Canberra Times*, 18 September 1986, p.6

"Gallery is missing 86 paintings, says report" *The Age* 3 December 1986

Stolen art and the damage done

"Restoration" *Compass* report, Geraldine Doogue (presenter), *ABC*, 23 December 2007

"Stolen paintings, brought back to life" *ABC Mid-West & Wheatbelt*, 11 August 2006

"Art thief apologises to monastery" *Canberra Times* 18 October 1986, p.12

"Art robbers jailed" *Canberra Times*, 15 November 1986, p.3

"Valuable religious paintings stolen" *Canberra Times*, 25 January 1986, p.9

Gavin Simpson "Monastery theft a mixed blessing" *Canberra Times*, 15 November 1989, p.27

"Man bailed on $3 million art theft charge" *The Sydney Morning Herald*, 8 February 1986

Paul McGeough "Man jailed over $1m art theft" *The Sydney Morning Herald*, 18 October 1986

Simon Kent "$2m art theft a 'national disaster'" *The Sydney Morning Herald*, 27 October 1986

"Stolen paintings go-between feared for his life" *Canberra Times*, 2 November 1986, p.6

"Interpol alerted after theft of paintings from Adelaide" *Canberra Times*, 27 October 1986, p.18

Australia's Most Wanted

Peter Schumpeter "Armed bandits raid Toorak house" *The Age*, 16 June 1988, p.3

"Farquhar 'had no suspicions'" *Canberra Times*, 13 March 1991, p.16

"Chemist tells court he arranged loan for Farquhar" *Canberra Times*, 8 March 1991, p.3

"Farquhar knew art was stolen, prosecutor says" *Canberra Times*, 5 March 1991, p.5

"Justice done says acquitted Farquhar" *Canberra Times*, 19 March 1991, p.1

The Sydney Morning Herald, 24 March 1991, p.18

"Stolen art now in safe custody" *Canberra Times*, 12 January 1990, p.4

"Farquhar sought loan of $50,000 chemist tells court" *The Sydney Morning Herald*, 8 March 1991

"Art theft Farquhar charged" *The Sydney Morning Herald*, 5 June 1989

Jennie Curtin "Farquhar trial judge queries jury's verdict" *The Sydney Morning Herald*, 18 May 1991

Karen Davey "Farquhar 'shocked' by news that Dobell painting was stolen" *The Sydney Morning Herald*, 10 March 1991

Karen Davey "Jury seeks more time in Farquhar painting trial" *The Sydney Morning Herald*, 17 March 1991

Anabell Dean "Farquhar had 'frightening suspicion' about the paintings." *The Sydney Morning Herald*, 7 March 1991

Anabell Dean "Farquhar on stolen art charge" *The Sydney Morning Herald*, 18 July 1989

"Farquhar bought stolen paintings: Crown" *The Sydney Morning Herald*, 5 March 1991

Jennie Curtin "Farquhar loan arranged in the street, court told" *The Sydney Morning Herald*, 12 March 1991

"Farquhar may face trial over four stolen paintings" *The Sydney Morning Herald*, 13 March 1990

Jennie Curtin "'Finally justice has been done'" *The Sydney Morning Herald*, 19 March 1991

"Art for art's sake" *The Sydney Morning Herald*, 7 June 1989

Anabell Dean "Farquhar sold art to fund business venture: witness" *The Sydney Morning Herald*, 6 March 1991

Janet Fife-Yeomans "Farquhar to stand trial over paintings" *The Sydney Morning Herald*, 14 March 1990

Sandra Harvey "Stolen artwork was under police noses" *The Sydney Morning Herald*, 11 January 1990

Keith Gosman, Candace Sutton, Cindy Jones and Karen Davey "Mystery remains over $1.5 million art heist" *The Sydney Morning Herald*, 24 March 1991

Hot Tucker

David Elias "Portraits of the artist as an old man" *The Age*, 8 February 1997, p.23

Robin Hughes "Interview with Albert Tucker" recorded: 15 February 1994 *Australian Biography project*

Justin O'Brien "'Remarkable mystic' the perfect muse for one of Australia's greatest artists" *Sydney Morning Herald*, 26 June 2015

Janine Burke "Albert Tucker: Portrait of the artist as a wronged man" *The Age*, 2 May 1998, p.126

Victoria Button, "Art offered for sale, court told" *The Age*, 6 February 1997, p.4

Victoria Button "Art Collector to stand trial over missing Tucker works" *The Age*, 8 February 1997, p.7

"Painting case" *The Age*, 7 February 1997, p.4

Victoria Button "Art collector ripped stolen works, court told" *The Age*, 4 February 1997, p.2

Victoria Button and Stephen Cauchi "The artist, the detective and the case of the missing paintings" *The Age*, 16 April 1998, p.3

Steve Butcher "Collector denies he stole artworks" *The Age*, 21 March 1998, p.5

Virginia Trioli and Stephen Cauchi "Finally, a verdict in the case that has shocked the art world" *The Age*, 8 April 1988, p.3

R v Joffe [1998] VSCA 101 (28 October 1998)

The cleaner

Olivia Hill-Douglas "Ex-cleaner admits owning stolen art" *The Age*, 3 December 2002

Copper-belly

Virginia Trioli *The Age*, 18 September 1996, p.17

Annika Smethurst, "$200,000 "Nesting" sculpture vanishes from Epping, believed to have been stolen" *Herald Sun*, 20 September 2012

Monique Hore, "Thieves nab $50,000 heritage statue from Fitzroy park" *Melbourne Leade*r, 24 March 2016

Simon Beaumont "WA sculptor Greg James has had four art pieces stolen in two years" *6PR882*, June 19 2020

The Australia Day art heist

Sue Cant and Rebecca Lancashire "Man tied up in $500,000 art grab" *The Age*, 28 January 1998, p.5

Mark Russell "Developer charged with stealing $3.8 million" *The Age*, 11 December 2005, p.6

Melissa Iaria "Developer jailed over $4.3m theft" *The Sydney Morning Herald*, 27 June 2008

The gloaters

Jeremy Kelly "Tucker painting kept in cellar" *Herald Sun*, 23 October 2002

"Man avoids jail for stolen art" *The Age*, 23 October 2002

Dewi Cooke and Henrietta Cook "Door opens on street artist's lost mural" *The Age*, 16 February 2013

Cassie May "History of Collingwood Technical School" *Culture Victoria*, 2017

Will Shank and Antonio Rava at "Conservation of Wall Paintings, Murals and Street Art – an international perspective" Australian ICOMOS (International Council on Monuments and Sites), 18 February 2020.

Turawan (Collingwood Technical College newsletter), #2 2/3/84 and #3 9/3/84

Anna Parlan "Keith Haring Mural" *Memo Review*, https://memoreview.net/blog/keith-haring-mural-melbourne-by-anna-parlane

The worst art thief in Australia

Sue Gardiner "Book proves Tweed man's $50m Cezanne painting is real" *Tweed Daily News*, 10 March 2014

"Mystery of the missing Cezanne" *The Sydney Morning Herald,* 28 February 2004

Greg Stolz, "'Cezanne' thief jailed", *CourierMail,* 16 May 2008

"Gold Coast man to stand trial over art theft" *The Northern Star,* 10 June 2006

David Fickling "Unknown 'Cézanne' stolen in outback" *The Guardian,* 28 February 2004

Peter Caton "Man appeals art heist sentence" *Daily Mercury,* 15 December 2009

Five-finger discounts

Andrew Taylor "A Cavalier approach: Investigation of Art Gallery of NSW's stolen painting mishandled" *The Sydney Morning Herald,* 6 June 2015

Richard Jinman and Clare Morgan "Masterpiece missing after gallery heist" *The Sydney Morning Herald,* 14 June 2007

Stolen Cavalier stolencavalier.wordpress.com

Paul Toohey "Aussie link to stolen masterpiece" *The Courier Mail,* 29 October 2011

"Heist from Art Gallery of NSW" *The Daily Telegraph,* 14 June 2007

Clare Morgan, "$1.4m Cavalier art theft probably an inside job" *The Age,* 15 June 2007

The stolen gods

"Dancing Shiva: National Gallery of Australia to return allegedly stolen statue to India" *ABC News,* 27 March 2014

Susan M Crennan "Review: Asian Art Provence Project" National Gallery of Australia

Madeleine Frith, Ece Velioglu Yildizci, Marc-André Renold, "Case Dancing Shiva Statue – India and National Gallery of Australia" *Platform ArThemis* (http://unige.ch/art-adr), Art-Law Centre, University of Geneva

Madras High Court, Subhash Chandra Kapoor vs Inspector of Police on April 3, 2012

Zachary Small "The Charges Against a Notorious Suspected Smuggler of Indian Artifacts" *Hyperallergic,* 19 August 2019

Patrick McDonald "Art Gallery of SA returns stolen Dancing Siva statue to India" *News.com,* 13 September 2019

Michaela Borland "Story of NGA's Cham Padmapani statue is shrouded in secrecy" *The Australian,* 16 February 2021

S Vijay Kumar "How an Australian museum ignores obvious red flags" *The New India Express,* 10 December 2020

VP Raghu "Idol smuggler Subhash Kapoor won't pay fine; finds comfort in prison" *DTNext*, 8 November 2022

False representations
"Alleged Art Forgery" *Brisbane Courier*, 29 November 1907, p.5
"Captain Cook's Miniature" *The Sydney Morning Herald*, 28 November 1907, p.4
"Works of art, alleged misrepresentation" *Examiner*, 28 November 1907, p.5
"Lovell, Cousins and Andrews miniature portrait trail" *Evening News*, 15 February 1908, p.8
"The antique – were they bogus miniature?" *Australian Star*, 14 February 1908, p.5
"Alleged bogus miniatures" *Daily Telegraph*, 15 February 1908, p.14
"Quarter Sessions" *Daily Telegraph*, 25 February 1908, p.10
"Metropolitan Quarter Sessions" *The Sydney Morning Herald*, 26 February 1908, p.7
"Who painted them? – Miniatures of celebrities" *Daily Telegraph*, 28 November 1907, p.8
"Alleged art swindles" *Townsville Daily Bulletin*, 28 November 1907, p.6
"Miniature portraits" *Evening News*, 13 February 1908, p.4
"Law Report Metropolitan Quarter Sessions" *Sydney Morning Herald*, 15 February 1908, p.7
"Miniature portraits" *Evening News*, 24 February 1908, p.4
"Alleged conspiracy – Jury disagrees" *Singleton Argus*, 27 February 1908, p.2
"Works of art forged" *Examiner*, 29 November 1907, p.6
"The Miniature Case" *Daily Telegraph*, 17 February 1908, p.5
"Alleged forgery of Miniatures" *Barrier Miner*, 26 February 1908, p.4
"Captain Cook's miniatures" *Sydney Morning Herald*, 29 November 1907, p.3
"Quarter Sessions" *Daily Telegraph*, 14 February 1908, p.10

Pro art forgers
Mail (Adelaide), 16 December 1950, p.3
"Faked Namatjiras, Abo art work 'being forged'" *Sunday Mail*, 23 November 1952, p.3
Peter Mohoney "Art world worried by thefts, forgeries" *Sydney Morning Herald*, 30 May 1976
"Dobell forgery unearthed" *The Age*, 25 August 1962, p.3
"Paintings in court not his work says Pro Hart" *Sydney Morning Herald*, 3 May 1977

"Art dealer has fake painting on his hands" *The Age*, 10 November 1976, p.4

"Hart fakes 'pathetic' but signature is good" *Sydney Morning Herald*, 1 February 1975

"Dobell Forgery Unearthed" *The Age*, 25 August 1962, p.3

"Forging of Native Art" *The Age*, 18 January 1954, p.3

"Artist angered by forgeries" *The Age*, 31 January 1975, p.10

Roff Smith "The art of faking it" *The Age*, 4 April 1993, p.31

Geoff Maslen and Janet Hawley "Fake the art forgery follies" *The Age*, 18 April 1987, p.115

"Painter on Fraud Charge" *The Age*, 11 April 1974

"Art work forged" *Canberra Times*, 23 September 1976, p.16

A dealer in 'Drysdales'

'Paid $35 "but wash machine still failed"' *The Age*, 1 March 1967, p.6

'Firm kept his frig., man claims' *The Age*, 3 March 1967, p.7

"Assault in raid cost L38" *The Sydney Morning Herald*, 29 August 1963

"Art dealer for trial over 'Drysdales'" *The Sydney Morning Herald*, 28 September 1976

"Art dealer knew 'Drysdale' works fake, court told" *The Sydney Morning Herald*, 20 April 1977

"Jailed for fake art sales" *The Sydney Morning Herald*, 27 April 1977

"Art dealer guilty of fraud" *The Sydney Morning Herald*, 23 April 1977

The fake dripper

Michael Kmetko "Altona High School – A Short History" coolnostalgia.bigpondhosting.com

"'Jackson Pollock' Exhibit to Be Checked" *New York Times*, 4 May 1978

Debora Hope, "Old masters: a meal-ticket for master cheats" *The Sydney Morning Herald*, 9 July 1984

Geoff Maslen and Janet Hawley "Fake the art forgery follies" *The Age*, 18 April 1987, p.115

"Art dealer stole $436,156" *Canberra Times*, 3 May 1979, p.12

"Jackson Pollock Exhibition in Australia" *Women's Weekly*, 19 April 1978, p.2-3

"Libel Action by Ledwij" *Canberra Times*, 17 May 1978, p.18

"Art dealer on theft charge" *Canberra Times*, 3 June 1978, p.8

"Three bought 'half-shares' in art" *Canberra Times*, 18 January 1979, p.9

"Art dealer stole $436,156" *Canberra Times*, 3 May 1979, p.12

"Perjury charge" *Canberra Times*, 22 May 1979, p.3

Blundell's innuendos
"What a bummer, an authentic fake" *The Sydney Morning Herald*, 8 May 1994

Matt Condon "Waterhouse in court battle over painting" *The Sydney Morning Herald*, 3 May 1987

Quentin McDermott "Fake: Fudging it in Australia's art world" *ABC News*, 8 June 2009

Geoff Maslen and Janet Hawley' Fake, the art forgery follies' *The Age* 18 April 1987

'Rogue's Gallery' *Four Corners ABC*, 10 May 1999

Ben Hills "What in a name?" *The Age*, 18 July 1998

Faking Possum
Tania Jonson "When is a Forgery Not a Forgery" *Journal of Indigenous Policy Issues* n.6

Statement of Clifford Possum Tjapaltjarri *Commercial Crime Agency Brief of Evidence: John Douglas O'Loughlin*, compiled 1999

Adrian Newstead *The Dealer is the Devil* (Brandl & Schlesinger, 2014)

The Toorak forgers
"Widow Warning to Motorist" *The Age*, 4 July 1964

Natasha Robinson' Serpent's head betrays art fakes' *The Australian*, 27 October 2007

Kim Akerman "Rover Thomas" *Artlink*, March 2000

The Cambridge Companion to Australian Art ed. Jaynie Anderson (Cambridge University Press, 2001, Cambridge)

Cheryl Hall' Toorak couple jailed for forging Aboriginal art' *Stateline ABC*, 9 November 2007

Susan McCulloch, 'Revealed: Black Art scandal', *The Australian*, 15 November 1997

Duncan Chappell and Kenneth Polk' Fakers and forgers, deception and dishonesty: an exploration of the Murky World of Art Fraud' *Current Issues in Criminal Justice* v20 #3

Victoria Laurie' Mary Macha, champion of Kimberley's indigenous art, dies aged 94' *The Australian*, 5 May 2017

Janet Thomas "The Incredible Journey of Rover Thomas" janetthomas.wordpress.com 20 June 2012

"The Delicate Art of Deception – revealing fakes and forgeries" Johnston Collection symposium October 2012

Geoff Maslen "Call for action on art forgeries" *The Age*, 22 February 1999, p.4

Robyn Sloggett and Stephen Nall "Considering Evidence in Art Fraud, An Australian Art Dealer's Perspective on Art Crime" in Duncan Chappell, Saskia Hufnagel ed. *Contemporary Perspectives on the Detection, Investigation and Prosecution of Art Crime: Australasian, European and North American Perspectives* (Routledge, 2016)

Sloggett, Robyn. "Slipping and Sliding: Blind Optimism, Greed and the Effect of Fakes on Our Cultural Understanding" *M/C Journal* 8.3 (2005)

Robyn Sloggett and Vanessa Kowalski "Building evidence for use in criminal cases – standard practice and methodologies – A case study in Australia" PDF

Natasha Robinson "Serpent's head betrays art fakes" *The Australian*, 27 October 2007

Kate Hagan "Forgers used sand for that desert finish, court told" *The Age*, 26 October 2007

Kate Hagan "And this is the Libertos, who thought they'd get away with it" *The Age*, 3 November 2007

Kate Ubergang "Jail for Toorak fake art couple" *Herald Sun*, 10 November 2007

Kate Hagan "Art-forging couple go straight to jail" *The Age*, 10 November 2007

Sarah Cascone "Court Case Claims Australian Art Market Is 30 Percent Forgeries" *Art Net News*, 22 July 2014

Senate Standing Committee on Environment, Communications, Information Technology and the Arts, Indigenous Art – Securing the Future Australia's Indigenous Visual Arts and Craft Sector (Commonwealth of Australia, 2007)

ACCC v Nooravi [2008] FCA 2021 29 August 2008

ACCC v Australian Dreamtime Creations Pty Ltd [2009] FCA 1545 21 December 2009

"Bonham's Strategic Entry into Aboriginal Art set to Reap Rewards" *Aboriginal Art Resources*, 9 June 2011

Pamela Liberto video *YouTube* https://www.youtube.com/watch?v=m29yZ4xLSIU (first accessed 12/7/14)

Quentin McDermott "Fake: Fudging it in Australia's art world" *ABC News*, 8 June 2009

Alexandra Taylor "Spotlight on Art Fraud and the Law in Australia" *Centre for Art Law*, 12 March 2018

Suzanne Spunner "Where's Rover? Indigenous Art Forgery and the victim impact" *Australian and New Zealand Law and History E-Journal* 2010

Suzanne Spunner "Problematic artworks or my doctor told me to take up painting to help me cope with the panic attacks" *Artlink*, September 2008

Corrie Perkins and Michaela Boland "Catalogue omission prompts suit over Thomas work" *The Australian*, 13 November 2008

The art of Investing
Michael Young "Art Fraud Case Grips Australia" *Art Asia Pacific*, May/June 2009

Erin Brady "Police investigate massive art fraud" *Daily Examiner*, 4 March 2009

Paul Bibby and Eamonn Duff"' Artful dodger' sentencing delayed again" *The Sydney Morning Herald*, 20 October 2013

Paul Bibby "Law finally catches up with artful dodger" *The Sydney Morning Herald*, 25 August 2013

Matt Carr "Man charged after fraud investigation" *Newcastle Herald*, 16 January 2012

"I'm a victim, pleads dealer hiding from art fraud case" *The Sydney Morning Herald*, 25 October 2009

Eamonn Duff "Search hots up for rogue art dealer" *Newcastle Herald*, 16 May 2009

Richard Noone "Australia's leading art dealer Ron Coles charged with allegedly masterminding one of our largest ever art frauds" *DailyTelegraph*, 17 January 2012

Eamonn Duff "Art dealer arrested over fraud" *Forbes Advocate*, 16 January 2012

How to frame a Brett Whiteley
Gabriella Coslovich *Whitely on Trial* (Melbourne University Press, 2017)

Gabriella Coslovich "Guilty verdict in Melbourne fake art scam" *Australian Financial Review Weekend*, 30 April 2021

Gabriella Coslovich "Fake art victim chases defacto as fraudster claims bankruptcy" *Australian Financial Review*, 27 October 2021

Pia Akerman "Brett Whiteley fraudster 'helped uncover another fake'" *The Australian*, 23 August 2016

Gant's gallery advertising in *The Age*, 5 December 1987, p.175 and *The Age*, 22 October 1988, p.76

"Rogue's Gallery" *Four Corners*, May 10, 1999 transcript

"Artists Beware of Dealers Selling Fakes" *Art + Law* 30 June 2010

Mark Russell "Brett Whiteley fake art: Dealer and conservator guilty of Australia's biggest art fraud" *The Age*, 12 May 2016

Patrick Durkin "Swans president seeks $2.5m from Brett Whiteley fraudsters" *Financial Review*, 12 September 2016

Stephanie Ferrier "Brett Whiteley: Mohamed Siddique and art dealer Peter Gant jailed over $3.6m art fraud" *ABC News*, 4 November 2016

Liam Mannix "Brett Whiteley art fraud case: Convictions sensationally quashed" *The Age*, 27 April 2017

Norman Lindsay and the Witch of Kings Cross

Art in Australia, number 35, December 1930

"'Art in Australia's, Norman Lindsay number" *Daily Advertiser*, 18 June 1931, p.1

"Norman Lindsay's Work" *The West Australian*, 9 July 1931, p.10

"Norman Lindsay's Work publishers in court" *The West Australian*, 11 June 1931, p.9

"Art in Australia" *Week*, 17 June 1931, p.35

"Is nude rude?" *Dubbo Liberal and Macquarie Advocate*, 18 June 1931, p.2

"Crude censorship" *Newcastle Morning Herald and Miners' Advocate*, 24 July 1931, p.8

"Australia disgusts" *Advocate*, 11 June 1931, p. 9

N.E. Geidhill "Art in Australia" *Daily News*, 19 June 1931, p. 6

"Norman Lindsay's Art summons Dismissed" *Herald*, 9 July 1931, p.30

N.R. Austin, "To the Editor of the Herald" *Sydney Morning Herald*, 22 March 1932, p.5

"Lindsay's Nudes police seize plates" *Wagga Wagga Express*, 13 June 1931, p.14

"Norman Lindsay deputation proposed" *Sun*, 19 June 1931, p.11

"Prosecution withdrawn Norman Lindsay's Art" *Telegraph*, 8 July 1931, p.2

"Woman Artist Fails to Appear" *The Age*, 13 August 1949, p.4

"Sydney Artist Charged" *Sun*, 4 August 1949, p.2

"Norton Paintings Held Not Obscenity" *The Age*, 20 August 1949, p.5

Nevill Drury *The Witch of Kings Cross* (Kingclear Books, 2002 Alexandria)

"Fine for Printing Book" *Sydney Morning Herald*, 7 March 1953, p.7

"Panther Embraces Girl in Weird Sex" *Mirror*, 13 September 1952, p.7

"P.M. Acts on Book by Artist" *Newcastle Sun*, 11 September 1952, p.1

"Egg and Panther in court melange" *Brisbane Telegraph*, 5 February 1953, p.19

"Pictures an 'offence to chastity'" *Sun*, 5 February 1953, p.2

The indecency of Mike Brown

Steve Meacham "Kind of blue" *The Sydney Morning Herald*, 12 November 2011

Richard Haese, "Mike Brown", *Fifty artworks from the Monash University Collection*, MUMA website

"Mike Brown Defence Fund" *Tharunka*, 28 February 1967, p.10

Richard Haese, *Permanent Revolution: Mike Brown and the Australian Avant-Garde*, 1953-97 (Miegunyah Press)

Warning signs
Paul Taylor (editor) *Hysterical Tears* (Greenhouse Publications, 1985)

Peter Wells "The 4th Biennale of Sydney" *Art New Zealand* #24 1982

Guy Brett and Roger Benjamin *Juan Davila* (The Miegunyah Press, 2006)

"Minister orders paintings returned" *The Canberra Times,* 16 April 1982, p.3

"Confiscated" *The Canberra Times,* 20 March 1973, p.11

Regional values
"Behind Cath Phillips" *The Age Good Weekend,* 15 July 1988

Trial by media
David Marr *The Henson Case* (Text Publishing, 2008)

David Marr *Panic* (Black Inc., 2011)

"Rudd revolted" *The Sydney Morning Herald,* 23 May 2008

"No charges for Henson" *The Age,* 6 June 2008

Virginia Trioli and Gus Goswell "Bill Henson model speaks out in defence of the controversial photographer" *ABC News,* 9 March 2017

Nick O'Malley "Hospital charity rejects exhibition over boy photo" *The Age,* 5 January 2011

A troll in St Kilda
Comments in *Port Phillip Leader,* 4 June 2013

http://www.vexnews.com/2013/05/big-stink-victorian-government-promotes-crap-art/

Ordinary Meeting of Council Minutes, City of Port Phillip, 28 May 2013

Dana McCauley, Wayne Flower, "St Kilda art gallery raided by police after displaying pornographic images involving children" *Herald Sun,* 1 June 2013

Rowena Orr SC and Georgie Coleman "Collage as child pornography and the limits to the right to freedom of expression – Case note" *Art Law Centre of Australia,* 23 February 2015

Stabbings in Melbourne
"Vandalism" *The Age,* 27 February 1897, p.10

"Vandalism" *Mount Alexander Mail,* Monday 1 March 1897, p.3

"The Premier's Portrait" *Mount Alexander Mail,* 27 November 1893, p.2

Shortlets, *Graphic of Australia*, 10 August 1917, p.32

Letters to the Editor, *Argus*, 14 November 1916, p.3

"Hoodlum at the Gallery Mars People's Treasure" *Herald*, 4 August 1917, p.6

Dickheads

Steve Martin and Zora Sanders "The gift of a god. The story of the University of Melbourne's God of Artemision" *University of Melbourne Collections*, Issue 23, December 2018

Lorinda Cramer and Lisa Sullivan, "Sculpture on campus", PDF & pamphlet, an initiative of the University of Melbourne's Collections Management Project, 2002

"Outdoor Artworks", PDF, City of Melbourne, October 2009

Charlotte Harper "Owl sculpture vandal clearly lacking in #BelcoPride" *Riot ACT*, 25 October 2016

Statue wars

Tom Worthington "Photos of Down by the Lake with Liz and Phil" www.tomw.net.au April 1995

Steve Evans "Dwindled to a dribble: What happened to Canberra's public art?" *Canberra Times*, 3 August 2019

Cressida Fforde, Jane Hubert and Paul Turnbull (eds.), *The Dead and Their Possessions: Repatriation in Principle, Policy, and Practice* (Routledge, 2002)

Paul Daley "The story of Yagan's head is a shameful reminder of colonialism's legacy" *The Guardian*, 31 August 2017

"Vandals cut off head of warrior's statue" *The Irish Times*, 8 September 1997

H. McGlade "The repatriation of Yagan: a story of manufacturing dissent" *Law Text Culture* v4 #1

Lily Mayers, "Australia Day: Malcolm Turnbull condemns Captain Cook statue vandalism as 'cowardly'" *ABC News*, 26 August 2017

"'Disgrace': Melbourne's Captain Cook statue vandalised ahead of Australia Day" *SBS News*, 25 January 2018

Aidan Wondracz "'Good Riddance': Vandals target Captain Cook's statue on the anniversary of his death and splatter it with paint in the colours of the Aboriginal flag" *Daily Mail*, 15 February 2019

Holy monkey thieves!

Jason Koutsoukis, Gareth Boreham and Rachel Gibson "Police refer Serrano work to censors" *The Age*, 9 October 1997, p.4

"Art or blasphemy: Serrano's work divides our city" *The Age*, 9 October 1997, p.1

Pell v Council of Trustees of the National Gallery of Victoria [1998] 2 VR 391

Peter Gregory, Jason Koutsoukis, Gareth Boreham, Rachel Gibson, Robin Usher reporting *The Age*, 9 October 1997, p.4

Elissa Hunt, "Andres Serrano' Piss Christ' triggers religious fury and court battle in 1990s trials" *Herald Sun*, 6 March 2013

George Pell "In respect of sacred symbols" *The Age*, 11 October 1997, p.43

Stephen Cauchi "Man gets bond for role in art attack" *The Age*, 17 April 1998, p.6

Jane Faulkner "Serrano show axed" *The Age*, 13 October 1997, p.1

"Gallery stands by its man" *The Age*, 14 October 1997, p.1

Tony Parkinson, Fergus Shiel and Robin Usher "Kennett urges Serrano to go home" *The Age*, 16 October 1997, p.3

Manika Naidoo "Vandal says he won't repent" *The Age*, 14 October 1997, p.6

Manika Naidoo "Vandal did not hate artwork, court told" *The Age*, 28 March 1998, p.8

Steve Butcher "Teenagers plead guilty to zoo monkey business" *The Age*, 27 August 1998, p.6

Angelique Chrisafis "Attack on 'blasphemous' art work fires debate on role of religion in France" *The Guardian*, 19 April 2011

Amanda Holpuch "Andres Serrano's controversial Piss Christ goes on view in New York" *The Guardian*, Saturday 29 September 2012

Jane Faulkner "Serrano show axed" *The Age*, 13 October 1997, p.1

Casey, D., Sacrifice, Piss Christ, and Liberal Excess, *Law Text Culture*, 5 (1), 2000

"Gallery stands by its man" *The Age*, 14 October 1997, p.1

Jonathan Jones "Andres Serrano on Donald Trump 'I never speak ill of people who've posed for me'" *The Guardian*, 4 April 2016

R. Mortensen "Blasphemy in a secular state: A pardonable sin?" (1994) *Media and Arts Law Review* 65.17

Bede Harris, "Should blasphemy be a crime? The Piss Christ case and freedom of expression" (1998) 22 *Melbourne University Law Review* 217

Andres Serrano "Protecting Freedom of Expression, from Piss Christ to Charlie Hebdo" *Creative Time Reports*, 30 January 2015

Taggers, Renks and 70K

S. D. Rokkatansky's *Road to Redemption – Life in the Fast Lane* (Carry Case Publishing, 2015)

Aisha Dow "Decrypting the 'mindless scribble' of Melbourne's illegal graffiti" *The Age,* 29 November 2015

Ashia Dow' Melbourne's graffiti pests. "If they only used their genius for good rather than evil"' *The Age,* 4 June 2016

The Ballad of Utah and Ether

Sean Irving 'Utah & Ether MUL' *Acclaim Magazine* Issue #28

Meribah Knight 'To Catch a Graffiti Artist' *The New Yorker,* 9 July 2016

Utah & Ether website http://utahether.com

Ether and Utah "No comment" *YouTube* https://youtu.be/RoxX3GzfLZM

'Techno DJ Abdulla Rashim arrested for graffiti on tour in Australia' *Fact Magazine,* 7 January 2016

Shannon Deery' Swedish musician vandalises trains in graffiti spree' *Herald Sun,* 6 January 2016

Nino Bucci and Bianca Hall' Graffiti artist Danielle Bremner slips police net as Jim Clay Harper jailed' *The Age,* 31 May 2016

The Encyclopaedia of Melbourne, ed. Andrew May-Brown and Shurlee Swain

S. D. Rokkatansky *Road to Redemption – Life in the Fast Lane* (Carry Case Publishing, 2015)

Banksy 'The Writing on the Wall' *The Guardian,* 24 March 2006

Alison Young *Street Art, Public City* (Routledge, 2014)

Matthew Lunn *Street Art Uncut* (Craftsman House, 2006)

Brendan Roberts' Three-months jail for graffiti vandal' *Herald Sun,* 23 August 2007

Nino Bucci' Notorious graffiti tagger Nost has his name up on sites but now he's carrying the can' *The Age,* 2 June 2017

Nino Bucci 'How Shane Newman, a brickie with an ice habit, became the notorious tagger Nost' *The Age,* 15 June 2017

Nino Bucci' US graffitist Jim Clay Harper captured in a headlock on Brunswick Street' *The Age,* 14 May 2016

Nino Bucci' Graffitists Nokier and Utah go to ground after Brunswick Street arrest of Ether' *The Age,* 17 May 2016

Bianca Hall' International graffiti artist who travelled to Melbourne to tag jailed for 6 months' *The Age,* 31 May 2016

Kaitlyn Offer "US vandal jailed by Melbourne Court" *News.com,* 31 May 2016

Nino Bucci "Notorious graffiti vandal blames prison officers for death of underworld figure" *The Age,* 1 July 2017

Cameron Houston and Chris Vedelago "Underworld figure Hizir Ferman dies after attack on guards at Loddon Prison, near Castlemaine" *The Age,* 29 July 2016

Elissa Hunt' Suspended jail term for US graffiti artist Jason Steven Williams, aka Revok' *Herald Sun,* 29 October 2009

The Communist in the cage
"Man Shot In Thigh" *The Argus,* 20 May 1933, p.21
Bernard Smith *Noel Counihan, Artist and Revolutionary* (Oxford University Press, 1993 Melbourne)
Bronwyn Watson "Painter Noel Counihan was a man of the people" *The Australian,* 4 May 2013
Lorena Allam 'Counihan's Cage' *Radio National,* 17 November 2013
"Speeches in Street" *The Argus,* 30 June 1933, p.13
"Speech from Cage" *The Argus,* 23 May 1933, p.5
Robert Smith, "Noel Counihan" *Australian Left Review* no.39

Beverley's body
Julie Copeland "Sunday Morning" *ABC Radio National,* 23 May 2004
"Painted Cows as 'edible art'" *The Canberra Times,* 2 December 1978, p.12
Michaela Boland "Art's in from the cold as the shock factor begins to fade" *The Australian,* 22 June 2012

Proudly unAustralian
Azlan McLennan, *Artist Statement,* December 2005
Clay Lucas "Art seizure fuels fire" *The Age,* 27 January 2006
"Socialists selling flag-burning kits" *The Age,* 18 February 2006
Dale Mills "Flagging Australia" *Altmedia.net.au,* 3 February 2010
Gabriella Coslovich "The politics of art" *The Age,* 14 May 2004
Michael Ashcroft "Footscray police in flag heist" *Green Left Weekly,* Issue 655, 17 November 1993

Courtroom Artists
Suzanne Carbone and Lawrence Money "Court artist gets caught out over her sketch" *Sydney Morning Herald,* 11 August 2009
Anna Krien "Drawn faces, the last of the courtroom artists" *The Monthly,* May 2012
"Familiar gangland faces gather in Carlton again" *The Sydney Morning Herald,* 7 April 2009
Steve Butcher "Rogues' gallery lands artist in court" *The Sydney Morning Herald,* 18 November 2009

Annabel Ross "Anthony Lister shrugs off criminal charges for graffiti in new Melbourne show" *The Sydney Morning Herald*, 5 March 2016
Steph Harmon "Anthony Lister found guilty of wilful damage over graffiti artworks" *The Guardian*, 28 January 2016